Leadership OS

Nik Kinley · Shlomo Ben-Hur

Leadership OS

The Operating System You Need to Succeed

Nik Kinley
Woking, UK

Shlomo Ben-Hur
Lausanne, Vaud, Switzerland

ISBN 978-3-030-27292-0   ISBN 978-3-030-27293-7   (eBook)
https://doi.org/10.1007/978-3-030-27293-7

This Palgrave Macmillan imprint is published by the registered company Springer Nature Switzerland AG
The registered company address is: Gewerbestrasse 11, 6330 Cham, Switzerland

To our families
—Connie, Lukas, Robin, Daniel & Arielle—
for being the OSs that enabled us to do this,
and pretty much everything else for that matter.

Preface

This book is the third part of a trilogy. The first, *Talent Intelligence*, was published in 2013. The second, *Changing Employee Behaviour*, was published two years later, in 2015. Now, nearly five years on, we have the last part.

We did not mean to write a trilogy. It just happened that way.

In *Talent Intelligence*, we explored how businesses can identify and measure talent. One of the ideas that emerged as we wrote the book was the critical role that context plays in determining whether someone is successful or not. We described the research showing that talent is not always transferable: just because you are a good fit for one role or business does not mean that you will be a good fit for another. And we ended up challenging the idea that there is such a thing as 'world-class' leaders, who can succeed anytime, anyplace, anywhere.

In *Changing Employee Behaviour*, we turned to how leaders and businesses can develop and change people's behaviour to improve performance. Again, we became interested in the role of context. We revealed research showing that the single biggest determinant of whether development initiatives succeed in changing behaviour is not the quality of the trainer or coach, or even the quality of material being taught, but the working context that people return to. You can attend a brilliant training course, but if your work environment does not support you to change and improve, then you probably won't. And since a person's boss is usually the most important part of this context, we went on to show leaders what they can do to support development and drive behaviour change.

We wrote *this* book largely because in our work with senior leaders around the world, we often felt that something was missing in the guidance they received. We felt that although many scholars and trainers were reciting the best theories of leadership, it was not the complete story. We kept seeing leaders who checked all the boxes on competency frameworks, yet ended up derailing because of the context they were in. This final part of the trilogy thus carries on from the two earlier books by looking further at how context affects leaders and how they can create useful working contexts for others, by developing what we call their Leadership Operating System (OS).

There were two other catalysts for writing this book. The first was our own experience in multinational corporates, both as leaders and followers. What we saw in both ourselves and the people we worked for was that while leadership models tend to present a straightforward 'follow-these-simple-steps-and-you'll-succeed' picture, the reality of leadership is messier. It is often about trial and error, about trying things to see if they work, and then experimenting with something else if they don't. We have endeavoured to reflect this in this book, and we believe the result is a more honest and realistic approach to how leadership works.

The final spark for this book was our children. You will find them in the pages that follow. They have been and remain a constant reminder for us that the world is changing, and with this evolution, the future is less certain. They remind us that our core job as parents is to provide an environment that helps them thrive and prepares them for the future. And they remind us that this job is not made any easier by the fact that we often feel one step behind the changing present and unclear about what exactly the future we are preparing them for will be like.

Leadership and parenting bear more than a passing similarity to each other, mostly because both share this central task of creating an environment in which others can thrive. What follows is the culmination of years of research on how leaders can best create this environment. If only we had such a guide for parenting.

In retrospect, of the three books in our accidental trilogy, we probably should have written this one first, since it is a foundation for everything else. But some things need time to mature. What follows is built on a review of over 1000 studies and articles about leadership and on our own research with more than 2500 leaders from a range of industries across the globe. We needed to do this, too, because the content of this book is a fundamental change in what we understand about how leadership works.

So the ideas presented here may have taken a little longer to germinate, but we believe that they are important, potentially liberating and worth getting right. We hope you agree.

Woking, UK   Nik Kinley
Lausanne, Switzerland   Shlomo Ben-Hur

Acknowledgements

Many people have been involved in writing this book. There are some without whom it would never have happened. There are others who have helped us develop our thinking. And then there are those who have helped us hone the text. It is a long list and we are grateful to them all.

Unfortunately, there is not enough space to name everyone, but there are some people we absolutely want to mention—people who have directly contributed time and effort to help us write this. Top of this list has to be our brilliant researcher, Noemi Dreksler. Without her, this book genuinely would not have been written. There just would not have been enough hours in the day. Special mention also needs to go to Brian Bolton, Associate Director of the Board Centre at IMD, for drafting the case studies that help bring the issues in each chapter to life. His skill in highlighting the key issues and producing engaging profiles brought colour and clarity to proceedings.

Thanks also need to go to Nathalie Wagner for the wonderful artwork and graphics. Lucy Kidwell and Liz Barlow at Palgrave Macmillan need thanks for their support, advice and encouragement. And an extra word of thanks is due to Lindsay McTeague, our wonderful copy editor, who yet again weaved magic with our words.

Finally, we want to thank all our students, coachees and clients for opening their lives to us and allowing us to learn so much from them.

Contents

About the Authors

Nikolas Kinley

Nik Kinley is a London-based Director of the global leadership consultancy YSC. His diverse experience over the past thirty years encompasses work with CEOs, factory-floor workers, life-sentence prisoners, government officials and children. He began his career in commercial roles, before spending the next decade working in forensic psychotherapy. He then returned to the corporate world, where he has held global leadership roles in talent management and leadership development for the likes of BP and Barclays. He currently works in advising firms across the globe on their leadership and people strategies, and as a coach with Boards, CEOs and senior execs with some of the world's largest firms. He has published award-winning research papers, authored multiple books, and is a regular speaker at global conferences.

Shlomo Ben-Hur is an organisational psychologist and a professor of leadership and organisational behaviour at the IMD business school in Switzerland. He is the Director of the school's flagship program for top executives, Cultivating Leadership Energy through Awareness and Reflection (CLEAR). Shlomo is the author and co-author of a variety of award-winning books, business cases and articles, and he advises a wide variety of organisations across the globe. Prior to joining IMD, Shlomo spent more than twenty years in the corporate world holding senior executive positions including at BP in London and DaimlerChrysler in Berlin. He earned his doctoral degree in Psychology from the Humboldt University in Berlin.

List of Figures

List of Tables

1

How Leadership Works

When our children were just two years old, they could use an iPhone. Not because they were especially smart (although as loving parents, we obviously believed they were). Nor because the phone was well built from quality components. It was because the operating system (OS) software on the phone was so well designed. It created an interface and environment that was so easy to navigate that our kids intuitively knew how to open apps and play games, without ever being shown how.

It was similar when the first personal computers came out, too. What enabled them to take off as mass products was the introduction of the Mac OS and Windows OS, which made them easy for even those new to computing to use. The hardware—the processors and drives—was important, but it was the operating systems that really made these products work well. And it is the same with leadership.

As a leader, having the necessary core components—the skills, characteristics and capabilities—is essential. Things like decisiveness, strategic thinking and influencing skills are critical, required ingredients. But they are also just foundations. Because as leaders rise to more senior levels, their jobs become less about doing things themselves that directly drive results, and more about directing and supporting other people to do so.

They do this by affecting things like what their team focus on, how motivated people are, what the levels of cooperation are, how decisions get made, and how empowered people are to speak up, challenge thinking and contribute new ideas. In other words, leaders create an operating environment, or system, for their people. And just as with the operating system on a phone or computer, it is this Leadership OS that is the difference between failure

© The Author(s) 2020
N. Kinley and S. Ben-Hur, *Leadership OS*,
https://doi.org/10.1007/978-3-030-27293-7_1

and success. Leaders can have all the core components and capabilities in the world, but if they do not create the right OS for their team or business, they will not succeed.

None of this should sound controversial or surprising. Yet amazingly, for the past 50 years, the leadership industry has more or less ignored these operating systems and has instead just focused on leaders' core components. There is an endless array of models describing the skills, qualities and behaviours that leaders need, and whole libraries of research into which of these components are most able to drive performance. This has undoubtedly been helpful. Today, we have a solid understanding of the skills that leaders need. But in focusing solely on these inner qualities, only half of the leadership story has been told, and leaders have been given only half the information they need to succeed. And the bit that has been missed is the most critical part.

This book is about that missing part of the story. It is not about the core capabilities you need to have, but about the operating systems you need to create. Based on over five years of research with thousands of leaders around the world, it describes what these systems are made of, explains why they are so important and reveals how they drive and enable performance. And it shows you how to identify the type of system you tend to create, and then optimise it to produce the best results.

Why Core Components Are Not Enough

For many years, the leadership industry has followed a kind of 'build-it-and-the-results-will-come' approach. It has developed leadership models that say, 'Be like this, do that': universal rules that leaders can follow in every situation, anytime and anywhere. The belief has been that if you get the behaviours, values and internal qualities right, then the performance will come.

But this approach is failing. Because the rules do not always work, and performance does not always come. In fact, every single major leadership model has been found not only to *not* help in some situations, but to actually make things worse and decrease performance.

Take what is probably the most famous model—transformational leadership. It describes four things leaders should do [1]:

- Act as a role model and walk the talk
- Motivate people with an inspiring goal
- Show genuine concern for people
- Push people to be creative and challenge accepted thinking.

As a model, it's a good one. Research has shown that if leaders follow these four rules, it can in many cases help them to improve their team's performance. Yet it is massively overhyped. Thousands of articles have been written about it, almost all describing it as *the* best way for leaders to deliver results, without any cautions or caveats. Indeed, reading these articles, you could be forgiven for thinking that transformational leadership is a kind of wonder drug that imbues leaders with amazing powers. Which would be fine, if it did. Except it doesn't.

In fact, there is a growing list of situations in which transformational leadership does not work so well. If a leader's team members are very goal-oriented, if they have a traditional view of organisational hierarchy or if they do not view the leader as 'one of them', then transformational leadership tends not to work so well [2]. There are also question marks over whether it can work in smaller organisations [3] and certain cultures [4]. And it can even *lower* creativity and performance in some types of followers [5].

So, far from being universally helpful, transformational leadership can in fact be *un*helpful in some situations. For all its benefits, in multiple scenarios, slavishly following its rules will sooner or later result in failure. And to make matters worse, there are no clear guidelines on when it is okay to use the model and when it is not. We know some things, but most of what we know is buried in arcane academic journals and hardly mentioned in mainstream articles.

This is not just a problem with transformational leadership, either. It is the same for models like charismatic leadership, empowering leadership, and even authentic and benevolent leadership [6]. And this is why this type of core component model of leadership is not enough if you, as a leader, want to fully understand what you need to do to succeed. For all these models can undoubtedly help in some scenarios, none of them will always work, and they can all have a negative impact in some situations. They are all limited, all unreliable.

The Power to Transform Taken Too Far: The Case of Elon Musk

Elon Musk is one of the most brilliant transformational visionaries of his time. His companies—PayPal, Solar City, Boring Company, SpaceX and Tesla—have not only disrupted industries but also redefined society. At the end of 2018, Tesla was worth $50 billion and had more than 40,000 employees. The company's mission—'to accelerate the world's transition to sustainable energy'—was arguably achieved years ago. The company changed

Fig. 1.1   Elon Musk

how automakers think about strategy and design, how regulators think about the future of the industry, and how consumers think about their role in society. The world is a better place with Elon Musk trying to change it. Any list of the world's most transformational leaders would have to feature him near the top (Fig. 1.1).

However, that is not all that Musk does. He is also massively engaged in social media. Here are some highlights of his 2018–2019 Twitter activity:

- He called a rescuer of a boys' soccer team trapped in a cave in Thailand a paedophile. Then he wondered why the man was taking so long to sue him.
- He posted a picture of himself smoking marijuana during a podcast.
- In August, he said that he was considering taking Tesla private at $420 a share, when the stock was trading at $340.
- That tweet prompted an investigation from the US Securities and Exchange Commission. In late September, Musk settled with the SEC,

agreeing to pay a fine and to step down as the chairman of Tesla's board, among other terms.

- One week after the settlement, he referred to the SEC as the 'Shortseller's Enrichment Commission'.
- The SEC settlement required Tesla to set up a board-level committee to review all executive-level public disclosures, including Musk's tweets. In February 2019, he falsely tweeted that Tesla would produce 500,000 cars in 2019. The SEC viewed this as a violation of the settlement and considered holding him in contempt. To this, Musk commented, 'Something is broken with SEC oversight.'

Much of what makes Musk such a brilliant visionary is his disregard for the status quo and the established way of doing anything. He views everything as a personal challenge and is both defiant and consistent in his rebelliousness. But he is not a teenager being told not to smoke. He is the CEO of a $50 billion company with more than 40,000 employees. And none of these employees has a clue what Musk will tweet tomorrow, or how the company will be performing in a year. Nobody ever knows what he is going to do next.

Thanks to this attitude, he has created several companies that most people did not even know the world needed. But ask yourself: Would you really want to work for him? Would you really want to work in the unpredictable environment he creates? Because given the reports that 41 senior executives left Tesla in 2018, it seems that at least some of Musk's employees did not want to. Having a provocative, world-changing leader can be inspiring in some situations. But having a leader who is *always* like that, seemingly regardless of the situation, can be frustrating, exhausting and, after a while, just plain limiting.

Why Capabilities Are Unreliable

The reason these traditional capability models are unreliable is that they are based on an over-simplistic picture of how leadership works. They focus extremely narrowly on how leaders behave and ignore all the other factors involved. And unfortunately, there are a *lot* of other factors. Things like business strategy, the behaviour of competitors, the culture of an organisation, the characteristics of teams and colleagues, and even cultural expectations of what leaders should be and do.

These are just a few of the factors involved, and they all do two things. They change the situations that leaders face, and thus also what leaders need to do to succeed. And they change the impact that leaders have by affecting how other people perceive and experience what they do. Contextual factors, then, are the reason you can behave the same way in two different situations and get entirely different results.

In light of this, one might think that leadership models would pay more attention to contextual factors. That instead of telling leaders to be a certain way, such as 'transformational' or 'authentic', they would say, 'Look out for contextual factors A, B and C, and then on the basis of these, behave in this way or that way'. But they don't. And unfortunately, they can't really.

The issue is that context is too complicated, with too many factors involved [7]. Trying to understand all of them, how they interact, and how they determine what leaders need to do and the impact they have is like trying to unravel a massive tangled ball of string.

To account for them all, you would not only have to say, 'Look out for contextual factors A, B, C, right through to Z and beyond', but you would also need to look at all the interactions between these factors. It is theoretically possible to do, but the resulting model would be unusably long. Imagine having to check 30-plus factors and their interactions before deciding what to do. It just wouldn't work.

There have been some models that have tried to simplify things and advise on how to behave in different situations (most famously, the situational leadership model) [8]. Yet inevitably, in trying to make themselves usefully brief, they over-simplified things and proved just as unreliable as all the other component models.

A Modern-Day Challenge

Left without an easy way to capture the complexities of context, the leadership industry has largely ignored them. As a result, its models are fundamentally limited—useful only in certain situations. And unfortunately, their failings have become increasingly exposed in recent years.

As the business world has become more global and the pace of change has increased, the role of contextual factors has expanded. They have become more complex and so more important in determining success. In a global company, what it takes to be a great influencer depends on where you are on any given day. In the US, you need different skills than you do in China. The same is true for how you manage, engage and motivate teams, how you can get the best from people of different generations, and how you operate in more or less digitised environments. Being able to operate in different contexts has become a required skill.

In the face of this, having the right core components is no longer enough for leaders. The impact of their personal characteristics and capabilities has become less reliable as the contexts they work in have become more complex and changeable. In today's world, over-simplified, one-size-fits-all models and approaches do not cut it!

The OS Solution

Leaders therefore need a new and different type of guidance to succeed. Something that does not ignore context and is more reliable.

The solution lies in our operating systems analogy. Because traditional models, with their narrow focus on leaders' capabilities, have ignored not only context but also the fact that as people rise to more senior levels, the mechanics of *how* they impact the business and drive performance changes.

At junior levels, people can directly drive results through what they do. They can make sure they do things well and work harder and longer so they do more of it. But as people move into leadership roles, their job becomes more about helping and getting *others* to do things. In fact, by the time someone becomes CEO of a large firm, there is little they personally do that *directly* impacts performance. Instead, they set the strategy, identify issues and resolve discussions. They focus people, motivate them and set the tone. And in doing so, they create a working environment—a kind of operating system—for their people.

So, to fully understand yourself as a leader and what you need to do to succeed, you need to understand the OS you create and how it affects your people and their performance.

What Is a Leadership Operating System (OS)?

The core components of leadership are your inner qualities, characteristics and capabilities—the things you can do and the ways you behave.

Your Leadership OS is the impact these things have on the people and processes around you, and the environment this creates. It is the relationships you have with the people around you—your team, peers and stakeholders—and the ways of working you establish with them.

On a computer, the operating system is software that is constantly running in the background, while you write documents, send emails or play games. Most of the time, you are not aware that it is there. But it is, and it is busy. It manages resources (the hardware components of the computer). It runs all your apps and programs. And it provides an interface for people to use the computer (think Windows or Apple's iOS). Your computer's OS is therefore critical. If it does not provide an optimal working environment for your apps, they will not run smoothly. And if it fails, your whole computer fails.

A Leadership OS is much the same:

- It manages resources, in that it enables (or limits) your ability to manage your people and get the best from them.
- It runs apps, in that it enables (or limits) your ability to make sure that work streams and projects run optimally, so objectives are met.
- And it provides an interface, in that it sets the tone for how people interact, work together and treat each other.

Just like a computer OS, your Leadership OS sits in the background, usually unnoticed behind the business of day-to-day activity. But it is there. And it can set you up for success or make achieving your goals nigh impossible.

How Context Plays a Part

Critically, Leadership OSs are not just the result of leaders' behaviour. Context is also an ingredient (Fig. 1.2). The operating environment around you is the result of both how you behave *and* contextual factors such as broader organisational and national cultures, the qualities and values that other people bring, and how others perceive and react to you.

Unlike capabilities, then, Leadership OSs *include* the influence of context. They are not something changed by context, but what is produced by it. So when we look at Leadership OSs, we are taking both leaders' qualities *and* contextual factors into account. We are looking at the outputs—the thing produced—rather than a few key ingredients. And as a result, Leadership OSs are better, more reliable indicators of what leaders need to do.

We are not saying that capabilities are unimportant. Having the right core components you need for leadership is essential. But committing to behave in certain ways is not a reliable path to success because contextual factors change both what you need to do and the impact of what you do. Operating systems, however, *are* the impact of what you do. And you are more likely to

Core component models present an oversimplified picture of leadership, in which behaviour directly drives results:

However, in reality, contextual factors change both what leaders need to do and the impact they have:

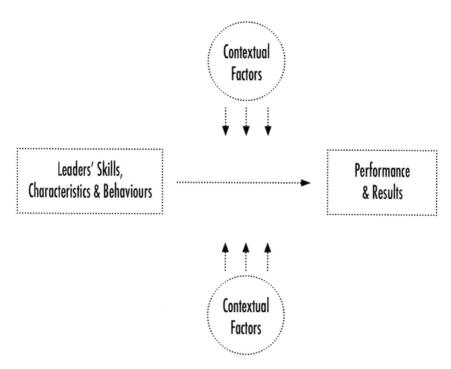

Fig. 1.2 Why core component models are not enough

succeed when you focus on achieving a certain outcome than when you try to behave in a certain way.

For this reason, we have spent the past five years researching Leadership OSs. What they are made of, how they work, and how leaders can use and optimise them to drive performance.

The Essential Elements of a Leadership OS

We began our investigation of Leadership OSs by scouring the past 50 years of research. And there, buried in the past, we almost overlooked the answer. In fact, the first time we saw it, we didn't even realise what we were looking at.

It is called Vertical Dyad Linkage Theory [9], and if there was a 'most-boring-theory-title' competition in 1975, it most surely would have won. As titles go, it is awful, providing no clue to what the theory is about. When we first heard of it, we guessed that it was something to do with electrical engineering, particle physics or genetics. As it turns out, though, we were wrong.

The theory explores leaders' relationships with their direct reports. It looks at how these relationships are formed. It examines both the impact that leaders have on their followers and the impact that these people have on leaders. And it tries to identify what kinds of relationships produce the highest levels of performance. It eventually became known by the friendlier title of Leader-Member Exchange Theory and has morphed into a whole body of research about the nature of leader–follower relationships. As such, it is a rich and fascinating resource for uncovering the nature of the OSs that leaders create.

It is a massive and diffuse body of work. In total, we reviewed over 1000 studies, including research from every continent. But even this was not enough. Most of what we looked at studied only the relationships between leaders and their direct reports. Yet we needed to understand how leaders interact with everybody around them—their boss, their peers, anyone they meet. This is because a Leadership OS extends to everyone leaders work with. Yes, it mainly concerns the environment they create for their direct reports—just because this is where they usually spend most of their time and have the biggest impact—but the OS that leaders create touches everyone they have dealings with.

So we looked further. As we did so, we had three key questions in mind. What is the impact that leaders have on the people and processes around them? What kind of working environment, or Leadership OS, does this create? And how does this affect people's performance?

Over the years, researchers have identified many different aspects of leaders' impact on the people around them that can affect performance. Things like how empowered people feel, whether they feel a strong sense of accountability, and whether they feel free to speak up and voice opinions. The list is long.

These points of impact—empowerment, accountability and all the rest—are essentially characteristics of leaders' OSs. Some leaders' OSs are characterised by people feeling empowered and motivated; other leaders' OSs by people having a strong sense of accountability and clear direction. And as we reviewed the research on these characteristics, we began to see a pattern. We saw that three OS characteristics reliably stood out as critical for success, three key aspects that leaders *must* create if they are to get the best from individuals, ensure work streams run optimally, and get people working together effectively. They are trust, clarity and momentum.

Trust

Trust stands out as possibly the single most important element of successful OSs [10]. It is a vital driver of both individual and team performance [11] and of organisational indicators such as sales figures and net profits [12]. And it is more important in driving these things than how motivated employees feel, how empowered they are or how much they enjoy their job [13].

Trust is crucial because of the types of performance it drives. Followers who trust their leaders show higher levels of *discretionary effort*—the extra mile people will go to ensure success [14]. They also show higher levels of *employee voice*—the tendency to speak up and challenge thinking. This is essential for innovation, good decision-making and risk management. And there is growing evidence that it becomes even more essential as businesses become busier, more changeable and more stressful.

Moreover, as we saw with Elon Musk earlier, trust is not only important for leaders' relationships with their direct reports but also critical for their relationships with their peers, bosses, customers, regulators and analysts. It needs to extend to everyone.

Clarity

The second key element of OSs is clarity. It is the understanding that exists about the strategy of the business, who is accountable for what, why certain things are important, and how things should be done.

Clarity is important because with it comes the essential alignment, unity and community that are critical for strategy implementation and business success [15]. And through these things, clarity also drives both better teamwork [16] and higher levels of employee commitment [17]. Little wonder, then, that a 2016 study of the most important leadership behaviours found that two of the top three were all about creating clarity (the third was about trust) [18]. And just as with trust, research suggests that as stress and uncertainty increase, so does the importance of clarity [19].

What is more, as with trust, clarity is important for every relationship a leader has. Think of Elon Musk's tweet about taking Tesla private and the confusion this sowed among his board. The need for clarity extends to every relationship.

Momentum

The final element of OSs is momentum—the energy and drive for sustained activity. This element includes motivation, confidence and empowerment, as well as the sense of connection, togetherness and team that people feel. Just as with trust and clarity, the importance of momentum lies in the results it is associated with. People who have higher levels of momentum are more likely to take the initiative, drive creativity and innovation, and show higher levels of entrepreneurialism [20, 21]. They have been shown to work harder and persist longer when they encounter difficulties [22, 23]. And they are more likely to show loyalty to the organisation and demonstrate commitment to it [24].

Again, we can point to Elon Musk's tweets as evidence of how a leader's OS extends beyond their team—his announcements have at times inspired people and at other times severely dented their confidence in both him and his companies.

Making a Model

These three essential elements—trust, clarity and momentum—do not encompass every aspect of a Leadership OS. But they are the features that research shows are most important for success. Taken together, they account for around 75–85% of how a leader's OS affects performance. So if you can get these right, you are doing well.

Importantly, they are also all things that you can take practical steps to improve. Thus, in what follows, we will focus on these three key elements—what they are, the role they play in your Leadership OS and what you as a leader can do to strengthen them.

As we will see in later chapters, trying to unpick exactly what each element is made up of is far from easy. As a simple example, ask a few people around you to define 'trust'. Chances are, you'll get as many different explanations as you ask people. By combing through the research, however, we have identified the most important components of each element, which we have combined to produce a comprehensive model of a Leadership OS (Figs. 1.3 and 1.4).

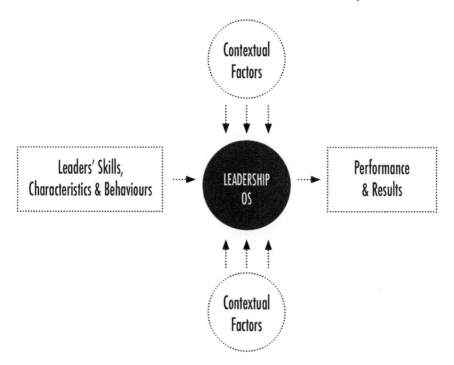

Fig. 1.3 OSs: The product of leadership qualities *and* contextual factors

Some aspects of these three elements may sound similar to what you have seen before in capability models. But there is a subtle yet fundamental difference. Capability models describe *how you should behave*. This new model of Leadership OSs describes *the impact you need to have*. This is not just semantics, either, or a play on words. Acting in a way you intend to be motivational is great, but it is not the same as creating an OS in which people *do* feel motivated. It is the difference between intending to be successful and actually being so.

The Importance of Operating Systems for Performance

Having identified these three principal elements of a Leadership OS, we set out to test whether they really do affect people's performance. To do this, we created a special survey tool that measures each element. We call it 'special' because it is fundamentally different from the hundreds of other surveys we have seen used in organisations. Rather than asking about how leaders

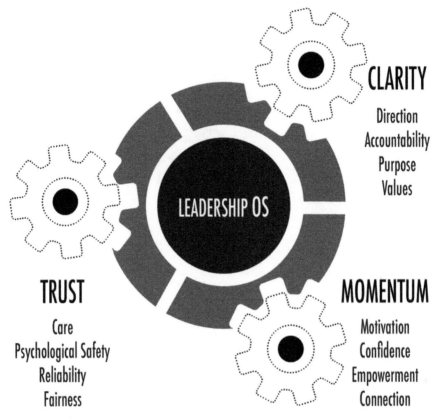

Fig. 1.4 The essential components of a Leadership OS

behave or the qualities they possess, it asks about the impact they have. For example, rather than asking if you listen, it asks whether the people around you feel safe and encouraged to speak up and voice their opinions, and whether when they do they feel heard by you. The survey is thus targeted at the environment or OS that you create, rather than the capabilities that you have.

We used this tool to survey more than 2500 senior leaders around the world. We then divided leaders into two groups: those rated high performing and those rated lower performing. Finally, we compared how the people who work around these high- and low-performing leaders described and evaluated their Leadership OSs. This led us to five key findings:

1. **Leaders' OSs are indeed different from their capabilities**. People rate leaders' OSs differently to how they rate their core components—their characteristics and capabilities. In fact, the pattern of responses we see

when we ask about leaders' impact on others is the opposite of what we see when we ask about their capabilities. When asked about how leaders behave, direct reports tend to rate individuals 9–13% *higher* than bosses do. But when direct reports are asked about the OSs leaders create and the impact they have on others, it is the opposite: direct reports rate leaders 4–6% *lower* than bosses do. So, having a strong set of capabilities is one thing, but having a positive impact on others and creating an OS that makes your team more effective is quite another.

2. **Your OS is personal to you, like a fingerprint.** Different leaders create different 'flavours' of OS, each with differing levels of the various components. Although your Leadership OS will probably vary over time and in different roles and businesses, there will be similarities. Looking back at the various OSs you have created in your career, therefore, you would see a pattern. A 'you'-type of OS: your own personal style and brand of leadership.

3. **High-performing leaders create better OSs.** The OSs created by high-performing leaders have significantly higher levels of trust, clarity and momentum than the OSs created by lower-performing leaders.

4. **This is true no matter where in the world you are.** Our study included leaders from around the world, from a variety of national and organisational cultures and a diverse range of industries. We found that the way leaders go about creating an OS appears to differ between countries. The balance between the three elements (which is rated highest, which lowest) can also vary. But no matter where people come from or where they operate, high-performing leaders produce higher levels of trust, clarity and momentum.

5. **What sets high-performing leaders apart is their ability to create high levels of the OS components that are more complex to create.** Ensuring high levels of accountability and empowerment (which are components of clarity and momentum, respectively) is an important minimum foundation for performance. You absolutely need to create them. But what really differentiates high-performing leaders is their ability to create OSs characterised by things like confidence, purpose and psychological safety (aspects of momentum, clarity and trust, respectively). And as we will see, these OS components are among the more complex to create.

Our research thus shows that Leadership OSs are critical levers for performance. To succeed in the increasingly complex context of a changing and global world, leaders need to look beyond traditional core component models of leadership. They are no longer reliable enough. So leaders need to think less about how to behave and more about the impact of their behaviour. Rather than setting out to be transformational or authentic, they need to focus on building a great OS and creating higher levels of trust, clarity and momentum. And this is the purpose of this book—to provide guidance and techniques for leaders to build an effective Leadership OS.

How to Use This Book

This book is a how-to guide. It is all about how to build the trust, clarity and momentum required for an effective Leadership OS. Each chapter has broadly the same structure. We first describe the research on each component of the model. These components are the levers through which you can build trust, clarity and momentum. We then explain how each is important for the three functions of a Leadership OS: getting the best from people, ensuring work streams run optimally, and getting people working together effectively.

For the most part, we focus on the impact that your OS has on your direct team and their performance. But we also show how your OS extends beyond this, to affect all the interactions you have—with boards, investors, regulators, customers and the media. To help do this, we present real-world case studies to bring the importance of each component to life.

Finally, for each component of a Leadership OS we present three or four techniques, or devices, that our research revealed to be useful in building it. Importantly, these techniques are not presented as over-simplified, 'follow-these-three-steps-to-guarantee-success' recipes. Instead, they are options that you can try. And because the people and situations you work with and encounter will vary, you will need to adapt and change which techniques you use in each scenario.

We understand that this is probably not what you are used to. The leadership industry is founded on core component and capability models that promise success if you behave in a certain way or follow certain steps. But in our experience—both as leaders and in our work with leaders—real life leadership is not like this. For all the promises of the 'follow-these-simple-steps' articles, leadership is, in reality, a case of considered trial and error. You try things and try your best to make them work. And when they don't, you try something else.

Our Leadership OS approach reflects this reality. We present a model that will enable you to take a more informed, structured and systematic approach to the trial and error of leadership. It does not promise the world in three easy steps, but it will yield better and more reliable results.

One final thing: there is a lot here. Three elements, each made up of four components. There are 15 chapters dedicated to the model and over 50 techniques described. Ideally, you would take the Leadership OS survey first and then focus on the components you are rated lowest on. If that is not possible, however, we recommend that you take each element in turn. Read the five chapters on trust first. Then maybe take a week or so to try some of the techniques we describe to boost trust. Only after that, come back to the book and do the same for clarity, before finally returning to look at momentum. In other words, take your time: like all strong foundations, Leadership OSs take time to build.

References

1. B. Bass, "From transactional to transformational leadership: Learning to share the vision," *Organizational Dynamics*, vol. 18, no. 3, pp. 19–31, 1990.
2. D. Wyld, "Transformation leadership: When is it redundant?," *Academy of Management Perspectives*, vol. 27, no. 2, https://doi.org/10.5465/amp.2013.0064, 2013.
3. O. T. C., A. Okwu, V. Akpa and I. Nwankwere, "Effects of leadership style on organizational performance: A survey of selected small scale enterprises in iko-si-ketu council development area of lagos state, Nigeria," *Australian Journal of Business and Management Research*, vol. 1, no. 7, pp. 100–111, 2011.
4. C. Robert, T. Probst, J. Martocchio, F. Drasgow and J. Lawler, "Empowerment was negatively associated with work and co-worker satisfaction in India but positively associated with supervisor satisfaction in the United States," *Journal of Applied Psychology*, vol. 85, no. 5, pp. 643–658, 2000.
5. S. Eisenbeiss and S. Boerner, "A double-edged sword: Transformational leadership and individual creativity," *British Journal of Management*, vol. 24, pp. 54–68, 2013.
6. N. S. Hill and K. M. Bartol, "Empowering leadership and effective collaboration in geographically dispersed teams," *Personnel Psychology*, vol. 69, pp. 159–198, 2016.
7. J. Barling, *The science of leadership: Lessons from research for organizational leaders*, New York, NY: Oxford University Press, 2014.
8. P. Hersey and K. H. Blanchard, *Management of organizational behavior 3rd Edition—Utilizing human resources*, Upper Saddle River, NJ: Prentice Hall, 1977.
9. F. Dansereau, G. Graen and W. J. Haga, "A vertical dyad linkage approach to leadership in formal organizations," *Organizational Behavior and Human Performance*, vol. 13, no. 1, pp. 46–78, 1975.

10. K. Dirks and D. Ferrin, "Trust in leadership: Meta-analytic findings and implications for research and practice," *Journal of Applied Psychology*, vol. 87, no. 4, pp. 611–628, 2002.

11. K. Dirks, "Trust in leadership and team performance: Evidence from NCAA basketball," *Journal of Applied Psychology*, vol. 85, pp. 1004–1012, 2000.

12. J. H. Davis, F. D. Schoorman, R. C. Mayer and H. H. Tan, "The trusted general manager and business unit performance: Empirical evidence of a competitive advantage," *Strategic Management Journal*, vol. 21, pp. 563–576, 2000.

13. R. Martin, Y. Guillaume, G. Thomas, A. Lee and O. Epitropaki, "Leader–Member Exchange (LMX) and performance: A meta-analytic review," *Personnel Psychology*, vol. 69, pp. 67–121, 2015.

14. N. Gillespie and L. Mann, "Transformational leadership and shared values: The building blocks of trust," *Journal of Managerial Psychology*, vol. 19, no. 6, pp. 588–607, 2004.

15. R. Stagner, "Corporate decision making: An empirical study," *Journal of Applied Psychology*, vol. 53, no. 1, pp. 1–13, 1969.

16. K. Dale and M. L. Fox, "Leadership style and organizational commitment: Mediating effect of role stress," *Journal of Managerial Issues*, pp. 109–130, 2008.

17. M. W. Johnston, A. Parasuraman, C. M. Futrell and W. C. Black, "A longitudinal assessment of the impact of selected organizational influences on salespeople's organizational commitment during early employment," *Journal of Marketing Research*, vol. 27, no. 3, 1990.

18. S. Giles, "The most important leadership competencies, according to leaders around the world," *Harvard Business Review*, 15 March 2016.

19. S. Hannah, M. Uhl-Bien, B. Avolio and F. Cavarretta, "A framework for examining leadership in extreme contexts," University of Nebraska Management Department Faculty Publications. Paper 39, 2009.

20. F. Walumbwa, B. Avolio and W. Zhu, "How transformational leadership weaves its influence on individual job performance: The role of identification and efficacy beliefs," *Personnel Psychology*, vol. 61, no. 4, pp. 793–825, 2008.

21. S. Hannah, B. Avolio, F. Walumbwa and A. Chan, "Leader self and means efficacy: A multi-component approach," *Organizational Behavior and Human Decision Processes*, vol. 118, no. 2, pp. 143–161, 2012.

22. D. H. Schunk and P. A. Ertmer, "Self-regulation and academic learning: Self-efficacy enhancing interventions," in M. Boekaerts, P. R. Pintrich, & M. Zeidner (Eds.), *Handbook of self-regulation*, San Diego, CA, Academic Press, 2000, pp. 631–649.

23. M. E. Gist, C. K. Stevens and A. G. Bavetta, "Effects of self-efficacy and post-training intervention on the acquisition and maintenance of complex interpersonal skills," *Personnel Psychology*, vol. 44, no. 4, pp. 837–861, 1991.

24. N. Kinley and S. Ben-Hur, *Changing employee behavior*, London: Palgrave MacMillan, 2015.

Part I

Building Trust

2

Trust

The Heart of an Effective OS

Deep within us all, there is a primitive and powerful biological trust system. The moment we sense something or someone, our brains and bodies react. And based on our previous experiences, we make a basic but fundamental decision: whether this thing or person is friend or foe, good or bad, safe to approach or best avoided; whether to trust them.

It happens when we greet people we know well and when we meet people we have never met before. And it happens every time someone meets you. On a physical, biological level, you react to them, and they respond to you. In fact, the system is so sensitive that you do not even have to be in the room for people to respond to you. Just showing them a picture of you or asking them to imagine you is enough to cause them to react [1].

Neuroscientists call it the X-system [2]. When we see people or experience social events, our brains automatically categorise them as positive or negative. Based on this, certain regions of the brain and certain neurochemicals are activated so we are better prepared to react. This happens automatically, with subtle physical and chemical changes in the body and brain that we are usually not even aware of [3]. And it operates lightning-fast—in a matter of milliseconds—often before we consciously recognise how we feel about someone.

Yet the effect is profound. As the system leaps into action, it activates processes throughout the body, readying us for different courses of action. It can activate parts of the brain used for friendly social interaction, or it

© The Author(s) 2020
N. Kinley and S. Ben-Hur, *Leadership OS*,
https://doi.org/10.1007/978-3-030-27293-7_2

can heighten our sense of attention and cause us to feel anxious and wary of other parties.

Like ripples on a pond, the impact of these changes sweeps through us, altering how we think, feel and act. On a broad level, it affects whether people respond to things positively or negatively. It can thus change how they interpret new information, making them more or less critical of it. It can change how much they cooperate with others. And it can change both whether a team believes what their leader says and their commitment to the leader's decisions.

Indeed, such is the influence of this potent biological trust system that it is *the* foundation of a successful Leadership OS, *the* most critical factor. In this chapter and the next four, we are going to show you how to build it and use it. We are going to break down exactly what trust is, reveal the effects it has, and share some techniques you can deploy to hack into this biological system and boost the trust in your team.

It is tough to do well because it usually works in the background, below your consciousness and beyond your control. It is an effect you have on others, often without you or them even realising it. But it is also an opportunity because this system means that you have a kind of superpower: you can literally turn parts of people's brains on or off.

The X-System

There is a phrase in English that you can be 'turned off' by someone. It is the idea that certain people can leave you feeling repelled, that the way they behave can turn off your interest in them. Well, it isn't just a saying. It actually happens.

In 2011, researchers ran an experiment with a group of middle-aged employees [4]. They asked them about their previous bosses, both those they felt they had had a good relationship with and those they had had a less positive relationship with. As they were describing their experiences with these different leaders, the researchers scanned their brains. When the employees described what happened with bosses they liked and trusted, parts of the brain known to be involved with social behaviour activated. But when they recalled events with less liked and less trusted bosses, these regions of the brain were shut down. Instead, other areas, known to be involved with narrowing attention, less compassion and more negative emotions, all lit up. So the basic biological decision that people make about whether to trust you or not activates or shuts down different parts of the brain.

This is the X-system at work. Keen to understand it further and its impact on us, researchers have found ways to replicate what happens when we trigger people's trust systems. They discovered that when people say they trust someone, not only do parts of the brain start up but they also release a chemical called oxytocin, which affects how the brain works [5]. So the researchers started giving people extra oxytocin, using a nasal spray, to see what would happen.

To start with, they found that it seems to make people pay more attention to social cues and better at detecting emotional facial expressions, especially happy ones [6]. As a result, they are better able to accurately read the mood and mental state of others [7]. It also makes people more positive about social cues and events, increasing how trustworthy they think others are [8]. It can reduce any social anxiety and wariness they may feel about others [9]. And this seems to be especially true when they see others as similar to them or as part of their group or team [10]. Finally, it also appears to make people behave in more pro-social ways [11]. It can lead them to say thank you more [12] and make them more generous [13].

This is the level on which trust occurs. It is a deep, biological thing. The mere thought of you can trigger physical reactions in other people that affect their behaviour in all sorts of ways. This is part of why it can be so powerful. There is another source of its influence, too, though: the role trust plays in your Leadership OS and what it does to how people work together.

What Trust Does

When we say that a leader has an OS characterised by high levels of trust, what we mean is that most people in a team feel that they trust their leader and the people around them. And when this happens, when a critical mass of people feels this way, trust does three things to the way your team work together (Fig. 2.1).

Fig. 2.1 The functions of trust in a Leadership OS

A. Channels Effort into Collaborative Activity

The first thing trust does is to channel activity by connecting people, so they are more likely to work together. When people are working in an OS with only low trust, motivation tends to be transformed into individual, siloed efforts. Where trust is high, however, motivation is converted into joint effort. So collaboration, cooperation and teamwork all increase [14].

B. Improves Information Flow

The second thing trust does is to increase communication and thereby information flow. When a Leadership OS is high in trust, people are more open and proactive about sharing knowledge, ideas and concerns [15]. As a result, decision-making improves as issues are discussed more effectively. Risk management is improved as potential problems are raised more quickly. And creativity and innovation also increase, as people discuss and share ideas more.

Indeed, in our research looking at the impact of Leadership OSs on performance, high levels of trust are the biggest differentiator between leaders rated as strong decision-makers and those rated as poor decision-makers. And trust is also what most separates leaders who are rated as strong innovation drivers from those seen as less innovative.

C. Adds a Protective Buffer

The last thing trust does is to act as a protective buffer against difficult times. It does this in two ways. First, it makes people behave more positively towards each other. When a Leadership OS is high in trust, people report a greater sense of connection. They are more courteous towards each other [16], demonstrate more empathy [17] and show higher levels of altruism. As a result, trust can reduce the negative impact of heavy workloads and stress on the way the team functions [18]. For example, in low-trust OSs, stress tends to reduce communication, but in high-trust OSs, this does not happen so much [19].

The second way trust adds a protective buffer is by making people view new information and events more positively. It can thus ensure that when heated debate and conflict occur—as they inevitably do in any team—this does not turn into more personal conflict [20]. It encourages people to remember that they are all 'in it together' and on the same side. In this vein, it can even reduce the often negative impact of organisational politics, as people are less inclined to view such politics negatively [21]. So trust basically acts as a kind of lubricant, keeping your team functioning effectively when the going gets tough.

These, then, are three ways trust can affect how your team work together. It helps you to get the best from your people, to ensure that everything runs smoothly, and it sets the tone for how people should interact and work together. And all of this pays off.

In Leadership OSs with high levels of trust, people demonstrate higher levels of commitment to the business, working harder, longer and with greater levels of effort [22]. They enjoy what they do more, too, reporting far higher levels of job satisfaction, accomplishment and loyalty to their business. Consequently, results improve. Strong levels of trust are related to higher sales and profits [23], better productivity [24] and even the percentage of wins in basketball teams [25]. This appears to be true across cultures, too, with researchers obtaining the same findings all over the globe [26–28]. Wherever you are in the world, trust is powerful stuff.

This is just as well, as our need for high-trust OSs appears to be increasing. As business becomes more global, finding ways to help people work effectively together is becoming ever more critical. As it becomes more complex and less predictable, having the information you need is becoming more essential. And as it becomes busier and more stressful, the buffering effects of trust are becoming more critical. Little wonder, then, that the most recent research suggests that the difference in performance levels between high-trust and low-trust OSs is growing bigger [29].

It is therefore rather unfortunate that the levels of trust in organisations seem to be so low.

A Crisis in Trust

The research on trust levels makes grim reading. Study after study has reported low levels of trust in all sorts of businesses around the world. Here are a few statistics, all from recent surveys:

- Only 7% of workers strongly agree that they trust senior leaders to look out for their best interests [30].
- Some 50% of people believe their organisation prioritises financial goals over ethics; 44% say the same of their line managers [23].
- Over half of employees do not trust their organisation to tell them the truth [31].
- Almost 60% of people say they have left an organisation due to trust issues [23].

And here is one more, the most staggering of all: nearly 60% of people say that they trust strangers more than they trust their own boss. That is worth thinking about for a second. If it does not constitute a crisis of trust, then what does?

The reaction of most leaders when we tell them these statistics is reliably consistent. They are a little surprised, but tell us that they know how important trust is and that they believe they are one of the 40% of bosses who *are* trusted more than strangers. Hardly anyone thinks they are part of the 60% less trusted!

But we remain concerned because we have seen from our research that leaders tend to overrate how positive their Leadership OS is, including its levels of trust. In fact, compared with feedback from direct reports and peers, leaders overrate it more than 80% of the time. So, even if the grim statistics on prevailing levels of trust are a little overstated, they are consistent enough to be believable and worrying. This begs an interesting question: if we all know trust is important, why do trust levels appear to be so low?

Finding Out Why

There are a number of ideas about how the situation got this bad. One is that it has always been this way, since there is a natural power difference between leaders and followers that inevitably leads to some degree of lack of trust. Another is that it used to be much better, and that trust has only dipped in the past 30 years as workplaces have become more changeable and jobs less secure. Events such as the global financial crisis of 2008 may also have reinforced this, since they have eroded trust across the board.

Both these ideas have merit, and both are probably involved to some extent. However, our research has led us to add another explanation to the list. *Leaders do not pay enough attention to trust, and in recent years it has become even harder for them to do so.* As a result, it is effectively unmaintained, unmanaged and left to develop or degrade on its own.

Most of the time, most leaders focus on deliverables and what needs to happen next. After all, objectives must be met. Few put time aside to focus specifically and systematically on trust. It is just not something that most leaders do in a deliberate and planned way.

Even if they want to, over the past 50 years it has become harder for them to do so. As workplaces have become more efficient, leaders' spans of control have expanded, so they now have more tasks to do and less time to focus on elements like trust. They are also more stressed, and most leaders' natural reaction to stress is to focus even more on tasks. This is why our research shows that trust is the element of leaders' OS most damaged by stress because it causes them to focus on the stuff that needs doing, rather than on the people they are doing it with.

This matters because when they are task-focused, leaders are less likely to behave in ways that create and support trust: researchers have shown that when you are task-focused, you use different parts of your brain than when you are engaged in social activities and issues [32]. So, when you are busy thinking about budgets, project plans or product specifications, you turn off the parts of your brain that are key to building trust.

This, then, is why leaders *must* make time for trust, why they must be deliberate and systematic in how they build and nurture it. Because otherwise, on a fundamental, biological level, they will not use the right parts of their brains to enable them to build trust.

When Trust Goes Bad: The Case of José Mourinho at Manchester United

José Mourinho is one of the best football managers of all time. If you don't believe us, just ask him—he'll certainly tell you so. Mind you, he has reason to because perhaps the only thing larger than Mourinho's ego is his trophy case. He has led teams to league titles in England, Spain, Italy and Portugal, and won the UEFA Champions League twice (Fig. 2.2).

When many people think of Mourinho, they think of his personality: mercurial, outspoken and arrogant. Many say his style of play is boring, but he doesn't care what people think: winning is what matters to him.

Mourinho's method is based on careful preparation, complete commitment and challenging his players to be the best they can. They speak of how he studies the game meticulously, and the phrase repeatedly heard is that 'he knows his stuff'. This knowledgeability gives his players confidence, as well as ensuring they are well prepared and well drilled in what they need to do. Then there are his drive and focus—the sense he exudes that he would give absolutely everything to ensure his team wins. It has proved to be infectious and inspiring, with players giving him their all in return. Finally, there is the way he pushes the people around him to be their best. His players have spoken of how they had to prove themselves to him every day, and how he seemingly had an ability to push them to give more than anyone else could.

From 2003 to 2015, Mourinho's teams won eight league titles in four of the top European leagues with this approach. He wasn't always the easiest manager to play for, but he managed to instil immense trust in his teams. Players saw him giving everything for the team and they wanted to do the same. They knew their hard work would be rewarded. And he turned groups of talented individuals into winning teams.

Fig. 2.2 Jose Mourinho

Then something changed. Some commentators have pointed to his time at the Spanish side Real Madrid as being the turning point. But it was publicly exposed in 2016, when he became the manager of Manchester United, the English Premier League's leading club. United had won 13 of the first 21 Premier League titles, but had not won since 2013 and seemed lost. Mourinho was supposed to be their saviour.

When he arrived in Manchester, almost everything was different from what he had encountered before. It was unlike all his previous managerial challenges. But Mourinho was Mourinho. He had never been one to change much, even announcing once, 'I am José Mourinho. I don't change.' The United fans learnt this the hard way.

What had worked at his previous clubs did not work at Manchester United. He did not adapt to his new situation. Messages that had challenged and inspired players earlier in his career seemed to intimidate and disengage the United players. And when his players failed to respond, he blamed them, publicly chastising them at times. As a result, the trust they had in him was undermined, until eventually—after it happened repeatedly—it was lost.

His players became risk-averse, subdued shadows of their former selves, scared of making mistakes. Self-conscious and possessed by their worries, they lost their ability to function as a team. The more the team lost, the more Mourinho became an exaggerated version of himself, pushing them more, challenging them more and continuing to criticise them in the press. And every time he did so, the trust in the team was further eroded. Eventually, United lost patience and parted ways with Mourinho.

One of Mourinho's players once said of his leadership style, 'Mourinho arouses feelings in people'. When those feelings are trust and confidence, you end up winning 8 league titles in 13 years. When they are fear and distrust, you end up looking for a new job.

José Mourinho remains one of the most successful football managers of all time. But his spell at Manchester United is a salutary lesson of the pivotal role played by trust in a Leadership OS. It is the core foundation that everything else is dependent upon. And so when Mourinho was unable to create an atmosphere of trust, everything else he tried failed. At the time of writing, Mourinho was still looking for the next management role. Only time will tell if he learned his lesson.

Installing Trust in Your OS

How, then, can you go about developing a Leadership OS with high levels of trust? The first point to make is that it *can* be done and that *you* can do it. In fact, you are the only person who can because trust is personal. Yes, some people are more trusting than others. And yes, contextual factors such as broader organisational culture can affect levels of trust. But leaders are the single biggest determinant of whether trust forms in their OS [16]. So whether there is a high level of trust in *your* OS is down to whether you personally evoke trust [33].

In the next four chapters, we are going to break trust down into its component parts and look at how you can install each in your Leadership OS. Over the years, there has been lots of research and debate on what these factors are. Indeed, one recent review found over a hundred different definitions of what trust is and what it involves [34].

However, in our research, as we compared many previous studies, we discovered four things that stand out as by far the most important in determining whether people feel a high degree of trust (Fig. 2.3). To build trust successfully, each is important and requires attention. The four are:

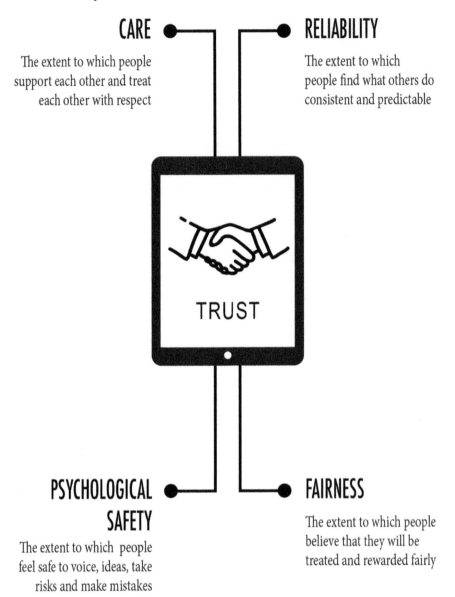

CARE

The extent to which people support each other and treat each other with respect

RELIABILITY

The extent to which people find what others do consistent and predictable

TRUST

PSYCHOLOGICAL SAFETY

The extent to which people feel safe to voice, ideas, take risks and make mistakes

FAIRNESS

The extent to which people believe that they will be treated and rewarded fairly

Fig. 2.3 The components of trust

1. Care—the extent to which people support each other and treat each other with respect.
2. Psychological safety—the extent to which people feel safe to voice ideas, take risks and make mistakes.

3. Reliability—the extent to which people find what others do consistent and predictable.
4. Fairness—the extent to which people believe that they will be treated and rewarded fairly.

When people see this list of elements, they often ask, 'What about honesty?' After all, if you ask people to define trust, they usually mention this. Research, however, suggests that honesty is more of a 'hygiene factor': something that is necessary, but not enough. Lack of honesty will kill trust, every time. But telling the truth is a minimum standard—a vital foundation, but not what makes the difference between high levels of trust and just average levels.

We will look at each of the four components of trust in turn. As we do, unlike traditional competency model advocates, our aim is *not* to tell you how to behave because, as we saw in the previous chapter, behaviour can have an uncertain impact, and what works in some situations may not work in others.

Instead, our model calls on you to focus on the impact you need to have on others and the Leadership OS you need to build. For example, when we say care is a key element, we do not mean that you should go around caring (although it is a good start). Rather, you have to find ways to ensure that other people feel cared for, ways to trigger their biological trust systems to activate correctly, with the right parts of their brains engaged. If you can get enough people in your team activated in this way, you will create a Leadership OS that channels effort into collaborative activity, improves information flow, and adds a protective buffer.

So, in each chapter we will first describe the impact you need to have and then provide a range of techniques you can try to achieve this. We will also show how you can tell if you have succeeded in installing each component in your OS. In order to make the techniques in the following chapters work, however, there are a couple of things you should do first, a few foundations that need to be built.

Three Foundations of Trust

Over the years, an almost endless number of suggestions have been made about how to build and maintain trust. Three, however, have emerged as critical foundations, essential for any deliberate, systematic attempt to build trust.

Foundation 1: KYP—Know Your People

You may have heard of KYC—know your customer. Well, this is KYP—know your people.

If you approach building trust the same way with every person in your team, you will not always succeed. Inevitably, you will be more successful with some than others. This is because people vary in both the degree to which they need trust and the pace at which they give it. For example, people with high levels of confidence have been found to give trust more readily. People from regions like the Middle East, meanwhile, take more time and require a greater sense of personal connection to build trust than people from Europe or the US. And people from younger generations are likely to feel trust more quickly than those from older generations.

People also differ in which of the four components they most need to build trust. This is why there is no one answer to the question, 'Which is the most important component?' For some, feeling cared for is most important. For others, reliability may be key. The challenge—and also the solution—is that you need to vary your approach. And to do that, you need to know your people and what they need from you.

One simple technique you can use to ensure you know your people and the best way to build trust with each of them is to check their history. Imagine someone has worked in a company for five years and during this time has had five different managers. Each of these bosses set a slightly different direction, started new initiatives and made promises. And each then left within a year, without any of these things having been achieved. Now imagine you come along as the sixth boss. How likely do you think they are to trust you?

Situations like these are common. Everyone brings some history with them that affects their starting position and attitude towards you as their leader. Finding out what that history is will help you to understand whether they are approaching you with their trust systems activated in the right way. It will help you determine whether the social parts of their brains are turned on and the oxytocin is flowing, whether they will assume the best of you or are likely to be more cautious and guarded.

So, one thing you should do with all your people is to put time aside to sit with each of them (it doesn't have to be long) and ask them about their history with previous bosses. How many bosses have they had? Who was the best? Who was the worst? What made them good or bad bosses? And what does all this mean for how the two of you can work best together?

Foundation 2: Stay Close to Your People

Trust requires a relationship. So, the second foundation of trust building is simple: stay close to your people and communicate, communicate, communicate.

The research on this is consistent. It shows that the more distant an employee feels from their boss, the less likely they are to trust them. Followers who have more frequent face-to-face contact with their bosses tend to trust them more than those who have less frequent meetings. And leaders with smaller teams tend to create more trust than those with bigger teams [35]. So simply staying close to people is an essential foundation of trust.

Organisation size plays a role here, too, because as size increases, trust falls. The average level of trust in leaders in firms with around 100 employees is about 25% higher than the average trust found in organisations with over 1000 employees [35]. So leaders in larger organisations, where visibility is harder to achieve, need to work harder to evoke trust in their people.

Yet staying close needs more than just physical proximity. It also requires communication. In fact, when you ask followers what behaviours in their boss help them to feel that they can trust them, the two most common responses—by far—are openness and communication [36]. So just meeting people is not enough.

One technique you can use to ensure you stay close to people is to systematically signal your availability to them. We are assuming here that you meet regularly with your people, with clear time set aside in the diary. We are suggesting that, in addition, you expressly and repeatedly let them know when and how you are available for them. Most leaders we know try to make themselves available for their teams. However, few deliberately and systematically signal this. It is essential to do so, though, because most followers say the one thing they would like to change about their relationship with their boss is to have greater access to them. And every time you signal your accessibility, you will be both addressing this common desire and directly trying to trigger your people's trust systems.

A second technique you can use is quick, easy and effective. Ask your people what they want to know, whether there is information they would like to receive regularly that they do not currently. When people have a request here, it is usually related to either their, the team's or the company's performance. And the beauty of this technique is that even if your people cannot think of anything they would like to have more information about, just by asking them you will be signalling your willingness to be open.

Foundation 3: Monitor Your Trust

Trust is not a constant. Unfortunately. It is not something that, once established, you can rely on forevermore. It changes over time and is fragile—easier to destroy than to build. So it needs maintaining. The easiest way to do this is to check in on it regularly, to monitor how people are feeling. Again, this is something that many leaders do sometimes, but few do consistently and systematically.

At the end of each of the following chapters on the core components of trust, you will find several questions you can ask yourself to check the level of trust in your team. Use them as a checklist. The questions are designed to home in on some of the signs that can tell you if people's trust systems are activated in the right way. And again, be systematic about it. Diarise it. Put it in a task list. Once every six months, or less if the team is going through a period of rapid change, use the checklist. That way, if things start to go awry, you are more likely to notice it before it is too late.

The Heart of an Effective OS

Trust is the beating heart of your Leadership OS. It channels effort into collaborative activity; it improves information flow; and it adds a protective buffer to the functioning of the team.

Developing it takes work. Not so much in terms of time, but in terms of deliberate and conscious focus. Two things can help you here. First, your superpower: the fact that you can trigger the biological trust systems that lie deep within your people. By doing this, you can stimulate reactions and behaviours in them that in turn create higher levels of trust.

The second thing helping you is the fact that trust is contagious. As people meet others whose trust systems are activated—with all the positive behaviours this engenders—this triggers their trust systems, too. So trust begets trust, and as more and more people start to feel trust, it ripples through the broader team. And this means that with just a little forethought and systematic focus, your Leadership OS can have a huge impact on the effectiveness of the people around you.

NIPs and PIPs: Borrowing a technique from psychotherapy

Psychotherapists have been studying patterns of behaviour between people for over a hundred years. Some therapists specialise in working with individuals, but others work with whole groups of people—often extended families. And one of the key tools of their trade is called NIPs and PIPs: Negative Interpersonal Patterns and Positive Interpersonal Patterns.

NIPS and PIPs are behaviour loops: a pattern in which Person 1 behaves in way that causes Person 2 to react in a certain way, which then leads Person 1 to respond to that reaction, and so on. A negative pattern (or NIP) is one in which the outcome is undesirable or harmful in some way, for example people being unhappy. A positive pattern (or PIP) is one in which the result is helpful or beneficial.

When people meet and their trust systems interact, NIPs and PIPs occur. For example, imagine you meet someone whose trust system is activated in a negative way, in that they are anxious or defensive. This could trigger your trust system to respond in a negative way, too. It would not be intentional because your brain would detect and respond to the cues the other person was emitting before you even realised it. But the more task-oriented centres of your brain could be activated, the social areas could go quiet, and your oxytocin levels could drop. As a result, you could smile less than normal, be less sensitive or speak more guardedly. The other person could then notice this, reinforcing their defensiveness. And before either of you are consciously aware of anything, you could find yourself in a negative pattern.

However, whenever you try to trigger a positive reaction in someone's trust system, you are attempting to create the opposite of this—a positive pattern. You are trying to activate the other person's trust system in a way that leads them to start interpreting events and responding more positively, so that this in turn can trigger positive responses in both yourself and others. And this is how trust can be contagious and ripple through a group—through NIPs and PIPs.

So next time you meet someone, ask yourself whether you think you are in a negative or positive pattern. It can be a useful question to ask, because it is not something you usually think about. This is especially true for negative patterns, as you can then take steps to intervene and stop the pattern from building further.

References

1. P. Vrtička, D. Sander and P. Vuilleumier, "Lateralized interactive social content and valence processing within the human amygdala," *Frontiers of Human Neuroscience*, vol. 6, no. 358, https://doi.org/10.3389/fnhum.2012.00358, 2013.
2. M. Lieberman, "Social cognitive neuroscience: A review of core processes," *Annual Review of Psychology*, vol. 58, pp. 259–289, 2007.
3. J. Ledoux, "The emotional brain, fear, and the amygdala," *Cellular and Molecular Neurobiology*, vol. 23, nos. 4–5, pp. 727–738, 2003.

4. R. E. Boyatzis, A. M. Passarelli, K. Koenig, M. Lowe, B. Mathew, J. K. Stoller and M. Phillips, "Examination of the neural substrates activated in memories of experiences with resonant and dissonant leaders," *The Leadership Quarterly*, vol. 23, no. 2, p. 25, 2012.

5. P. J. Zak, R. Kurzban and W. T. Matzner, "Oxytocin is associated with human trustworthiness," *Hormones and Behavior*, vol. 48, no. 5, pp. 522–527, 2005.

6. L. Schulze, A. Lischke, J. Greif, S. C. Herpertz, M. Heinrichs and G. Domes, "Oxytocin increases recognition of masked emotional faces," *Psychoneuroendocrinology*, vol. 36, no. 9, pp. 1378–1382, 2011.

7. G. Domes, M. Heinrichs, A. Michel, C. Berger and S. Herpertz, "Oxytocin improves "mind-reading" in humans," *Biological Psychiatry*, vol. 61, no. 6, pp. 731–733, 2007.

8. A. Theodoridou, A. Rowe and I. R. P. Penton-Voak, "Oxytocin and social perception: Oxytocin increases perceived facial trustworthiness and attractiveness," *Hormones and Behavior*, vol. 56, pp. 128–132, 2009.

9. P. Kirsch, C. Esslinger, Q. Chen, D. Mier, S. Lis, S. Siddhanti, H. Gruppe, V. Mattay and A. Meyer-Lindenberg, "Oxytocin modulates neural circuitry for social cognition and fear in humans," *Journal of Neuroscience*, vol. 25, no. 49, pp. 11489–11493, 2005.

10. C. De Dreu, L. Greer, G. Van Kleef, S. Shalvi and M. Handgraaf, "Oxytocin promotes human ethnocentrism," *Proceedings of the National Academy of Sciences of the United States of America*, vol. 108, no. 4, pp. 1262–1266, 2011.

11. E. Andari, J. Duhamel, T. Zalla, E. Herbrecht, M. Leboyer and A. Sirigu, "Promoting social behavior with oxytocin in high-functioning autism spectrum disorders," *Proceedings of the National Academy of Sciences of the United States of America*, vol. 107, pp. 4389–4394, 2010.

12. J. A. Barraza, N. S. Grewal, S. Ropacki, P. Perez, A. Gonzalez and P. J. Zak, "Effects of a 10-day oxytocin trial in older adults on health and well-being," *Experimental and Clinical Psychopharmacology*, vol. 21, no. 2, p. 85.

13. P. J. Zak, A. A. Stanton and S. Ahmadi, "Oxytocin increases generosity in humans," *PLOS One*, vol. 2, no. 11, p. e1128, 2007.

14. K. Dirks, "The effects of interpersonal trust on work group performance," *Journal of Applied Psychology*, vol. 84, no. 3, pp. 445–455, 1999.

15. Y. Gong, S. Cheung, M. Wang and J. Huang, "Unfolding the proactive process for creativity: Integration of the employee proactivity, information exchange, and psychological safety perspectives," *Journal of Management*, vol. 38, no. 5, pp. 1611–1633, 2012.

16. K. Dirks and D. Ferrin, "Trust in leadership: Meta-analytic findings and implications for research and practice," *Journal of Applied Psychology*, vol. 87, no. 4, p. 611, 2002.

17. P. Zak, "The neuroscience of trust," *Harvard Business Review*, January–February, pp. 84–90, 2017.

18. B. Gilbreath and P. Benson, "The contribution of supervisor behaviour to employee psychological well-being," *Work & Stress*, vol. 18, no. 3, pp. 255–266, 2004.
19. S. Hannah, M. Uhl-Bien, B. Avolio and F. Cavarretta, *A framework for examining leadership in extreme contexts*, University of Nebraska Management Department Faculty Publications, Nebraska. Paper 39, 2009.
20. T. Simons and R. Peterson, "Task conflict and relationship conflict in top management teams: The pivotal role of intragroup trust," *Journal of Applied Psychology*, vol. 85, no. 1, p. 102, 2000.
21. E. Vigoda-Gadot and I. Talmud, "Organizational politics and job outcomes: The moderating effect of trust and social support," *Journal of Applied Social Psychology*, vol. 40, no. 11, pp. 2829–2861.
22. B. A. De Jong and T. Elfring, "How does trust affect the performance of ongoing teams? The mediating role of reflexivity, monitoring, and effort," *Academy of Management Journal*, vol. 53, no. 3, pp. 535–549, 2010.
23. K. Dirks and D. Skarlicki, "Trust in leaders: Existing research and emerging issues," *Trust and Distrust in Organizations: Dilemmas and Approaches,* vol. 7, pp. 21–40, 2004.
24. R. Nyhan, "Changing the paradigm: Trust and its role in public sector organizations," *The American Review of Public Administration*, vol. 30, no. 1, pp. 87–109, 2000.
25. K. Dirks, "Trust in leadership and team performance: Evidence from NCAA basketball," *Journal of Applied Psychology*, vol. 85, no. 6, pp. 1004–1012, 2000.
26. A. Ozturk, M. Hancer and Y. Wang, "Interpersonal trust, organizational culture, and turnover intention in hotels: A cross-level perspective," *Tourism Analysis*, vol. 19, no. 2, pp. 139–150, 2014.
27. Q. Miao, A. Newman and X. Huang, "The impact of participative leadership on job performance and organizational citizenship behavior: Distinguishing between the mediating effects of affective and cognitive trust," *The International Journal of Human Resource Management*, vol. 25, no. 20, pp. 2796–2810, 2014.
28. R. Costigan, R. Insinga, J. Berman and G. Kranas, "A four-country study of the relationship of affect-based trust to turnover intention," *Journal of Applied Social Psychology*, vol. 42, no. 5, https://doi.org/10.1111/j.1559-1816.2011.00880, 2012.
29. K. Atuahene-Gima and H. Li, "When does trust matter? Antecedents and contingent effects of supervisee trust on performance in selling new products in China and the United States," *Journal of Marketing*, vol. 66, no. 3, p. 61, 2002.
30. K. Illes and M. Mathews, "Leadership, trust and communication leadership, trust and communication: Building trust in companies through effective leadership communication," Westminster Business School, London, 2015.
31. K. Dirks and D. Skarlicki, "Trust in leaders: Existing research and emerging issues," in R. M. Kramer and K. S. Cook (Eds.), *The Russell Sage Foundation*

series on trust: Trust and distrust in organizations: Dilemmas and approaches, New York, NY, Russell Sage Foundation, 2004, pp. 21–40.

32. A. Jack, A. Dawson, A. Ciccia, R. Cesaro, K. Barry, A. Snyder and K. Begany, *Social and mechanical reasoning define two opposing domains of human higher cognition*, Cleveland, OH, Case Western Reserve University, 2010.

33. G. Alarcon, J. Lyons, J. Christensen, K. Klosterman, M. Bowers, T. Ryan, S. Jessup and K. Wynne, "The effect of propensity to trust and perceptions of trustworthiness on trust behaviors in dyads," *Behavior Research Methods*, vol. 50, no. 5, pp. 1906–1920, 2018.

34. M. Walterbusch, M. Gräuler and F. Teuteberg, "How trust is defined: A qualitative and quantitative analysis of scientific literature," in *20th Americas Conference on Information Systems, AMCIS*, 2014.

35. I.L.M., "Index of leadership trust," Institute of Leadership & Management, London, 2011.

36. I.L.M., "The truth about trust: Honesty and integrity at work," Institute of Leadership & Management, London, 2014.

3

Care

This chapter is about the first component of trust: care. It may not be quite what you expect because it is a great example of how thinking about your Leadership OS is different from thinking about your skills or how you should behave.

There is no shortage of stories of how great caring leaders act. One of the most inspiring is that of the explorer Ernest Shackleton. In the autumn of 1914, Shackleton set out with a team of 28 men on an epic expedition: to become the first to walk across the continent of Antarctica. One hundred years later, the story of what happened on that trip is lauded as one of the finest examples of leadership. Not because the group succeeded—because they never made it as far as Antarctica. Their ship became trapped in sea ice then sank, leaving Shackleton and his men stranded on the ice with just three small lifeboats, several tents and meagre supplies. The story is acclaimed because two years later, when Shackleton finally got back to land, every single one of his men was still alive.

What happened during those two years is a saga of surviving repeated disasters and resourcefully adapting to terrible conditions. He was not a perfect leader—historians have pointed to mistakes he made—but through it all, Shackleton held his men together, inspiring them to defy the odds while keeping spirits up and teamwork constant.

Reading his diaries, you can see a clear turning point that marks the moment he stepped into this role. At the beginning of the trip, he was impatient for progress, singularly focused on his mission. But when the group abandoned ship, something shifted in him. He lay aside all hope of reaching

© The Author(s) 2020
N. Kinley and S. Ben-Hur, *Leadership OS*,
https://doi.org/10.1007/978-3-030-27293-7_3

Antarctica and applied himself instead to getting his men back to civilisation, giving everything he had to the care of his men.

When his courage or confidence flagged, he made sure never to show it. He worked tirelessly to keep his men in the right mindset, maintaining routine and discipline, and creating opportunities for fun whenever he could. And when one of his team lost their gloves, he gave the man his own and suffered the resulting frostbite in brave silence. He improvised, used every resource at hand and, for two long years, never once took his eyes off his all-consuming goal of saving his men. And they knew it. They knew that he would give his all—give his life if need be—to save theirs.

It is an almost archetypal story. A perfect example of a leader who was able to inspire people by caring for them. As a result, it has been told to leaders across the globe as a way to help them think about how they, too, can care for their people.

Yet as inspirational as Shackleton's story might be, it is about as far removed as it could be from most modern-day leaders' challenge of caring. In fact, strange as it may sound, Shackleton had it easy. There was an undisturbed primal purity to his task. There was no paperwork, administrative process or politics to worry about. His men were all he had to focus on, and there was only one outcome metric that mattered: the number left alive.

For most leaders these days, however, life is not so straightforward. The objective is usually not simply to survive. The context is more complex, and making people feel cared for is more complicated. It can be hard to demonstrate genuine care through all the mechanics of deadlines, appraisals and succession planning. And even when you do manage to find a way to show that you care, you may not have the impact you expect—or hope for.

Consider this. Sitting on a train the other day, we overheard a woman complaining about her boss. She had just had her annual performance review meeting and was unhappy with how it had gone. The performance rating she received had been okay. And she thought her boss had been fair. It was just that she felt he was, well, too nice. 'It's awful. He's so fluffy. It's great he cares, but it's in the wrong way and it's too much. It's all "Let's reflect on this" and "How do you feel about that?" And when he gives you feedback, you can't believe it because it's all too positive. It's patronising, as if he is trying to parent me when all I want is an adult conversation about what I need to do. If he really cared, that's what he'd focus on. Not merely having a chat that leaves him feeling good about himself.'

It is a story we have heard many times: a disconnect between a well-meaning people-oriented manager and a task-focused employee. For all the manager's good intentions, there is a clash of styles that leaves at least one of them unhappy, and almost always it's the direct report. As we have seen before, just because you try to behave in a certain way does not mean that you will obtain a particular outcome.

This is why creating a caring Leadership OS is not about the degree to which *you* are caring and respectful, or whether *you* have emotional intelligence and empathy. It is about whether *other people* feel cared for and respected. It's about the actual impact you have.

Sometimes, how you act and your impact are mostly the same. In Shackleton's simple scenario it largely was. He cared, they were cared for and they survived. But today, they are often not the same, and ensuring someone feels cared for may not involve the sorts of things you might expect.

What Feeling Cared for Means

When looking at the research on what feeling cared for means, the first thing that stands out is just how little there is on the subject. There is no end of advice on how to *act caring*. Yet there are surprisingly few studies on what *feeling cared for* consists of and what it does to people. Fortunately, what does exist is clear. It shows that feeling cared for usually means one or both of two things: feeling supported and feeling respected.

Feeling Supported

Ask most people what feeling cared for is, and support will probably be at the top of the list. Often this is emotional support, such as feeling that your boss can empathise with you and understand how you feel. They may praise you, say they believe in you or express sympathy after something negative happens. Either way, you feel their emotional support, they are on the same side as you emotionally.

At other times, support can be more practical. Your boss might provide advice, give feedback or help you access resources you need. For many people, the idea of 'support' conjures up emotional aspects. But, interestingly, the research reveals that practical support tends to be more impactful than emotional support. And this seems to be true no matter where in the world you are.

There are three reasons for this. First, practical support is more likely to solve problems and move things forward than emotional support. Second, although practical help can be experienced as emotional support as well, the reverse is seldom true [1]. Finally, emotional support is a lot harder to get right. This is because—as we saw in the example of the employee on the train—what counts as emotional support varies more from person to person than what counts as practical support [2].

This variation in what emotional support means is perhaps most evident when considering the differences between people from different cultures and regions. For instance, a recent study in China described a case where a worker said they had the utmost respect for their boss because 'he does real things'. They told of how, when their mother fell ill, their boss told them to take care of her and reduced their workload by taking on part of their duties himself [3].

Another example comes from a senior executive we worked with in Saudi Arabia. When an employee's father fell ill, the executive went to the hospital to visit him, even though they had never met before. And later, when the father passed away, the leader drove for three hours to attend the funeral.

These are not the only two cultures in which the meaning of feeling cared for extends beyond how someone acts towards you personally. There are reports of it across the Asian and Arabian peninsulas and in parts of South America, too. Readers from these cultures probably see the examples above and think, 'Of course that's what a good leader should do'. Yet many Western readers probably think these leaders were overinvolved in their employees' lives and perhaps even not respecting their privacy enough.

This is not to say that emotional support is unimportant. On the contrary. For many people, it may be more important than practical support. But the practical side of support tends to have a bigger impact because it can also act as emotional support, and it tends to be easier to get right because it does not vary as much between people.

Feeling Respected

The second half of feeling cared for is about feeling respected [4]. Feeling that you, your expertise and your contribution are valued. It is partly to do with how you feel about yourself and your sense of self-worth. And it is partly to do with what you think others think of you—your reputation and credibility.

Again, there are cultural differences here that reveal how difficult it can be to get it right. Ask what 'feeling respected' is about in the West, and people will usually reply that it is having your opinion heard and valued, or something about the way others talk to you and treat you. For you as a leader, this means you sometimes have to be careful about how you phrase things to your direct reports. It is why you may have been told that when giving feedback, you should sandwich a negative message between two positive points. It is to protect your team members' sense of feeling respected.

In much of Asia, however, things are a little different. Feeling respected is all about having face. This is similar to the Western idea of respect, in that it is about people's reputation and feelings of prestige. But the amount of respect that people need to show is more closely tied to their position in the company hierarchy. So while showing kindness to subordinates is part of maintaining face, Asian leaders are also generally freer in how they can talk to their employees than people from Western cultures. This is simply because people at lower levels have 'less face' that needs protecting, and because speaking with authority is part of what being a senior-level leader with high levels of face is all about.

What Feeling Cared for Does

So, feeling cared for consists of feeling both supported and respected, and in today's increasingly global business world, it is harder to get this right. There are undoubtedly moral arguments for why leaders should nonetheless make an effort to do so and ensure their people feel supported and respected. But we want to focus on the practical arguments because when a Leadership OS—the environment that a leader creates for people to work in—leaves people feeling cared for, this has a positive effect on the way people work together (Fig. 3.1).

A. Increases Collaboration

The key thing a Leadership OS high in care does is to increase collaborative activity. It does this through a number of routes. It boosts employees' sense of commitment to their leader and colleagues [5], and thus makes them more likely to go along with their requests [6]. It helps create a sense of

Fig. 3.1 The functions of care in a Leadership OS

unity and common identity between team members, and so improves cooperation [7]. And it creates a more positive mood in the team [8], increasing helping behaviours [9] and reducing conflict [10].

B. Protects Against Stress and Pressure

The second, related, thing a Leadership OS high in care does is to act as a protective buffer for the team, keeping them functioning smoothly when things around them get rough. There are two reasons for this. First, because feeling cared for seems to limit the impact of stress [11]. And second, because it can be reciprocal, in that if I feel cared for by you, I am more likely to try caring for and supporting you, too. The combined effect, therefore, is that the team creates a protective, caring buffer around themselves against stress and pressure. The impact of this is that they are more able to bring their strengths to bear for more sustained periods of time.

C. Improves Debate and Discussion

The final thing a Leadership OS high in care does is to improve the level and quality of debate and discussion in the team. It does this is by making people more likely to be courteous and treat each other with respect. As a result, they are more likely to share information [12] and to listen to each other when they do [13]. It also means that when people disagree, they are less likely to take the disagreement personally.

Creating Care: Emperor Akihito of Japan

When he was a child, Tsugu Akihito was separated from his parents and raised by chamberlains and tutors. It was deemed appropriate for a direct descendant of the sun goddess Amaterasu (Fig. 3.2).

Akihito was the son of Hirohito, the god-like emperor who reigned over Japan during its nearly 15-year expansion across Asia in the 1930s and 1940s. Hirohito was the longest-reigning monarch in Japan's history and a distant figure to the Japanese public, neither seen nor heard. When he made a national radio broadcast to announce Japan's surrender on 15 August, it was the first time most Japanese people had heard his voice. In a second historic broadcast, made in January 1946, Hirohito renounced the traditional divine status of Japan's emperors. Akihito was 12.

Fig. 3.2 Emperor Akihito

Hirohito's reign lasted another 43 years. During this time, he tried to move the monarchy closer to the Japanese people, appearing in public more and even becoming the first Japanese monarch to go on an overseas trip. But although Hirohito was revered by many, he remained a generally distant leader, and it was Akihito who was to revolutionise the monarchy.

Even before he came to the throne, Akihito had a reputation for being different. In 1959 he had broken a 1500-year-old tradition by marrying a commoner. There were rumours that when the couple's children were born they had declined hired help—the traditional chamberlains—and had instead insisted on raising the children themselves. There were even rumours they made them pack their own school lunches.

When Akihito succeeded to the Chrysanthemum Throne upon his father's death in January 1989, it was an optimistic time for Japan. The country was rich, at the height of its post-war economic boom. Sony was about to buy Columbia Pictures, and Mitsubishi was on the verge of buying the Rockefeller Center in New York. The talk was of Japan as a new superpower.

But a year into Akihito's reign, disaster struck. An asset bubble burst and the Tokyo stock market collapsed, losing 35% of its value. The result was a prolonged period of economic stagnation. Indeed, 30 years on, Japanese stocks and land prices are still below 1990 levels.

Then, in January 1995, a 6.9-magnitude earthquake ripped through the city of Kobe, toppling buildings and starting fires that burned for days and turned the sky black. Around 6000 people died. In 2011, an even more devastating quake hit just off the north-east coast. At magnitude 9, it was the fourth largest earthquake ever recorded. It unleashed a giant tsunami that smashed into the coast of northern Japan, sweeping away whole towns and killing nearly 16,000 people.

At that point, Akihito did something no emperor had ever done before. He sat down in front of a TV camera and spoke directly to the Japanese people. He told them of his grief for those who had lost their lives and of his concern for the survivors. He told them that he cared.

Two weeks later, he and his wife—Empress Michiko—arrived at an evacuation centre in a stadium outside Tokyo. People were camped on the floor, with what little was left of their possessions piled around them. They had left almost everything behind, unsure of when—or even if—they would be able to return to their homes. When Akihito walked in, they were not quite sure what to expect. And what he did surprised everyone. Akihito, the direct descendant of the sun goddess Amaterasu and generations of emperors who had ruled over their people without ever being close to them, knelt on the ground in front of a family and quietly spoke with them. He asked them how they were, what had happened to them and their families, and whether they were being taken care of. He told them that everything possible would be done to help them. After a while, he stood up and went around each family in that building in turn, gently speaking with them. This was not a politician posing for photos, waving and leaving; this was someone quietly taking their time to speak with people and console them.

Japanese people had never seen an emperor behave like this before. It was unheard of. To conservatives, it was a shock and some even disapproved. But for many more Japanese people, it was a deeply moving act of empathy that cemented a special relationship between him and the people that has persisted.

Akihito does not look like a revolutionary. He is small and softly spoken. But throughout his three-decade rule, he rejected his father's reclusive and ceremonial style of rule to become a much more present and active monarch. Most famously, he engaged in multiple overseas visits to countries like South Korea and China, apologising for Japan's behaviour in the war, and again earning the ire of conservative critics.

More recently, Akihito publicly—if politely—rebuked Japanese Prime Minister Shinzo Abe. In 2015, on the 70th anniversary of the end of World War II, Mr Abe gave a speech in which he said that the peace and prosperity that Japan enjoyed then was due to the sacrifice of the three million Japanese who died during the war. The next day, Akihito made a speech saying the prosperity was due to the hard work and sacrifice of the Japanese people after the war.

In 2017, Akihito broke with precedent and announced he would abdicate in 2019, becoming the first Japanese emperor in two hundred years to do so, thus ending his reign in much the same way he had spent it. He will be remembered for connecting with his public in a way that no other Japanese monarch before him ever did. His TV speech and visit to the refugee centre in 2011 may have changed nothing on a practical level, but to the Japanese populace they made a world of difference.

In taking his time with people and kneeling with them, he didn't just express concern, he made people feel cared for. It was not a grand gesture, but a simple act. But then that's the point about making people feel cared for. It is usually rooted in the simple things.

The Neuroscience of How Care Works

The effects of feeling cared for are rooted in the neuroscience of the body's biological trust system. When people feel cared for, it activates their X-system. The social parts of the brain are engaged, so they both pay more attention to social events—becoming more empathetic—and respond more positively to them [14]. Oxytocin levels are boosted, buffering the impact of stress and anxiety (both of which decrease oxytocin levels) [15]. This has a positive effect on a range of thinking and decision-making skills. It increases the attention people pay to positive options, decreases the attention they pay to negative options, and makes it more likely that they will positively inter-pret ambiguous options [16]. In other words, it makes them more positive and optimistic.

Moreover, recently, neuroscience has revealed why it is so important for leaders to actively and consciously focus on making people feel cared for, rather than leaving it to natural skill and chance.

In 2016, a team of researchers from leading neuroscience institutions, including Harvard and Stanford universities, discovered that when people become leaders, something inside them changes. They found that in both men and women, ascending to a leadership position causes levels of a chemical called testosterone to rise [17].

Importantly, this was not some laboratory study. These were real executives in real jobs receiving real promotions. And the bigger the promotion they received—as measured by the number of reports in their team—the higher their level of testosterone.

This was an incredible finding because testosterone inhibits the brain's ability to produce oxytocin, making people less generous, less trusting and less empathic. This means that one of the side effects of being promoted into a leadership role is that—on a biological level—it makes you less able to gauge the feelings of your people accurately.

This makes your task of ensuring that your team feel cared for all the harder because you have a built-in blind spot for how they are feeling. Fortunately, the extra effort is worth it.

The Benefits of Feeling Cared For

The impact of creating a Leadership OS high in care is well recorded. One of our favourite studies was undertaken at the International Islamic University in Islamabad, Pakistan [18]. Participants were asked to enter data into a computer in return for a stated wage and split into different groups. One group was paid the wage and nothing more. A second group was told just before the work began that they would be paid 17% more than advertised. And a third group received the wage plus a letter simply stating that the experimenters cared about the participants. Compared with the wage-only group, the people who were awarded the unexpected raise were 21% more productive. Which sounds good. Except the group where participants received the basic wage plus a simple message saying they were cared for was 23% more productive.

This wasn't a one-off laboratory result, either. Research from across industries and cultures shows that organisations that promote caring create more value [19]. When they feel cared for, employees show more commitment, higher levels of performance, and greater productivity [20, 21]. They demonstrate better levels of teamwork [22]. They work harder, with greater conscientiousness [23] and can manage higher levels of workload [24]. They are less stressed [25], report higher levels of job satisfaction [26] and have lower levels of absenteeism [21] and turnover [27]. And they show higher levels of initiative [28], innovation [29] and entrepreneurialism [30].

So care might sound soft and fluffy, but it isn't. A little care can go a long way.

It Has to Be You

There is one other critical thing that the research has revealed: it *has* to be you as the leader who does this. Feeling cared for by colleagues is important and can have a positive effect. But the impact is nothing like as strong as the effect of feeling cared for by your boss [31]. You matter like no one else and, as a result, this is one task you cannot delegate.

The more senior you become, the more important this is because research shows that the effects of feeling cared for trickle down through layers of management [32]. If your direct reports feel cared for, it is more likely they will act in a way to ensure that their people feel cared for, as well, and so on.

Unfortunately, there is also evidence that the task is getting harder in modern organisations. As teams become more dispersed, employees are reporting lower levels of support [33]. And as teams become more diverse, it is becoming harder for leaders to know what they need to do to ensure people feel cared for.

Luckily, there are things you can do.

Installing Care in Your OS

We began this chapter by saying that care is a great example of how building a Leadership OS is different from thinking about how you behave or the competencies you need to have. This is because the aim is not for you to behave in a certain way, but for you to have a certain impact and create a certain type of OS. The focus is not on you and what you need to do, but on other people and what they need to feel.

Obviously, what you do is important—it is how a Leadership OS is created. And if you want to build a caring OS, it helps to have a few techniques. So we are going to present four basic devices, or techniques, you can use to build a sense of being cared for in your people (Fig. 3.3). It is not a prescriptive list. Since the impact of how you behave changes from person to person and situation to situation, the techniques are more like menu options than a strict schedule of things you must do. And while none of them is

Fig. 3.3 Four techniques to increase care

likely to be new or revelatory to you, they are all things that, in our experience, leaders often do not do as much as they should.

Indeed, our research with thousands of leaders worldwide shows that around *70% of leaders overestimate the degree to which their direct reports feel cared for.* Yet it is clearly something worth investing in. Because our research also showed that *the direct reports of high-performing leaders rate themselves as nearly 20% more cared for* than the direct reports of low performing leaders. So, ensuring people feel cared for is something that leaders who are rated as high performing do more of.

To decide which techniques to use, you need to approach the list with two things in mind. First, you need to be purpose ful and systematic. Creating a sense of being cared for is harder than it might sound and definitely not as easy as just trying to appear caring. So you need to put time aside to think about this and make a deliberate effort to do it. Otherwise, the time pressures of day-to-day activity will take over and the building of care will be left to chance.

Second, as we said in the previous chapter, you need to know your people. Before you act, think about the story of the employee on the train. Think about whether your people have the same style and needs as you do. Think about their cultural background, their confidence levels and the degree to which they appear to need to feel cared for.

As an example of why this is important, imagine for a second the difference between how a trading manager might go about making sure people feel cared for and how a school principal might. You would expect greater emphasis on practical support with the traders and a more aggressive feedback culture. With teachers, by contrast, you might expect emotional support to play a bigger role, and it is likely that any feedback given would be less direct. So, which of the techniques below is the right one will depend on the individuals you are dealing with and the situation. But if you put time aside to think about this and you know your people, you will know what to do.

Systematically Show Interest

The first technique is a classic example of something we all know we should do, but probably do not do as much we should. Showing interest in people and their lives helps them feel cared for. A recent Google study showed that when leaders regularly express an interest in team members, performance levels go up [34]. And although it sounds like an obvious thing to do, research suggests that at least half of leaders are not naturals at it because they are more task-focused than relationship-focused. They naturally gravitate towards task-related issues, and under time pressure or stress, they do so even more. As a result, they don't show interest in others as much as they should.

This is why it is important not only to take an interest in your people and their lives but also to show it systematically. By far the easiest way to do this is always to spend the first five minutes of any one-on-one meeting with your direct reports asking them about their lives. With people you think will respond well to this, ask a few questions, and with those more like our example employee on the train, maybe restrict it to one. If you know they have kids, ask them how their kids are doing. If you know they are having work done on their house, ask them how it's going. Or if you know they commute, ask them how their commute is. What you ask does not matter as much as you might think. The important thing is to ask something, and in doing so, show an interest.

One last thing: no matter what you ask, make sure you understand how your people feel about it. Having a conversation in which they tell you they are having a new heating system installed at their house is one thing. Having a conversation in which they tell you how disruptful it is and the stress it causes at home is quite another. The objective is not just some tickbox, reflex, bland, 'How was your weekend?' sort of conversation in which you don't really care about the answer. The goal is to be curious and expand what you know about your people—to make sure that they feel that you care about what they say.

Offer Career Management

The second thing you can do is invest time in your people's careers. Studies show that when leaders demonstrate an interest in employees' career development, people's perceptions of being cared for increases [35]. This is not about creating a list of training programmes they can attend, but setting aside regular time with them to help them develop. The sorts of things you can do include regularly reviewing development plans, setting 90-day learning goals or requiring your team to tell you about an interesting article they have read each month. The objective is to make learning a norm within your team, an expectation that you have of everybody. It will signal to everyone that you care and help people perform better.

Give Praise, Respect and Feedback

The third technique you have at your disposal is to give praise, respect and feedback. The emphasis here is on doing all three. There is plenty of research showing that praise helps boost trust. You do not want to overdo it because otherwise it can become meaningless. But studies suggest that most leaders overestimate the amount of praise they give. So it is worth questioning yourself on how praising or critical you really are and then looking for opportunities to increase the amount of appreciation you show. For example, how often do you say thank you to your direct reports? The point here is not whether *you* think you say it enough, but whether *they* think you do.

Every time you offer praise, you also offer respect. But respect is sometimes worth handing out on its own, too. Adding some simple language to the way you talk to your direct reports can help here, for example, 'I respect the way you did that.' Even something as basic as that can go a long way.

Less advertised is the importance of feedback. We may not immediately equate constructive criticism with feeling cared for, but studies show that it can be especially important to more experienced and task-focused workers. Since these groups are aware that things are rarely perfect, merely relying on praise risks coming across as undiscerning or insincere. And, remember, whether you are focusing on praise or feedback, the science shows that you will be more effective if you praise in public and give feedback in private.

Make People Feel Heard

The final thing you can do is to make sure that your people feel heard and understood. Some of this is simple stuff, like not interrupting them or not looking at your phone when they are speaking, both of which signal that you are focused on something other than them and what they want to say.

Yet the task is not as easy as this may make it sound. Every time you talk with a direct report, both your and their biological trust system kicks in. As a result, they will detect and respond to social cues that you make before you are even aware that you have behaved in a certain way. It could be the way that you sit, your tone of voice or the degree of eye contact you make. Every slightest movement you make is judged.

Obviously, it is not possible to control every aspect of your behaviour. But what you can do is to make sure that after the trust systems have done their work, you take extra steps to reassure your people that you understand them. Reflect what they have just said back to them to show that you have heard and understood. Ask questions to clarify. And in all of this, push yourself to ensure that you understand their perspective. Why they want the things they do, think the things they do and feel the way they do.

The Importance of Sincerity

Creating a Leadership OS in which people feel cared for is a foundation, a basic, an essential. Without it, not much else is possible, at least, not sustainably. If people do not feel cared for, then sooner or later they will withdraw, first in terms of effort and then, eventually, physically too.

We sometimes feel a little self-conscious telling leaders they need to do this. After all, it is obvious. But as the business world becomes less stable and more diverse, it is something that is also becoming more complex and harder to do. And it is something that the majority of leaders overestimate their ability to do.

The only way to address this is deliberately, consciously and systematically, to ensure that you are doing what you need to do in order to create a Leadership OS high in care. Yet there is a hidden challenge here, because how do you, as a leader, balance doing things systematically with also being sincere? How do you create little routines and processes you can follow to ensure that you invest in making people feel cared for, and yet at the same time make it appear something natural and sincere to your followers? For most leaders, *that* is the real challenge of making people feel cared for.

We will see more of this challenge as we dig deeper into what trust means and how to create it. As we progress, we will offer some solutions, beginning in the next chapter, as we turn to look at one of the most pivotal and complex aspects of trust: psychological safety.

Summary + Checklist

See Table 3.1.

Table 3.1 Summary of care

	OS function	Techniques to build it
Care	• Increases collaboration • Protects against stress and pressure • Improves debate and discussion	• Systematically show interest • Offer career management • Give praise, respect and feedback • Make people feel heard

Table 3.2 Have you installed care in your Leadership OS?

	✓	✗
Do people feel that their skills and abilities are respected by you?	☐	☐
Would everyone in your team say that you reliably give them recognition or praise for doing good work?	☐	☐
Do people believe that you feel a sense of responsibility for their well-being?	☐	☐
Do people feel that you take an interest in their lives?	☐	☐
Do people believe that you invest in their development and will help them progress their career?	☐	☐

Checklist

To help you think about whether you have successfully installed care in your Leadership OS, ask yourself how the people around you—your direct reports, peers and stakeholders—would respond to the following questions (Table 3.2).

References

1. N. Semmer, A. Elfering, N. Jacobshagen, T. Perrot, T. Beehr and N. Boos, "The emotional meaning of instrumental social support," *International Journal of Stress Management*, vol. 15, no. 3, pp. 235–251, 2008.
2. C. Tardy, "Counteracting task-induced stress: Studies of instrumental and emotional support in problem-solving contexts," in B. R. Burleson, T. L. Albrecht and I. G. Sarason (Eds.), *Communication of social support: Messages, interactions, relationships, and community*, Thousand Oaks, CA, Sage, 1994, pp. 71–87.
3. P. Fu, "Chinese leadership and culture," in R. J. House and J. Chhokar (Eds.), *Cultures of the world, A GLOBE anthology of in-depth descriptions of the cultures of 14 countries*, New York, NY, Lawrence Erlbaum Associates, 2008, pp. 877–908.
4. G. Greguras and J. Ford, "An examination of the multidimensionality of supervisor and subordinate perceptions of leader–member exchange," *Journal of Occupational and Organizational Psychology*, vol. 79, pp. 433–465, 2006.

5. F. Stinglhamber and C. Vandenberghe, "Organizations and supervisors as sources of support and targets of commitment: A longitudinal study," *Journal of Organizational Behavior*, vol. 24, no. 3, pp. 251–270, 2003.

6. N. Arshadi, "The relationships of perceived organizational support (POS) with organizational commitment, in-role performance, and turnover intention: Mediating role of felt obligation," *Procedia-Social and Behavioral Sciences*, vol. 30, pp. 1103–1108, 2011.

7. R. Eisenberger and F. Stinglhamber, *Perceived organizational support: Fostering enthusiastic and productive employees*, Washington, DC: American Psychological Association, 2011.

8. N. Madjar, G. Oldham and M. Pratt, "There's no place like home? The contributions of work and nonwork creativity support to employees' creative performance," *Academy of Management Journal*, vol. 45, no. 4, pp. 757–767, 2002.

9. N. Telle and H. Pfister, "Positive empathy and prosocial behavior: A neglected link," *Emotion Review*, vol. 8, no. 2, pp. 154–163, 2016.

10. C. Sulea, D. Virga, L. Maricutoiu, W. Schaufeli, C. Zaborila Dumitru and F. Sava, "Work engagement as mediator between job characteristics and positive and negative extra-role behaviors," *Career Development International*, vol. 17, pp. 188–207, 2012.

11. J. Xu and H. Cooper-Thomas, "How can leaders achieve high employee engagement?," *Leadership and Organization Development Journal*, vol. 32, no. 4, pp. 399–416, 2011.

12. M. Sharifirad, "Can incivility impair team's creative performance through paralyzing employee's knowledge sharing? A multi-level approach," *Leadership & Organization Development Journal*, vol. 37, no. 2, pp. 200–225, 2016.

13. J. Decety and C. Lamm, "Human empathy through the lens of social neuroscience," *The Scientific World Journal*, vol. 6, pp. 1146–1163, 2006.

14. J. Decety, "The neural pathways, development and functions of empathy," *Current Opinion in Behavioral Sciences*, vol. 3, pp. 1–6, 2015.

15. M. Heinrichs, T. Baumgartner, C. Kirschbaum and U. Ehlert, "Social support and oxytocin interact to suppress cortisol and subjective responses to psychosocial stress," *Biological Psychiatry*, vol. 54, no. 12, pp. 1389–1398, 2003.

16. C. Hartley and E. Phelps, "Anxiety and decision-making," *Biological Psychiatry*, vol. 72, no. 2, pp. 113–118, 2012.

17. G. Sherman, J. Lerner, R. Josephs, J. Renshon and J. Gross, "The interaction of testosterone and cortisol is associated with attained status in male executives," *Journal of Personality and Social Psychology*, vol. 110, no. 6, pp. 921–929, 2016.

18. P. Zak, "The Neuroscience of Trust," *Harvard Business Review*, January–February, pp. 84–90, 2017.

19. D. Bhanthumnavin, "Perceived social support from supervisor and group members' psychological and situational characteristics as predictors of subordinate performance in Thai work units," *Human Resource Development Quarterly*, vol. 14, no. 1, pp. 79–97, 2003.

20. J. Harter, F. Schmidt and C. Keyes, "Well-being in the workplace and its relationship to business outcomes," in C. L. Keyes and J. Haidt (Eds.), *Flourishing: The positive person and the good life as well as well-being in the workplace and its relationship to business outcomes: A review of the gallup studies*, Washington, DC, American Psychological Association, 2003, pp. 205–224.

21. A. Pazy and Y. Ganzach, "Pay contingency and the effects of perceived organizational and supervisor support on performance and commitment," *Journal of Management*, vol. 35, no. 4, pp. 1007–1025, 2009.

22. M. Griffin, M. Patterson and M. West, "Job satisfaction and teamwork: The role of supervisor support," *Journal of Organisational Behaviour*, vol. 22, pp. 537–550, 2001.

23. R. Eisenberger, P. Fasolo and V. Davis-LaMastro, "Perceived organizational support and employee diligence, commitment, and innovation," *Journal of Applied Psychology*, vol. 75, no. 1, p. 51, 1990.

24. S. Kirmeyer and T. Dougherty, "Work load, tension, and coping: Moderating effects of supervisor support," *Personnel Psychology*, vol. 41, pp. 125–139, 1988.

25. G. Prati and L. Pietrantoni, "The relation of perceived and received social support to mental health among first responders: A meta-analytic review," *Journal of Community Psychology*, vol. 38, no. 3, pp. 403–417, 2010.

26. P. Brough and J. Pears, "Evaluating the influence of the type of social support on job satisfaction and work related psychological well-being," *International Journal of Organisational Behaviour*, vol. 8, no. 2, pp. 472–485, 2004.

27. R. Eisenberger, F. Stinglhamber, C. Vandenberghe, I. Sucharski and L. Rhoades, "Perceived supervisor support: Contributions to perceived organizational support and employee retention," *Journal of Applied Psychology*, vol. 87, no. 3, pp. 565–573, 2002.

28. I. Onyishi and E. Ogbodo, "The contributions of self-efficacy and perceived organisational support when taking charge at work," *SA Journal of Industrial Psychology*, vol. 38, no. 1, pp. 1–11, 2012.

29. H. Vinarski-Peretz and A. Carmeli, "Linking care felt to engagement in innovative behaviors in the workplace: The mediating role of psychological conditions," *Psychology of Aesthetics, Creativity, and the Arts*, vol. 5, no. 1, p. 43, 2011.

30. L. Zampetakis, P. Beldekos and V. Moustakis, "'Day-to-day' entrepreneurship within organisations: The role of trait emotional intelligence and perceived organisational support," *European Management Journal*, vol. 27, no. 3, pp. 165–175, 2009.

31. T. Ng and K. Sorensen, "Toward a further understanding of the relationships between perceptions of support and work attitudes: A meta-analysis," *Group & Organization Management*, vol. 33, no. 3, pp. 243–268, 2008.

32. L. Shanock and R. Eisenberger, "When supervisors feel supported: Relationships with subordinates' perceived supervisor support, perceived organizational support, and performance," *Journal of Applied Psychology*, vol. 91, no. 3, p. 689, 2006.

33. C. O'Donnell, H. Jabareen and G. Watt, "Practice nurses' workload, career intentions and the impact of professional isolation: A cross-sectional survey," *BMC Nursing*, vol. 9, no. 2, 2010.
34. C. Duhigg, "What Google learned from its quest to build the perfect team," *The New York Times*, 25 February 2016.
35. K. Illes and M. Mathews, *Leadership, trust and communication: Building trust in companies through effective leadership communication*, London, UK: Westminster Business School, 2015.

4

Psychological Safety

On 10 May 1996, tragedy unfolded on the slopes of Mount Everest. A group of 23 people, led by two of the world's most skilled and experienced high-altitude climbers, were overcome by a storm as they tried to descend the mountain. The two leaders and three other members of the expedition died. The rest barely made it back.

Investigations of the incident focused on the behaviour and decision-making of the two experienced climbers, Rob Hall and Scott Fischer. Both had impressive reputations, both had been to the summit before, and Hall had guided 39 climbers to the top in the previous 6 years. The expedition was well organised and well resourced; it followed a well-known and well-trodden route. Any journey to Everest has its dangers, however, and what matters then is how people respond. And it is here that things went wrong [1].

Interviews with survivors revealed two critical points of failure in Hall and Fischer's decision-making as the storm approached. The first was over-confidence and a consequent downplaying of the risks. The second was the most damaging, however. First-hand accounts reveal that the team did not discuss the problems facing them openly, and group members did not feel comfortable expressing concerns or dissenting views. Neal Beidleman, a more junior but still experienced guide on the tour, stated afterwards that he had had serious reservations about some of the decisions made. He did not express them, though, as he was conscious of his 'place in the pecking order'. This had been reinforced by a speech Rob Hall gave at the start of the expedition, in which he said he would tolerate no dissension and emphasised

© The Author(s) 2020
N. Kinley and S. Ben-Hur, *Leadership OS*,
https://doi.org/10.1007/978-3-030-27293-7_4

how his word would be absolute law. As one of the other survivors noted afterwards, passivity on the part of the group had been encouraged and reinforced right from the beginning.

The consequence of all this was an absence of what psychologists call *psychological safety*. People did not feel free to speak up, and so doubts were not raised, problems were downplayed and concerns were kept quiet. The result was a tragedy. And although your day-to-day life at work may be a world away from the slopes of Mount Everest, the importance of creating psychological safety for your people is no less vital. Because make no mistake: if you do not have a Leadership OS high in psychological safety, then sooner or later, something bad will happen. It is just a matter of time.

What Psychological Safety Is

Psychological safety was first studied by researchers in the 1960s. It drifted out of focus for a few decades, before interest in it re-emerged in the 1990s. Today, it is one of the most studied aspects of leadership.

It is defined as people's perception of the consequences of taking interpersonal risks in a particular group or situation [2]. In other words, what people think will happen if they do things like speak up, voice opinions and question others' thinking. Just as with care—the first component of trust—what matters is not what would really happen, but what people *believe or feel* is the case. If they think it is safe, they are more likely to communicate openly, seek out and give honest feedback, collaborate, take risks and show initiative—all critical elements of high-performing organisations. If they do not think it's safe, they are less likely to do these things.

Shortly after the financial crisis of 2008, we published research showing how decision-making and risk-taking could have a catastrophic impact if not done right. We showed how executives and board members of the financial institutions at the centre of the crisis talked afterwards of how they did not speak up in meetings, did not raise concerns and did not present contradictory data because of fears of how it would be perceived. Psychological safety—or the lack of it—was at the centre of a financial catastrophe that echoed through global economies for a decade [3].

It has long been known that because of fear of either being viewed negatively or of damaging relationships, people are often reluctant to tell bad news at work. The psychological safety research has added to this, noting that people stop communicating *good* ideas and news as well [4].

Studies have also highlighted how psychological safety is nearly invisible. After all, how do you know if someone does not speak up? If they hold something back? It is almost impossible to know. This means that if your Leadership OS is high in psychological safety, it can be a powerful source of competitive advantage: those that do not have it, usually do not know it, and so cannot do anything about it. They just miss out on all its benefits.

What Psychological Safety Does

The effect of having a Leadership OS high in psychological safety can be dramatic, since it extends into almost every aspect of how your team functions. It affects your capacity to get the best from your people; impacts your ability to ensure that work streams run smoothly; and sets the tone for how people interact with each other. And it does all this through three key functions it performs in your Leadership OS—three key effects it has on how people work together (Fig. 4.1).

A. Enables Employee Voice

Possibly the most crucial thing psychological safety does is to allow information to flow freely. Like the oil in your car engine, it acts as a kind of lubricant, making it easier for information, opinions and know-how to move through your team. It does this by enabling what is known as *employee voice*—people's willingness to say things. This can range from stating concerns or challenging viewpoints to sharing knowledge or offering ideas on how to improve processes, services and products [5]. When people feel safe, things get said and so information flows. Decisions are generally better when based on a full spread of facts. Risks are more effectively managed when concerns are more readily raised. And creativity and innovation flourish when more ideas are exchanged.

Fig. 4.1 The functions of psychological safety in a Leadership OS

B. Makes Conflict Useful

Inevitably, when opinions are expressed, sooner or later there is disagreement. When this happens, one of two things tends to occur. Either the debate takes on a sharper, sometimes more personal or defensive edge, which hinders people's ability to appreciate each other's viewpoints and collaborate. Or the disagreement remains focused on the task or issue at hand. People do not take things personally, do not become defensive and so continue to work effectively together.

We see these two paths in the research about what happens when there is task conflict—disagreement over a work issue. If psychological safety is high, then creativity and performance increases follow. If psychological safety is low, however, disagreement tends to lead to decreases in creativity and performance [6, 7]. So psychological safety is what enables disagreement and conflict to become something positive and useful.

C. Turns Diversity into Performance

The final thing psychological safety does come as a result of the previous two effects. It enables diverse people and expertise to come together and become something more than just the sum of their individual parts.

If people have a voice and engage in more open, less defensive conversations, this allows people from diverse backgrounds both to make their expertise heard and—critically—to combine these different contributions, to find points of agreement and create common ways forward. There is lots of talk in the media about how diversity is great for performance. Yet there is a caveat that is rarely mentioned: diversity only leads to higher performance when psychological safety is high [8].

Reaping the Benefits

The list of benefits that these three effects of psychological safety have on the Leadership OS is much-studied and long. Psychological safety leads to better decision-making by protecting against biases and mistakes. It leads to higher levels of creative problem solving [9], process improvement [10] and innovation [11]. And it leads to greater levels of effort [12], initiative [13] and engagement [14]. Teams are better able to adapt to change successfully [15]. They are more likely to raise disagreement and give candid feedback

[15] and, as a result, are more able to learn from failure and mistakes [16]. They are also more likely to report errors and so maintain a stronger quality control, error management and safety culture [17, 18]. And in Leadership OSs where psychological capital is high, there are also higher levels of ethical behaviour [19], lower levels of workplace bullying [14] and so better levels of talent retention [20].

Little wonder, then, that psychological safety has been shown to improve both productivity levels [12] and firm performance measures such as return on assets [21]. In fact, a recent long-term study by Google's People Analytics Unit identified psychological safety as *the* number one characteristic of successful high-performing teams [22]. And to round it off, these effects appear to be just as true in both public and private sector organisations, and all over the world [21, 23, 24].

When Psychological Safety Goes Missing: The Case of Jürgen Schrempp and DaimlerChrysler

In November 1998, Chrysler and Daimler-Benz merged in what was then the largest corporate merger in history—worth $36 billion. The combined company, DaimlerChrysler, became the fifth largest automobile company in the world (Fig. 4.2).

Chrysler, the American company led by CEO Bob Eaton, had enjoyed outstanding performance during the 1990s. It was an innovative renegade in terms of both products and processes. It essentially eliminated corporate hierarchy and had a true matrix structure using 'platform teams', which were autonomous businesses with representatives from all functional areas working on a single project. Employees wore jeans, travelled in economy class, and called each other by their first name.

The German company Daimler-Benz, led by CEO Jürgen Schrempp, was just the opposite. Its reputation was built on luxury and quality. It had a traditional hierarchical business structure, with multiple business units and rigid reporting responsibilities. Employees wore suits and ties, travelled in business class, and never called anyone by just their first name.

Until 1995, the financial performance of the two companies was as different as their cultures. While Chrysler was thriving, Daimler-Benz was struggling. The company had made a number of diversifying acquisitions in the 1980s and 1990s and had become inefficient and unfocused.

Then, in May 1995, Jürgen Schrempp was appointed CEO and immediately began making the company his. Focusing on value creation, he

Fig. 4.2 Jürgen Schrempp

eliminated projects that did not create a 12% return on capital. The number of business units decreased from 35 to 23. He even took on the labour unions—and won, leading to a 10% cut in headcount.

Schrempp's focus on shareholder value was very un-German; typically, all stakeholders in the country were viewed as integral to a company's success. He would regularly quiz colleagues on what Daimler's current stock price was; if they didn't know, he would make a note of it. Initially, his approach produced results. By 1997, Schrempp had turned the company around, with Daimler-Benz posting record levels of revenue and profits.

The company's success in 1997 led to more challenging goals for 1998—larger scale, greater efficiency and bigger profits. This is where the merger with Chrysler comes in. It was promoted as 'a merger of equals made in heaven.' Structurally, though, this wasn't quite the case. Daimler-Benz owned 57% of the new company and Chrysler owned 43%; 10 of the 18 management board positions were held by Daimler executives. Upon consummation of the merger, Schrempp and Eaton were appointed as co-CEOs, with the expectation that they would share the role for at least three years. Eaton, however, became a lame duck when he announced his retirement shortly after the merger, and he left the company in March 2000, leaving Schrempp in charge.

With Eaton's departure, any pretence of a merger of equals fell apart, as Schrempp started to impose his and Daimler's way of doing things across the whole company. Whereas Chrysler used one design platform for multiple vehicles, Daimler had a unique platform for each model. Believing Daimler's model to be best, Schrempp moved to convert the Chrysler lines to the Daimler way. And he did not understand Chrysler's matrix structure, so made changes to try to dismantle it. Tellingly, despite providing half of the company's revenue, Chrysler became a business unit inside DaimlerChrysler within only 18 months of the merger.

Through all of this Schrempp maintained a hierarchical style. Described as charismatic by some, he was perceived as impatient and unwilling to hear debate by others. It was 'his way or the highway'. And when things weren't going well, he was quick to pull the trigger and replace those he saw as responsible. As a result, a culture of fear soon emerged.

Before the merger, Schrempp had spoken of his and Daimler's desire to learn from Chrysler and take the best of both companies. But it quickly became apparent that he had little interest in learning anything from them. Within a year of the merger, the integration team contained only Daimler staff. And with his exclusive focus on financial performance, Schrempp took little notice of cultural integration. Rather than taking the best of both companies' cultures, he tried to impose Daimler's values and way of working on Chrysler. And it was here that things started breaking down.

Unhappy with his approach, senior Chrysler executives started leaving. Hamstrung by attrition, a loss of morale and Schrempp's imposed operating models, Chrysler experienced a dip in business performance. Schrempp's response only served to make things worse, as he fired key members of Chrysler's executive team, stripping the business further of leadership experience. He also began cutting costs, but cut hard and deep, negatively impacting quality and thereby hurting sales further. By the fourth quarter of 2000, the heady profits of 1998 and 1999 had evaporated into a $1.2 billion loss.

Chrysler's losses damaged Schrempp's status with his board and shareholders and, eventually, they lost patience. In late 2005 the board sacked Schrempp. The share price rose in the following days, but the damage had been done. In the three years following the merger, the combined company had lost more than 50% of its stock price. And when Daimler sold the Chrysler business to a private equity group in 2007, it was for a fraction of the price it had effectively paid for it less than 10 years earlier.

There were many causes of the merger's failure, but Schrempp's leadership style, and the culture of fear and discontent that developed around him, was certainly one of them. He did not appreciate the importance of cultural integration. He did not manage to get the best out of his people and retain key talent. And he did not listen to others' views and advice enough.

Throughout his career, Schrempp earned the nickname 'The Rambo of Europe' for his willingness to fire employees and cut business units. And he was proud of it, he liked being called 'Rambo'. But part of this reputation was his willingness to *uber leichen gehen*—to walk over people to achieve any goal. And unfortunately, many of his 420,000 employees ended up fearing that was exactly what he would do to them. As a result, psychological safety was conspicuously absent.

The Fight-or-Flight Response

Like care, psychological safety is rooted in our biological trust system. In fact, it is based in some of our most primitive neurological pathways—the parts of our brains dedicated to keeping us alert to physical dangers. In pre-historic days, these kept us alive by keeping us out of reach of hungry carnivores. If we saw danger, our bodies would instantly respond, providing us with the energy needed for sudden activity. Hence the well-known name of these neural pathways—the fight-or-flight response.

These days, there are fewer hungry carnivores to prey on you. But the neural pathways are still active, warning of all sorts of potential dangers. At work, this could be potential arguments, disapproval from your boss or even your colleagues thinking poorly of you. Precisely what triggers your pathways depends on things such as how generally anxious you are and your personal experiences. For example, if you have had two or three toxic bosses in the past, you are likely to be highly alert to the next one and may have accumulated frustration and defensiveness.

So, we all have triggers, waiting to set off the fight-or-flight response at the slightest hint of danger. And because this primal response uses many of the same parts of the brain as the trust system, when our fight-or-flight response is triggered, so is our trust system.

The result is that, under threat, we become more trusting of those we see as friendly, and less trusting of those we see as unfriendly, unknown or just different to us and not part of our group. And as we have seen before, this can happen in the blink of an eye and without us even knowing. How we perceive the world and respond to it can change without us even being aware.

Intriguingly, as scientists learn more about how the brain works, there is growing evidence that this connection between the fight-or-flight response and the trust system may be stronger in women than in men. Women's fight-or-flight response may be more likely to be set off by social triggers [25], and when the response is set off, it may be more likely that the trust system is also activated [26]. One consequence of this is that when managing women, you may need to work harder to establish psychological safety.

Woman or man, though, the connection between the fight-or-flight response and the trust system is there. Under threat, we become more cautious, more risk-averse and more defensive. Our ability to empathise with and understand others drops, and we become less objective and calm in how we manage conflict. We become less trusting.

Your Role in Creating Psychological Safety

This neurological link to the fight-or-flight response is why your role as a leader in creating psychological safety is very different than your role in instilling a sense of care.

Care is all about making people feel something positive—cared for. With psychological safety, however, it is not so much about keeping people feeling positive and safe as about making sure they do not feel unsafe—making sure their flight-or-flight response is not activated. Indeed, in this sense, creating a Leadership OS high in psychological safety is like a war on anxiety.

You are absolutely critical in this, too. Broader organisational culture can, of course, affect how safe people feel, as can differences in how anxious individuals are. But studies show that it is the impact of a person's leader that has the greatest effect on their feelings of safety [27]. This puts you in a powerful position. It means that the way you act is the most important determinant of whether one of leadership's most critical components is formed or not.

Fortunately, a number of techniques have been demonstrated to enhance the level of psychological safety in your Leadership OS (Fig. 4.3). As before, this is not a prescriptive list for you to follow slavishly. It is a menu of options that you can pick and choose from, depending on your situation and personal style.

Fig. 4.3 Three techniques to increase psychological safety

Reduce Sensitivity to Triggers

The first thing you can do is to target some of the factors that can cause people's fight-or-flight response to become more sensitive. These are contextual factors—sometimes physical, sometimes psychological—that make it more likely that the fight-or-flight system will be triggered. Studies show that it pays to be aware of three such contextual factors in particular.

Pressure and Stress

The first sensitising factor is time pressure, workload and other similar sources of stress [28]. If people start a conversation when they are feeling under pressure and stressed, their nervous system is already half activated, so they are naturally more sensitive to potential triggers. In today's business world, there is only so much you can do about such stressors. But you can try to create some space away from them, where it is easier for psychological safety to flourish. For example, a regular face-to-face meeting, with time for a general chat as part of the agenda, or some relaxants at team meetings, such as a pleasant environment with warm décor and comfortable chairs. Anything that signals to people that they are among friends can help in this respect.

Hierarchy

The second sensitising factor is hierarchy [29]. If you work in a business or national culture in which there is a strong sense of hierarchy and respect for authority, people tend to be more wary of upsetting senior leaders. The structure of hierarchy can make people who are used to it feel more psychologically safe. But it can also make them more sensitive to breaking the 'rules' of this hierarchy, by speaking up, for example, or questioning the views of more senior leaders.

To reduce these negative aspects of hierarchy on people's sensitivity, you need to go out of your way to invite people to contribute, show that you value their input and reward those who cut across the hierarchy with clear opinions [21]. In fact, you have to go beyond this and turn your invitations for input, as well as your team's contributions and your way of responding into what are called *social norms*. These are standard ways of operating or shared expectations of how everyone should behave. For example, one of your authors is English, and for him, it is a social norm to open doors for other people, in particular when he reaches the doorway first.

If you can establish this kind of routine way of behaving around how and when people voice opinions and ideas, it can help to counter hierarchy and encourage psychological safety. Doing this requires actively and publicly seeking out others' views regularly and persistently. You need to make sure that you respond positively, even when the views you receive may seem biased or ill-informed. And you have to show people that you genuinely value them contributing in this way.

We are reminded of one leader who did this incredibly effectively just by continually asking people, 'What do you think?' He then always made sure to thank them for their input and to ask at least one question to show he was genuinely interested in what they said (even if it was a simple, 'Tell me more').

Other techniques to try here include softening the power cues you display that can reinforce hierarchy. So, avoid sitting at the head of the table at team meetings if you can. Or try rotating who chairs the meeting between team members.

Another technique is to create what are called *practice fields*—safe zones where you create debates that people are expected to contribute to, but where there is little consequence if they make a mistake or say something stupid. We know one leader who does this by asking his people to go and investigate a topic once every quarter and then setting aside 15 minutes at the end of a team meeting for people to discuss the issue and how it is relevant to their work.

One final aspect to be aware of here is the hidden hierarchies that can exist between team members [30]. We have observed many teams in which some of the newer or more junior members defer to the opinions of the more established or senior team members. Just as over-reverence for you as the team leader can create a strong sensitivity to threat and thereby kill psychological safety, so can this kind of hidden hierarchy. It is thus important to cut across it when you see it happening by directly asking the quiet team member to voice their opinions.

Dispersion

The final key sensitising factor is dispersion—the growing tendency for teams to have members who work in different places. We are often told that such virtual teams are the new, agile way of working in the twenty-first century. And this may be so. But the fact remains that it is a lot harder to build a sense of psychological safety when people rarely meet face to face.

Again, there are physical limits to what you can do about this, but studies show that four things can help reduce the impact of dispersion. The first is obvious: bring the team together physically as much as possible and definitely a few times a year [9]. The second is to constantly remind people they are a team. One recent study, for example, showed that simply by using the word 'we' as much as possible, leaders can encourage people to speak up [31]. The third approach is to consider applying shared team rewards. Using them has been found to promote team unity even when the group members are dispersed [32]. And finally, leaders must do all they can to make their team feel that they are available. If you sit behind a closed door most of the day, or if people require a formal, diarised meeting to see you, or you are not available on the phone, or not responsive to emails, you will reinforce hierarchy. It is far better instead if people know they can drop into see you and chat things through at any time. And if they are in a different office or different country, they need to feel they can call and speak to you at any time [33].

These three issues—pressure and stress, hierarchy and dispersion—can all be potential causes of heightened sensitivity to threat. By directly tackling each of them, you can significantly increase the chances that psychological safety will take hold in your Leadership OS. Sometimes, however, just reducing sensitivity is not enough. And for these moments, there are other techniques that can help.

Address Specific Triggers

In every team, there are specific triggers that exist. These are issues or topics that, the minute they are raised—or even look as if they are about to be raised—cause people to close up and become cautious. It could be a political issue within the firm; the performance of other teams; the behaviour of a particular senior leader; the value of a change initiative; or differences in interpersonal styles within the team. Every time an issue like this exists, it acts like a cholesterol plaque blocking an artery. It stops the flow of communication.

So, when you identify these topics, it is important to step in and stop them from acting as triggers. The only way to do this is to force a conversation about them and make sure it goes well. The objective of this is two-fold. First, just to have the conversation. Even if people do not come up with a long list of trigger topics, merely by having the conversation, you will be signalling that you want open communication. Second, to identify what the 'undiscussables' are and whether you should be concerned about any of them.

There are two approaches to this. One is to throw in a casual question related to the issue. Something like, 'It feels like this has become an undiscussable for us. What do you think?' The second is to approach it more systematically with semi-formal discussions, first with each team member individually, and then with the team as a whole. If you like, try this step-by-step guide.

- Speak to your team members individually first. Start the conversation by saying how important it is for the team to feel they can speak freely on things. Set the tone, saying you need their help with this. Introduce the topic by suggesting that every team has undiscussables. Tell them that sometimes this is okay (for example, how much everyone is paid), but that sometimes it is not (for example, concerns about the value or quality of things).
- Then ask each individual what they think the undiscussables are in the team. When they offer ideas, ask open-ended questions to encourage them to expand (e.g., 'Tell me more').
- After the individual discussions, set aside some time in a team meeting. Start the conversation by reminding people why it is important not to have undiscussables and ask for their help. Ask the same question you asked in the individual sessions about what people think the undiscussables are.
- When people speak, ask open-ended questions that help to clarify what they are saying. And be willing to share some of your own thoughts and experiences on the matter.
- Remember, if you come up with a list of trigger topics that is great. But the objective is not to create a list. Rather it is simply to signal, by having this sort of conversation, that you want open communication.

Do this well once, and you will find that other undiscussables may disappear because every time you address one such trigger, you make it easier for people to address every such trigger.

Coach Styles and Reactions

The final core technique you can use to improve the level of psychological safety in your Leadership OS is to help your team members become more aware of what their personal triggers are and how they tend to respond to them.

To do this, all you need to do is to have a conversation with each of your team. Again, you can adopt a step-by-step approach:

- Set aside 20–30 minutes during a one-on-one meeting with them.
- Prepare for the talk by thinking first about what you believe their triggers are—the moments when you see them closing up and getting defensive.
- Begin by telling them about the importance of people not getting triggered, and explain that it is something you discuss with all your reports.
- Give them an example relating to yourself—what kind of things trigger you to become defensive.
- Ask them what they think triggers them and the effect it tends to have on them.
- Once they have identified a few things, start giving them feedback on what you observe about them in these situations.
- Finally, you can help them think through what they can do to try to respond more positively.

The War Against Anxiety

The war against anxiety is not an easy one. The struggle to stop natural, biologically based systems from kicking in is to a certain degree insurmountable. You will never succeed one hundred per cent. But if you succeed in getting three-quarters of the way there, it can make a dramatic difference to the Leadership OS within which your team functions. Information will flow more easily. Disagreement and conflict can be turned into a positive force. And diversity can be transformed into a tangible performance advantage.

Psychological safety is not a cure-all, of course. It will not solve every problem. As we will see later in the book, it is most powerful when combined with clarity. Yet it is a sufficiently critical foundation for performance to be worth investing in. And as with care, the best way to ensure it is an integral part of your Leadership OS is to be systematic about how you develop it.

In the previous chapter, we raised the question of how leaders can balance being deliberate and systematic about trying to develop trust with being sincere. With care, it is not easy. But psychological safety *is* an area where being systematic and consistent can help create a sense of sincerity. There is a caveat, however, and it's a big one.

You need to walk the talk. It is not enough to say that you value people speaking up. You need to act like it, too. If someone says something foolish, you should not punish them for it. Point out what is wrong, by all means. But make sure you also thank and praise them for speaking up. You cannot be seen to hold it against people forever when they get things wrong. And you have to be consistent in this.

It is here, then, that psychological safety helps point us towards an answer to that tricky question of balance between being deliberately systematic *and* genuine. The answer lies in what the experts call *behavioural integrity*: practising what you preach so you act in a way that is consistent with what you say. As long as you are reliable predictable in this way, being deliberate and systematic *can* be authentic. And so it is to this third essential component of trust that we now turn: reliability.

Summary + Checklist

See Table 4.1.

Table 4.1 Summary of psychological safety

	OS function	Techniques to build IT
Psychological safety	• Enables employee voice • Makes conflict useful • Turns diversity into performance	• Reduce sensitivity to triggers • Address specific triggers • Coach styles and reactions

Checklist

To help you think about whether you have successfully installed psychological safety in your Leadership OS, ask yourself how the people around you— your direct reports, peers and stakeholders—would respond to the following questions (Table 4.2).

Table 4.2 Have you installed psychological safety in your Leadership OS?

	✓	✗
Do people feel that you enable and encourage them to question your thinking and disagree with you?	☐	☐
Do people feel that you make it easy to raise tough and difficult issues with you?	☐	☐
Do people believe that you want them to bring new ideas to you?	☐	☐
Do people believe that you will support them if they make mistakes and not hold it against them?	☐	☐

References

1. M. Roberto, "Lessons from everest: The interaction of cognitive bias, psychological safety, and system complexity," *California Management Review*, vol. 45, no. 1, pp. 136–158, 2002.
2. A. Edmondson, "Psychological safety and learning behavior in work teams," *Administrative Science Quarterly*, vol. 44, pp. 350–383, 1999.
3. S. Ben-Hur and N. Kinley, "Coaching executive teams to reach better decisions," *Journal of Management Development*, vol. 31, no. 7, 2012.
4. F. J. Milliken, E. W. Morrison and P. F. Hewlin, "An exploratory study of employee silence: Issues that employees don't communicate upward and why," *Journal of Management Studies*, vol. 40, pp. 1453–1476, 2003.
5. J. Liang, C. Farh and J. Farh, "Psychological antecedents of promotive and prohibitive voice: A two-wave examination," *Academy of Management Journal*, vol. 55, pp. 71–92, 2012.
6. B. Bradley, B. Postlethwaite, A. Klotz, M. Hamdani and K. Brown, "Reaping the benefits of task conflict in teams: The critical role of team psychological safety climate," *Journal of Applied Psychology*, vol. 97, no. 1, p. 151, 2012.
7. J. Fairchild and S. Hunter, "'We've got creative differences': The effects of task conflict and participative safety on team creative performance," *The Journal of Creative Behavior*, vol. 48, no. 1, pp. 64–87, 2014.
8. L. Martins, M. Schilpzand, B. Kirkman, S. Ivanaj and V. Ivanaj, "A contingency view of the effects of cognitive diversity on team performance: The moderating roles of team psychological safety and relationship conflict," *Small Group Research*, vol. 44, no. 2, pp. 96–126, 2013.
9. A. Carmeli, Z. Sheaffer, G. Binyamin, R. Reiter-Palmon and T. Shimoni, "Transformational leadership and creative problem-solving: The mediating role of psychological safety and reflexivity," *The Journal of Creative Behavior*, vol. 48, no. 2, pp. 115–135, 2014.
10. J. Lee, M. Swink and T. Pandejpong, "The roles of worker expertise, information sharing quality, and psychological safety in manufacturing process innovation: An intellectual capital perspective," *Production and Operations Management*, vol. 20, pp. 556–570, 2010.

11. C. Post, "Deep-level team composition and innovation: The mediating roles of psychological safety and cooperative learning," *Group & Organization Management,* vol. 37, no. 5, pp. 555–588, 2012.

12. S. Brown and T. Leigh, "A new look at psychological climate and its relationship to job involvement, effort, and performance," *Journal of Applied Psychology,* vol. 81, no. 4, pp. 358–368, 1996.

13. M. Baer and M. Frese, "Innovation is not enough: Climates for initiative and psychological safety, process innovations, and firm performance," *Journal of Organizational Behavior,* vol. 24, no. 1, pp. 45–68, 2003.

14. R. Law, M. Dollard, M. Tuckey and C. Dormann, "Psychosocial safety climate as a lead indicator of workplace bullying and harassment, job resources, psychological health and employee engagement," *Accident Analysis & Prevention,* vol. 43, no. 5, pp. 1782–1793, 2011.

15. A. Newman, R. Donohue and N. Eva, "Psychological safety: A systematic review of the literature," *Human Resource Management Review,* vol. 27, no. 3, pp. 521–535, 2017.

16. B. Sanner and S. Bunderson, "When feeling safe isn't enough: Contextualizing models of safety and learning in teams," *Organizational Psychology Review,* vol. 5, pp. 224–243, 2015.

17. N. Keith and M. Frese, "Enhancing firm performance and innovativeness through error management culture," *Handbook of Organizational Culture and Climate,* vol. 9, pp. 137–157, 2011.

18. H. Leroy, B. Dierynck, F. Anseel and T. Simons, "Behavioral integrity for safety, priority of safety, psychological safety, and patient safety: A team-level study," *Journal of Applied Psychology,* vol. 97, no. 6, pp. 1273–1281, 2012.

19. M. Pearsall and A. Ellis, "Thick as thieves: The effects of ethical orientation and psychological safety on unethical team behavior," *Journal of Applied Psychology,* vol. 96, no. 2, p. 401, 2011.

20. J. Kruzich, J. Mienko and M. Courtney, "Individual and work group influences on turnover intention among public child welfare workers: The effects of work group psychological safety," *Children and Youth Services Review,* vol. 42, pp. 20–27, 2014.

21. R. Hirak, A. Peng, A. Carmeli and J. Schaubroeck, "Linking leader inclusiveness to work unit performance: The importance of psychological safety and learning from failures," *The Leadership Quarterly,* vol. 23, no. 1, pp. 107–117, 2012.

22. B. Bergmann and J. Schaeppi, "A data-driven approach to group creativity," *Harvard Business Review,* 12 July 2017.

23. Q. Gu, G. Wang and L. Wang, "Social capital and innovation in R&D teams: The mediating roles of psychological safety and learning from mistakes," *R&D Management,* vol. 43, no. 2, pp. 89–102, 2013.

24. P. Guchait, A. Paşamehmetoğlu and M. Dawson, "Perceived supervisor and co-worker support for error management: Impact on perceived psychological

safety and service recovery performance," *International Journal of Hospitality Management,* vol. 41, pp. 28–37, 2014.

25. L. Stroud, P. Salovey and E. Epel, "Sex differences in stress responses: Social rejection versus achievement stress," *Biological Psychiatry,* vol. 52, no. 4, pp. 318–327, 2002.

26. F. Youssef, R. Bachewa, S. Bissessara, M. Crockett and M. Faber, "Sex differences in the effects of acute stress on behavior in the ultimatum game," *Psychoneuroendocrinology,* vol. 96, pp. 126–131, 2018.

27. A. Edmondson and Z. Lei, "Psychological safety: The history, renaissance, and future of an interpersonal construct," *Annual Review of Organisational Psychology and Organisational Behaviour,* vol. 1, no. 1, pp. 23–43, 2014.

28. D. Chiaburu, S. Marinova and L. Van Dyne, "Should I do it or not? An initial model of cognitive processes predicting voice behaviors," in *Academy of Management Proceedings,* Briarcliff Manor, NY, Acade, 2008, pp. 1–6.

29. I. Botero and L. Van Dyne, "Employee voice behavior: Interactive effects of LMX and power distance in the United States and Colombia," *Management Communication Quarterly,* vol. 23, no. 1, pp. 84–104, 2009.

30. I. Nembhard and A. Edmondson, "Making it safe: The effects of leader inclusiveness and professional status on psychological safety and improvement efforts in health care teams," *Journal of Organizational Behavior,* vol. 27, no. 7, pp. 941–966, 2006.

31. M. Weiss, M. Kolbe, G. Grote, D. Spahn and B. Grande, "We can do it! Inclusive leader language promotes voice behavior in multi-professional teams," *The Leadership Quarterly,* vol. 39, no. 3, pp. 389–402, 2018.

32. G. Chen and D. Tjosvold, "Shared rewards and goal interdependence for psychological safety among departments in China," *Asia Pacific Journal of Management,* vol. 27, no. 3, pp. 1–20, 2012.

33. A. Edmondson, "Speaking up in the operating room: How team leaders promote learning in interdisciplinary action teams," *Journal of Management Studies,* vol. 40, no. 6, pp. 1419–1452, 2003.

5

Reliability

Do you know which prison officers are hated most by prisoners? It is not the ones you might imagine. One of your authors used to work in prisons, trying to change the behaviour of dangerous offenders. Observing the relationships between prison officers and inmates, he saw something that we have both since seen replicated time and again in the relationships between leaders and their people.

The prison officers who were hated most were not the bullies. Not the violent ones. Not the vindictive. It was the unreliable ones. The unpredictable ones, who would act like your friend one day and your worst enemy the next.

When we asked a prisoner why this was, we were told, 'Because you can't manage them. The mean ones? You know they're going to be mean. You know what to do. But the unpredictable ones, you never know what to do. You can't manage them. It's like playing Russian roulette every time you deal with them: you never know what you're going to get'.

And it is the same with leaders. Being predictable, being reliable, is one of the most vital cornerstones of any effective Leadership OS.

This is a short but important chapter. It is short because what it takes to be reliable is straightforward. Acting it out day to day may not always be easy and, in fact, might be fraught with difficulties, but what you *ought* to do is clear. So the chapter is short. But it is also important because it contains some very big words. Not big as in long; but big in meaning. Things like integrity and authenticity. Words that carry a certain weight and that

© The Author(s) 2020
N. Kinley and S. Ben-Hur, *Leadership OS*,
https://doi.org/10.1007/978-3-030-27293-7_5

have huge implications for both your reputation as a leader and the impact you have on your people and your business.

Why We Hate the Unpredictable

The philosopher and cognitive scientist Daniel C. Dennett once pointed out something that at the time seemed counterintuitive, and yet, once seen, changed the nature of research into the workings of the brain. He suggested that the function of memory—the reason it exists—is *not* to help us remember things. After all, there is little survival value in just remembering. Instead, he argued, the function of memory is to help us *predict* things. To help us predict our environments: which foods won't poison us, which animals won't hurt us, which paths will lead us home. In fact, Dennett said, the human brain could be thought of as one big prediction machine [1].

Thirty years later, progress in neuroscience has largely borne out Dennett's ideas. We can see it in the inner workings of our biological trust system. In the chapters on trust and care, we showed how the biological trust system detects subtle social cues to classify people and situations as trustworthy or not. In the chapter on psychological safety, we saw how this trust system is connected to a deeper biological detection system—one designed to keep us safe by watching out for potentially threatening situations and then triggering a fight-or-flight response. Dennett's system lies even deeper.

This deeper-seated system is a first level of processing, completed before our lightning-fast trust system even gets involved. It is so fundamental to the way brains work that it has been found in newborn human babies [2], dogs [3], cats [4], rats [5], frogs [6] and even sea slugs [7]. Almost every type of brain does it.

As might be expected from something found in even sea slugs, what this system does is very simple. It classifies sensory information entering the brain as either novel or known [8]. As what we see and hear enters our heads, it reaches a part of the brain called the amygdala. It is there that this classification occurs. If something is labelled as new, certain pathways in the brain start-up so we can focus on it, and our threat-detection systems kick in and check whether it is something we need to worry about. And in doing so, they also trigger our trust system, classifying whatever it is we have encountered as potentially untrustworthy.

It is because of this system that the prison officers who are hated most are the unpredictable ones. Because whenever our brains detect something new, or different, or just not as predicted, we become alert and edgy [9].

We can see this in a recent study on the effects of how leaders treat their direct reports on people's physical stress levels [10]. The researchers divided leaders into three groups. One group was consistently fair to people. A second was consistently unfair. And the final group was changeable—sometimes fair, sometimes not. The researchers then measured the levels of stress hormones in the direct reports of these leaders. They found that the employees with the highest levels of stress hormones were those with changeable leaders. On a purely biological level, being sometimes fair is worse for people than being consistently unfair. Deep, deep down, we are hardwired to prefer the predictable and at a biological level we do not trust the unpredictable or unreliable.

A Different Sort of Integrity

The phrase psychologists use to describe this kind of reliability in leaders is *behavioural integrity*. When they study it, they look at two things:

1. Do leaders create a sense of reliable consistency for others? For example, do people feel leaders are steady in their moods, consistent in the decisions they make and unvarying in the messages they give out? [11]
2. Do people believe that leaders walk the talk and align what they do with what they say? This is in terms of both whether leaders act in accordance with the values they promote and—potentially trickier—whether the way they act is aligned with company values and policy [12].

When leaders do these two things, they create a predictable environment that increases trust. When they don't, when they are inconsistent, people's novelty-detection system is triggered, and so trust falls.

This is probably not what most people think of when they hear the word 'integrity'. Usually, they think of honesty and telling the truth. And this kind of moral integrity certainly grabs the headlines, especially in these days of increasing focus on leaders' ethics.

Yet although moral integrity receives all the attention, researchers have found that behavioural integrity has a far greater impact on leaders' ability to drive high performance [13]. Telling the truth is crucial. And if you get caught *not* telling the truth, it can kill performance. But if you want to build performance, behavioural integrity is even more important. And to understand *why*, we need to see what behavioural integrity does to a Leadership OS.

What Reliability Does to an OS

Research shows that creating a sense in others that you are reliable, that you have behavioural integrity, serves three functions in a Leadership OS (Fig. 5.1).

A. Prevents Stress

The first thing reliability does is to stop people's novelty-detection system in the brain from activating. As a result, people who work for reliable leaders report lower levels of stress [14]. This, in turn, leads to lower levels of absenteeism and burnout [15] and higher levels of job satisfaction [16] and engagement [17].

B. Creates Belief

The second thing reliability does is to support people's belief in both you and your business. If you are not seen to walk the talk with your team, they are less likely to believe in what you say and what you do. When they hear you say something, they will wait until they see you act on it before they believe in it. And when they see you take action, they will wait until they see the outcome before believing that it was the right decision to make. This can significantly limit your ability to create clarity about what is important and needs focusing on [13]. It can also considerably reduce your people's confidence in both your and their ability to succeed. Combined, all these factors can have important knock-on effects on your ability both to drive change and to ensure high performance.

It is similar with your stakeholders, too—be it peers, the board or investors. Their belief in you is critical to their support for you. And to believe in you, they need to see you as solid, dependable and reliable. In fact, this is particularly important for CEOs and senior executives because belief trickles up [18]. When people believe in you, it also boosts their belief in your

Fig. 5.1 The functions of reliability in a Leadership OS

business: hence the particularly negative impact we saw in Chapter 1 and the case of Elon Musk's erratic, unpredictable tweets. They have affected not only people's belief in him but also their belief in his businesses.

C. Encourages Reliability in Others

The final thing about reliability in a Leadership OS is that it is contagious. Studies show that where leaders are perceived to be low in behavioural integrity, their people tend to follow suit and act the same way. They say one thing but do another. Where leaders are seen as behaving consistently and walking the talk, though, their people are more consistent as well [19]. So as a leader, your behavioural integrity sets the tone for what other people do. If you are reliable, your people are more likely to be reliable, and that in turn releases all sorts of positive behaviours that are needed to drive performance.

The impact of these three Leadership OS functions on the performance of your people and your business can be profound. Leader reliability has been shown to increase creativity levels in people, increase the amount people collaborate and help each other, and decrease factors like cynicism and resistance to change [20].

The reason for this link is grounded in the hard neuroscience and hardwiring of the brain. When people create a Leadership OS high in reliability, their novelty-detection systems is less likely to be triggered. And as a result, they are more likely to trust, more likely to be open, sociable and positive, and less likely to be guarded and wary [21].

In light of this, it is perhaps no surprise to find that leader reliability is a strong predictor of both individual performance [22] and team performance [23] across a range of industries [24] and countries [25].

Reliability: The Controversial Case of Josh Silverman at Etsy

Etsy has a mission. It is to be an inclusive alternative to companies that only put profit before purpose. Founded in 2005 in Brooklyn, Etsy quickly grew to become an online community of creative entrepreneurs, thoughtful consumers and passionate employees. Its headquarters has gender-neutral bathrooms. The company progressively embraces a vibrant gay and transgender community. It offers generous parental leave and free organic food. Pets roam freely around headquarters. And as a result of all this and more, it was one of the largest companies to be a certified as a *B Corp*, a title granted only to firms committing to the highest social and environmental standards (Fig. 5.2).

Initially, it looked like a promising business, too. From 2012 through 2014, Etsy's revenues increased 150% as their number of active buyers and sellers doubled. In 2014 revenues reaches $195 million. Like many technology-driven companies, the firm was not profitable, but it hoped that investing in scale would eventually lead to profitability. And to help accelerate this growth, the company became publicly listed in April 2015, raising $200 million in the process. Etsy's stock price quickly jumped from $16 to over $25.

One year later, revenues had grown to over $360 million. But expenses had doubled, and losses were increasing. Investors became worried, and the stock closed 2016 under $12 per share. When early 2017 showed no sign of this pattern changing, the Board decided to act. In May 2017, they fired the CEO, Chad Dickerson, who many viewed as the heart and soul of the firm

Fig. 5.2 Josh Silverman

and who had been instrumental in creating Etsy's mission and culture. In his place, they appointed Josh Silverman, a 48-year-old private equity guy, who although a Board member was largely unknown by employees.

Silverman's transition to CEO was a difficult period for the business. Not only had it lost Dickerson, but 80 other employees were fired on Silverman's first day, and another 140 would lose their jobs within a month. Projects were cancelled. The 'Values-Aligned Business' team was shuttered, and the firm's B Corp status allowed to lapse. And the open and enthusiastic culture that so characterised the company, suddenly felt to many like it was becoming became less open and enthusiastic.

Silverman, though, knew what he had gotten himself into and knew what he was doing. On his first day as CEO, he introduced himself to the staff, then made it clear that there would be changes. Moreover, he didn't just say what needed to change, he tried to explain why as well. He had a number of core messages, and on that first day and in the months that followed, he was deliberate and systematic in trying to communicate them clearly and consistently.

Most important of the messages was the idea of 'the vital few and the worthless many'. This was the notion that while there were hundreds of things the business could do, there were very few that would add significant value. Backing this, he quickly clarified the company's strategy, distilling it down to just four areas: better search tools on the website, improved customer trust, new marketing capabilities for sellers, and enhanced platforms for sellers. He then eliminated non-core projects and focused on just 30 initiatives that were aligned to the new strategy and had the greatest opportunity for growth.

Silverman was equally clear in his commitment to the twin themes of innovation and accountability. Employees were encouraged to be more innovative and to take more risks, but once committed to objectives were then held more accountable. To help this, he used the early layoffs to redesign and professionalise the company's organisational chart.

During the Q&A portion of that first meeting in May 2017, one employee asked how they could trust leadership now, which suddenly felt decidedly cold and un-Etsy-like. Silverman replied, 'Trust is earned, not granted. Keep an open mind, and we'll get to know each other'.

In the two years or more since Silverman took over, there have been accusations and complaints that he destroyed the Etsy that was, the culture that made it unique. There has even been a *New York Times* article in which the tale of Silverman's impact on Etsy was used to highlight concerns about capitalism more broadly.

Yet for every negative comment on Silverman's impact, there are also positive reports about improvements he wrought, such as the greater focus on empowering people to innovate. Many of the company's great benefits are still in place, and the firm was recently lauded for its continuing commitment to diversity and inclusion. 55% of its employees are women, as are nearly two-thirds of its management team, and the company has also achieved gender parity on its Board. What's more, the proportion of engineers in the firm who are female has increased during Silverman's tenure, to 32%.

So the firm's mission has not been forgotten and its culture not wholly changed in Silverman's time. And whichever side of the debate you sit on—whether you view his impact as positive or negative—two things appear unquestionable. First, in the two years before Silverman took over as CEO, Etsy suffered losses of $90 million; in the two years since he took over, it enjoyed profits of $160 million. And the stock price increased from $10 to almost $70.

Second, Silverman was a man of his word. He said he would make changes, he told everyone what those changes would be, and then he made them. And in doing so, he worked to answer that question asked of him on his first day, to earn people's trust. They may not have liked the changes he made, but everyone knew what he was asking of them, everybody know where they stood. He saw his business through a period of transformational change by being consistent, being reliable. And the results speak for themselves.

Creating a Sense of Reliability

Unfortunately, creating a sense of reliability for others is not always straightforward. In our experience, it is yet another aspect of leadership that is becoming harder to do well. The business world has become more changeable, making consistency harder and creating a broader culture in which unpredictability is almost expected. The psychological contract between businesses and employees has shifted in the last 30 years, with lower levels of consistent loyalty—in both directions. And the increased visibility of executive behaviour in this age of the internet and social media has helped stoke a rising general cynicism about all leaders.

Against this background, your challenge is to find ways to create a sense of consistency for others and be seen to walk the talk. The good news here is that research shows that the most significant determinant—by far—of whether a sense of reliability exists within your Leadership OS is you. For all the background cultural noise, it is the personal impact that you have on others that makes the biggest difference to whether people feel that they are operating within a reliable, predictable environment [24].

As before, what you need to do differs between people. But in general, there are four techniques that the research shows can help to create a sense of reliability (Fig. 5.3).

Avoid Surprising Communication—Good or Bad

If you want to avoid triggering people's novelty-detection system, the best way is to avoid surprising them. Surprises can be great at birthday parties, less so at work. This is evident in the working of company boards.

A lesson learnt fast by many first-time CEOs is that while boards predictably hate surprise bad news, they tend to be quite suspicious of surprise good news, too. The reason is that if something is a surprise, it means it hasn't been foreseen. And if it hasn't been foreseen, it isn't under control. So the mere existence of a surprise—good or bad—can undermine the degree to which others see you as reliable.

So, the first thing you can try to do is to avoid surprises, and the easiest way to do that is through regular, transparent communication. Schedule regular updates. Provide as much information about the performance of your team, unit or business as you can. Give people a chance to question you about it. And in so doing, create a sense of transparency—the feeling in others that nothing is hidden and that there are no surprises lurking around the corner.

Practise Self-Control

Although self-control is perhaps not something most people would immediately associate with reliability and integrity, it has repeatedly been shown by

Fig. 5.3 Four techniques to increase reliability

researchers to be critical in this regard. Simply put, leaders with higher levels of self-control are viewed as more consistent than leaders with low levels of self-control [10]. This is because when your self-control is low, you are more likely to react emotionally, to let frustration, irritation and anger show, and in so doing surprise people with your reaction. And every time you do that, you trigger their biological trust system to be wary of you.

Fortunately, self-control is something you can get better at. In fact, there is a whole science to it, with books full of advice. Broadly speaking, there are three main approaches. The first focuses on relaxation or reducing background stress levels. You will find a lot here on tools like breathing techniques and meditation. The second approach focuses on awareness or mindfulness—helping you to become more alert to the things that will trigger you to lose self-control, and thereby more able to avoid them. And finally, there is a range of techniques focused on improving self-discipline through simple practice exercises. This last approach builds on the research showing that practising simple exercises of self-discipline, such as writing a diary, can improve people's self-control more generally [26]. So, if you think people are often surprised by your reactions, try one of these approaches because the appearance of self-control boosts people's belief in your reliability.

Say It, Do It, Repeat It

If you tell people that you are going to do something, tell them when you will do it, and then always, always report back to them afterwards and confirm that you did indeed do it. It sounds simple, but doing it consistently takes deliberate effort and systematic focus. In the rush of day-to-day activity, it is all too easy to forget to do. This is why, in our experience, it is something that all leaders know they *should* do, and most leaders do sometimes, but few do all the time. It is worth the small investment, though, because there is no easier way to build others' confidence and belief in you than by actually doing something when you say you will.

Create Routines

The final technique involves creating a sense of consistency by using routines. These are simple sequences—ways of talking or behaving—that you deliberately repeat time and again. In the previous chapter, we gave the example of a leader who always asked, 'What do you think?' It was like a calling card—something that was seen as uniquely them and that they would reliably do. Other examples would be leaders who always begin or end their team meetings with the same routine questions. Or those who repeatedly use the same phrases when they speak—something that can be particularly important when working with boards and investors.

The idea is simple. By creating these consistencies, you create a sense of predictability. You quite literally put people's brains at ease, as they classify what they see and hear you doing as something known. So, think about the way that you do things, the way you talk to people and the phrases you use. Then identify just a few that you can start using as your own personal routine.

Differentiating Reliability

The third pillar of trust, then, is reliability. It is relatively straightforward in terms of what it is and how it functions. It is deeply practical, grounded in the impact leaders have on the people around them, day in day out. And like the other components of trust, it is grounded in the neuroscience of the brain.

Yet it is also a bit different from care and psychological safety. It touches upon bigger, more nebulous aspects: how much integrity people think you have; whether they think you act with authenticity; how much they believe in you. And it is this aspect of reliability that makes it so important.

There is also a difference in terms of how people judge your reliability. With care and psychological safety, people mostly assess you on how you behave towards them personally. But studies show that people's perceptions of your reliability are also heavily grounded in how they see you behave towards other people [27]. Seeing you surprise someone else or act inconsistently with them is just as likely to trigger a person's biological trust system as if you surprised them personally.

And it is here, in people's perceptions of how you treat others, that we find the fourth and final component of trust: fairness.

Summary + Checklist

See Table 5.1.

Table 5.1 Summary of reliability

	OS function	Techniques to build it
RELIABILITY	• Prevents stress • Creates belief • Encourages reliability in others	• Avoid surprising communication • Practise self-control • Say it, do it, repeat it • Create routines

Checklist

To help you think about whether you have successfully installed reliability in your Leadership OS, ask yourself how the people around you—your direct reports, peers and stakeholders—would respond to the following questions (Table 5.2).

Table 5.2 Have you installed reliability in your Leadership OS?

	✓	✗
Do people feel that they know where they stand with you (the leader)?	☐	☐
Do people feel that they can predict how you will respond to things?	☐	☐
Do people believe that when you say you will do something, you *always* do it?	☐	☐
Do people believe that there are *never* any surprises with you?	☐	☐

References

1. D. Dennett, *Consciousness explained*, London: Penguin Books, 1993.
2. N. Turk-Browne, B. Scholl and M. Chun, "Babies and brains: Habituation in infant cognition and functional neuroimaging," *Frontiers in Human Neuroscience*, vol. 2, p. 16, 2008.
3. A. Prichard, P. Cook, M. Spivak, R. Chhibber and G. Berns, "Awake fMRI reveals brain regions for novel word detection in dogs," *Frontiers in Neuroscience*, vol. 12, p. 737, 2018.
4. K. Lee, K. Lee, K. Min, Y. Zhang, J. Shin and H. Lee, "Hierarchical novelty detection for visual object recognition," in *IEEE/CVF Conference on Computer Vision and Pattern Recognition (CVPR)*, 2018.
5. M. Albasser, C. Olarte-Sánchez, E. Amin, M. Brown, L. Kinnavane and J. Aggleton, "Perirhinal cortex lesions in rats: Novelty detection and sensitivity to interference," *Behavioral Neuroscience*, vol. 129, no. 3, pp. 227–243, 2015.
6. E. J.P. and W. Kehl, "Configurational prey-selection by individual experience in the toad bufo bufo," *Journal of Comparative Physiology*, vol. 126, pp. 105–114, 1978.

7. C. Bailey and M. Chen, "Morphological basis of long-term habituation and sensitization inaplysia," *Science*, vol. 220, pp. 91–93, 1983.

8. N. Balderston, D. Schultz and F. Helmstetter, "The human amygdala plays a stimulus specific role in the detection of novelty," *NeuroImage*, vol. 55, no. 4, pp. 1889–1898, 2011.

9. P. Whalen, "The uncertainty of it all," *Trends in Cognitive Science*, vol. 11, pp. 499–500, 2007.

10. F. Matta, B. Scott, J. Colquitt, J. Koopman and L. Passantino, "Is consistently unfair better than sporadicallyfair? An investigation of justice variability," *Academy of Management Journal*, vol. 60, no. 2, pp. 743–770, 2017.

11. W. Ouchi and A. Jaeger, "Type Z organization: Stability in the midst of mobility," *The Academy of Management Review*, vol. 3, no. 2, p. 305, 1978.

12. S. Worden, "The role of integrity as a mediator in strategic leadership: A recipe for reputational capital," *Journal of Business Ethics*, vol. 46, no. 1, pp. 31–44, 2003.

13. T. Simons, H. Leroy, V. Collewaert and S. Masschelein, "How leader alignment of words and deeds affects followers: A meta-analysis of behavioral integrity research," *Journal of Business Ethics*, vol. 132, no. 4, pp. 831–844, 2015.

14. D. Prottas, "Perceived behavioral integrity: Relationships with employee attitudes, well-being, and absenteeism," *Journal of Business Ethics*, vol. 81, no. 2, pp. 313–322, 2008.

15. J. Jiang, "Leader–member relationship and burnout: The moderating role of leader integrity," *Management and Organization Review*, vol. 10, no. 2, pp. 223–247, 2014.

16. R. Moorman, T. Darnold and M. Priesemuth, "Perceived leader integrity: Supporting the construct validity and utility of a multi-dimensional measure in two samples," *The Leadership Quarterly*, vol. 24, no. 3, pp. 427–444, 2013.

17. G. Vogelgesang, H. Leroy and B. Avolio, "The mediating effects of leader integrity with transparency in communication and work engagement/performance," *The Leadership Quarterly*, vol. 24, no. 3, pp. 405–413, 2013.

19. R. Kannan-Narasimhan and B. Lawrence, "Behavioral integrity: How leader referents and trust matter to workplace outcomes," *Journal of Business Ethics*, vol. 111, no. 2, pp. 165–178, 2012.

20. D. White and E. Lean, "The impact of perceived leader integrity on subordinates in a work team environment," *Journal of Business Ethics*, vol. 81, no. 4, pp. 765–778, 2008.

21. H. Peng and F. Wei, "Trickle-down effects of perceived leader integrity on employee creativity: A moderated mediation model," *Journal of Business Ethics*, vol. 150, no. 3, pp. 837–851, 2018.

22. M. Palanski and G. Vogelgesang, "Virtuous creativity: The effects of leader behavioural integrity on follower creative thinking and risk taking," *Canadian Journal of Administrative Sciences*, vol. 28, no. 3, pp. 259–269, 2011.

23. M. Palanski and F. Yammarino, "Impact of behavioral integrity on follower job performance: A three-study examination," *The Leadership Quarterly*, vol. 22, pp. 765–786, 2011.

24. M. Palanski, S. Kahai and F. Yammarino, "Team virtues and performance: An examination of transparency, behavioral integrity, and trust," *Journal of Business Ethics*, vol. 99, no. 2, pp. 201–216, 2011.

25. A. Davis and H. Rothstein, "The effects of the perceived behavioral integrity of managers on employee attitudes: A meta-analysis," *Journal of Business Ethics*, vol. 67, pp. 407–419, 2006.

26. G. Martin, M. Keating, C. Resick, E. Szabo, H. Kwan and C. Peng, "The meaning of leader integrity: A comparative study across Anglo, Asian, and Germanic cultures," *The Leadership Quarterly*, vol. 24, no. 3, pp. 445–461, 2013.

27. M. Muraven, "Building self-control strength: Practicing self-control leads to improved self-control performance," *Journal of Experimental Social Psychology*, vol. 46, pp. 465–468, 2010.

28. D. Den Hartog and A. De Hoogh, "Empowering behaviour and leader fairness and integrity: Studying perceptions of ethical leader behaviour from a levels-of-analysis perspective," *European Journal of Work and Organizational Psychology*, vol. 18, no. 2, pp. 199–230, 2009.

6

Fairness

Just for a second, think back to when you were a child. Think back to sometime in your upbringing—the younger, the better—when you felt let down. When a promise was not fulfilled. Or you thought something was *unfair*. Do you remember that feeling, the physical sensation it produced? What it felt like for something to be unfair?

Some people report it as being an almost tingling sensation of discomfort. Of suddenly feeling restless, or of something not being quite right. Others refer to it as an inner burning. And for others still, it just kicks straight into anger and outrage. Such is the primal, visceral power of fairness.

We may not be children anymore, and we may have learned to control these reactions and feelings, but they are still there. And they still affect us, as adults, as employees and as leaders.

The last of our four components of trust is fairness. It is like a wrapper for the other three, in that it is all about whether you can create a sense of care, psychological safety and reliability in a *fair and just manner*. It is the perception others have of whether you treat people in a reasonable, even-handed and proper way, without favouritism or discrimination. And this applies not just to how you treat them as individuals themselves but also to how they see you treat people in general [1].

Fairness acts as a wrapper for the other three components because it is also the sense others have of whether their trust in you as their leader will pay off. Whether, if they put in the work and achieve the results, you will do your bit for them and make sure they are treated and rewarded appropriately. Fairness, then, is part of the core psychological contract that exists

© The Author(s) 2020
N. Kinley and S. Ben-Hur, *Leadership OS*,
https://doi.org/10.1007/978-3-030-27293-7_6

between you and the people around you. It may not be written down, it may never be explicitly said, but this contract is there nonetheless, waiting to be fulfilled—or broken, and with it, the whole notion of trust.

A Psychological Contract

If fairness were a legal contract, it would have clauses. Lots of them. It would lay out different conditions that need to be met for fairness to be said to exist. Psychologists have tried to identify and categorise these conditions. They have come up with three, each a different type or aspect of fairness:

- Procedural fairness—whether the processes used to make business and HR decisions are believed to be fair.
- Distributive fairness—whether pay and rewards such as salaries, bonuses, holidays and training are viewed as fair.
- Interactional fairness—whether people feel they are treated fairly in terms of the respect they are given and how things like decisions and appraisals are communicated.

Create a perception of all three, and people will see you and your Leadership OS as fair. Fail to do so, and they will see the contract as broken. And with it, their trust in you and the system you create.

A Powerful Response

The power of fairness comes from the neurology of it, from where it is based in our brains, and what it does there. In a wonderful, if slightly low-tech experiment, scientists recently showed in which parts of the brain our sense of fairness is based. They did this by asking participants to make a simple decision—how to split £20 between themselves and a second person. They gave the participants a couple of options. They could split the money equally, giving themselves and the other person £10 each. Or they could split the money unfairly. The experimenters gave the participants several choices here. They could give themselves £12 and the other person £8. They could give themselves £14 and the other person £6. Or they could give themselves £16 and the other person just £4.

After they had run this experiment once, the experimenters asked the participants to do it again. This time, however, they attached magnets to people's heads to disrupt functioning in the part of the brain called the right dorsolateral prefrontal cortex. Then they checked to see if the magnets changed how people made decisions about how to split the money. And sure enough, with the magnets activated and brain functioning disrupted, people made more unfair decisions, suggesting that the right dorsolateral prefrontal cortex is indeed the home of fairness [2].

What makes the fact that fairness is based in this part of the brain particularly interesting is the degree to which it is connected to our emotional system. We might think of fairness in terms of 'justice' and objective and rational decisions. However, when we perceive something as unfair, it is the emotional centre of the brain that activates far more than the thinking parts [3]. This is why fairness can be such a powerful motivator of how we behave, why it feels like it matters so much to us. Because it triggers something quite primal and emotive in us.

This explains why studies have repeatedly shown that people can react in powerful and aggressive ways to perceived breaches of fairness. Even when they respond more mildly, it is evident that fairness is of real value to them. Indeed, studies show that people would rather be paid an average amount and feel that things are fair than be paid more but feel they are not treated fairly [4]. Fairness matters.

A Trigger for Trust

The workings of this fairness part of the brain are also tied to the operation of our biological trust system [5]. In fact, activity in these circuits acts as a cue that can trigger the trust system [6]. When we feel that things are fair, our trust system becomes activated. Oxytocin levels increase, and we become more sociable, positive and empathetic [7]. When we think things are unfair, however, the oxytocin decreases, and we become less sociable, positive and empathetic [8].

So, on a basic biological level, fairness functions as a clause or condition for trust. It can trigger a sense of trust or distrust and, with it, powerful reactions within us. And as with the trust system, all this can happen in the blink of an eye without us even being aware of it.

What Fairness Does in an OS

In light of this, it is not surprising that fairness plays an important part in any Leadership OS. It serves three functions in particular (Fig. 6.1).

Fig. 6.1   The functions of fairness in a Leadership OS

A. Encourages Effort, Initiative and Innovation

The most obvious thing fairness does is to promote positive behaviour: whatever people think is going to be rewarded [9]. That could simply be hard work [10]. It could be high standards and quality control. Or it could be coming up with creative solutions [11]. It is whatever you—as their leader—ask of them and focus them on. Fairness is the lever—the clause in the psychological contract—that makes your objectives work. And as a result, when Leadership OSs are high in fairness, employees show greater levels of engagement [12], higher levels of commitment [13] and are more willing to go beyond the call of duty to achieve results [14].

B. Promotes Cohesion

The second thing fairness does is less obvious, and perhaps even surprising. You might think that the basic connection between fairness and reward would focus people on individual achievement. Yet a finding that occurs repeatedly in the research is that it is, in fact, the other way around. When people believe that fairness does not exist, they become more focused on what they personally want and need. So, they become less socially minded and more guarded. When a sense of fairness prevails, however, they work together better [15].

There seem to be many reasons for this, all of which stem from people's trust system being activated in a positive way. So, when fairness is seen to exist, people become more trusting and sociable and say that being part of a team is more important to them [16]. They are more likely to accept group goals [17] and show commitment to these shared objectives [14].

People collaborate more [18]. They are more likely to share resources and knowledge [19]. They help each other more [20] and are more likely to treat each other ethically and respectfully [21]. They have less conflict with colleagues [22], and when disputes *do* arise, they are more likely to compromise to resolve them [15]. As a result, teams are more cohesive and better able to function as a group [23]. They are more than just the sum of the individuals who make up the team.

Furthermore, recent research has revealed that an additional effect of this cohesion is that teams are more agile and adaptable [24]. This is because they are less focused on themselves and what they want, and therefore more open to what others and the business in general wants and needs, such as change. So, as with the other components of trust, the social and interpersonal effects of fairness mean that its impact is far beyond what might be expected.

C. Prevents the Negative Impact of Unfairness

The final thing fairness does is to stop people from feeling that situations are unfair. This may sound obvious, but it is critical because when people think that things are unfair, they don't tend to respond well.

At the most basic level, unfairness is a negative feeling [25]. It makes people more likely to feel stressed [26], report higher levels of anxiety and emotional exhaustion [21], and even more physical health complaints [25]. And as a result, they are more likely to be absent, burn out or leave [27].

Just as damagingly, when people do not leave, they are more likely to neglect their duties [27] and engage in what are referred to as *counterproductive work behaviours* [28]. These may involve theft, absenteeism or bullying—general unethical behaviour. So, preventing a sense of unfairness is vital.

Add these three functions together, and it is no surprise that Leadership OSs high in fairness are associated with impressive business results. Both individual task performance [29] and team performance increase [20], in terms of overall performance ratings *and* hard commercial numbers, like sales figures [30]. And with this, trust and belief in you, as a leader, also go up [31]. So creating a Leadership OS high in fairness is worth the investment of time and effort. The question is, how?

Ensuring Fairness: The Case of John Mackey at Whole Foods

Whole Foods Market was founded in 1980 by John Mackey and friends. They wanted to create a grocery store focused on fresh, organic and natural products as an alternative to the food that lined the shelves of the large mass-market grocery chains. Mackey grew up in Texas at the tail-end of the 1960s counterculture, but his business acumen was formed by his father, an accounting professor and CEO. With Whole Foods, Mackey wanted to blend liberal social values with conservative fiscal values. And the place where these two core values most famously met was in Whole Foods' compensation policy (Fig. 6.2).

In 1986, just six years after founding the company, Mackey instituted two radical changes to the company's benefits. His goal was to help employees understand why some people were paid more than others. He figured that if workers understood what types of performance earned people more money, then they would be more motivated to work hard.

First, he put a cap on cash compensation, limiting the amount that any one person could earn relative to the average employee salary. Initially, this was eight times the average salary. This number has risen with time, of course, and in 2017 it was 19 times the average salary. But the limit has remained, and from the time the company was publicly listed in 1992, the

Fig. 6.2 John Mackey

compensation limit has been made public in the company's annual statement to all investors.

The second change Mackey made was even more radical. He made all salaries visible to all employees. Any worker could search a database to see what their colleagues were earning. A cashier could find out how much more their store manager made than they did; and a store manager could find out how their salary compared to that of every other store manager.

Obviously, not everyone was happy with what they saw. A store manager in Texas, where the cost of living was relatively low, might understand why a store manager in New York City made more money, but they were less understanding when they saw a store manager a few miles down the road making more. Mackey's response when questioned about this was always the same: he paid people for performance, and people who performed better got paid more.

Crucially, Mackey backed this up with data. He trusted his people and wanted them to trust him and the business. Whole Foods posted each store's sales data daily, each region's data weekly, and once a month it sent each store a detailed report on sales and profitability at each of the chain's locations. In fact, it gave its people so much data that in the late 1990s the Securities and Exchange Commission classified all of the company's employees as 'insiders'.

What Mackey did was radical. Behind all of it was his belief in the importance of fairness to the relationship between the business and its employees. So Whole Foods invested far more time and effort in creating a culture of mutual trust and fairness than most other listed companies. But it worked. In 1998 Whole Foods had 15,000 employees; in 2017 it had over 90,000. The company was on *Fortune* magazine's Best Companies to Work For list for an amazing 20 consecutive years, from 1998 to 2017. And the price Amazon paid to acquire the business in 2017? $13.7 billion. Fairness, it appears, can pay huge dividends.

Creating Fairness

As with every aspect of a Leadership OS, a sense of fairness is created by a complex combination of factors. There are national cultural influences, in that different countries have distinct ideas about what counts as fair and what does not. The same goes for specific businesses. More results-focused firms may tolerate slightly more aggressive behaviour than organisations that place greater emphasis on relationships and consensus.

Fig. 6.3 Three techniques to increase fairness

There are factors linked to location, too, in that the more physically distant an employee is from their leader, the less likely they are to trust their fairness. Then there is the fact that fairness is relative, in that people judge how fair or not you are towards them by comparing this with how you treat other people. There is also evidence that some people are simply more sensitive to potential breaches of fairness than others [32].

These contextual factors show that what matters most is not what you do, but the impact that it has and how it is perceived. What counts is not whether you are objectively fair or not, but what other people believe.

This does not mean, of course, that what you do does not matter. Because it does. Just as with the other components of a Leadership OS, the most significant contributor to a sense of fairness is usually the leader. This is why the degree of fairness in an OS can vary hugely within the same firm, from team to team [33]. Every leader and the OS they create is unique.

Research shows that three techniques can be particularly useful in creating a sense of fairness in your Leadership OS (Fig. 6.3) [34]. How you go about applying them will depend on your situation, the people you are dealing with and your personal style.

Explain the Process

One challenge that every leader faces sooner or later is that people tend to judge fairness by the outcome[35]: by whether they think their pay rise or bonus is fair; by whether they feel appreciated and praised; or by whether they think they have received enough training or been awarded the promotion they believe they deserve. And you may not have any control over some of these aspects.

In these complex situations, creating a sense of fairness matters most because it is at these times that it can make the biggest difference to how people feel and react [36]. Research shows that the best way—by far—of ensuring that people feel fairness at such moments is to help them understand *how* decisions were made. The procedure or process that was followed, the information that was considered, and how this is consistent with what you have done before or with other people.

For example, one of your authors recently received a smaller bonus than in previous years despite obtaining a good performance review. But he knew that it was because the company as a whole had done less well that year due to a broader economic downturn, and that everyone was getting a smaller bonus as a result. Knowing that this was what was behind the decision to give him a smaller bonus made all the difference to how he perceived it: it made it seem fair.

The important thing in all of this is not to try and justify *why* decisions were made and outcomes chosen. It is to help people understand that even if the outcome was not what they wanted, the decision-making process was fair. Studies of brain activity in these moments show that different neural pathways are activated when people understand the processes followed and view them as fair [37]. Research also shows that regardless of whether people obtain the outcome they want, if they are given a credible explanation of the process, they are far more likely to respond positively [38]. Even if the broader context is unequivocally unfair, you—in your relationships and your Leadership OS—can still create fairness.

Use Appraisals to Create Trust

There is so much written about how to run appraisals effectively that we do not want to add to the mountain of advice given elsewhere. But you do need to get performance appraisals right.

Appraisals are the single most important fairness-related process in the working calendar. If people do not think you are fair in appraisals, they will not think you are fair with anything else. Moreover, an extra challenge here is that official company processes often do not help. They are by nature formal tick-box processes, a series of things that need doing and must be said. This structure is there to help ensure fairness. It may well do so, too, but it does not help *convey* fairness. It does not help you to connect with the biological trust system of your direct reports. If anything, it gets in the way.

This is why research shows that when companies go to great lengths to codify appraisal procedures, this can have an inadvertently *negative* impact on people's sense of fairness. Because it is all about the process and does nothing to help people to connect and trust. As a result, it can generate cynicism more than a sense of fairness.

The solution is not to rely only on the process, on the who needs to complete what form or have which conversation, by when. Instead, you need to focus on *how* you do all of this, and how you can do it in a manner that creates a positive reaction in the trust system of your direct reports. If you think about the other components of trust we have covered, this means paying attention to things such as:

- How you can convey to your direct reports that you *care* about their appraisal and want them to do well in it. This could be by simply telling people this. It could be by spending more time with them at the start of the year, setting them up for success with good objectives. Or it could be by making sure that you allocate a generous amount of time for appraisals conversations, and make sure you never cancel them at the last minute.
- How you can help people to feel *psychologically safe* during the process. For example, by making sure that you give them the opportunity to have a voice in the process. You can do this by asking them what they think or giving them an opportunity to comment on things. It is simple stuff, but research shows that when leaders take the time to do this, employees are more likely to feel psychologically safe and have a greater sense of fairness [39]. In fact, psychological safety appears to be a condition for fairness—something that needs to exist for a sense of fairness to emerge.
- How you can avoid surprising people. In other words, how you can be perceived as being *reliable*. The key thing here is to avoid—as far as possible—introducing new information or data in the final appraisal meeting. And the only way to do this is to ensure that you give people feedback on their performance continually, throughout the year.

So, invest in your performance appraisals. Do not just follow the process, but deliberately and systematically think about how you can do so while also triggering a trust reaction in your direct reports.

Improve How You Treat People You Don't Value

The final technique is an important but tricky one. Although we have never met you, we're guessing that you're human. And because you are human, we know that you are—in some way—biased. You are not an unfeeling computer, approaching new situations without memory or desire. There are things you like and value, and things you don't. And no matter how hard you try to be rational and objective, sometimes these preferences will be apparent and affect what you do and how you do it. And as we have seen from the operation of our trust system, this can happen without you even being aware of it. This is true when you look at a new set of business results for your area. It is true when you go to a meeting and are introduced to new people. And it is true of how you treat the people around you, day in day out.

You have your preferences. You have your favourites, or the people you like or warm to or just value slightly more than others. And it will show. People will know, even if you are not aware of what these preferences are. And as we have learnt with fairness, people judge you not only on the basis of whether you are fair with them personally but also whether they think you are fair with others.

So, the last technique is this: think of the direct report you like or value the least. Think of the peer, stakeholder or board member you like or value the least. Now think about how you behave differently towards them compared with everyone else. You may need help, you may have to ask a trusted other, because it can be hard to see. But there *will* be differences.

Some of these differences may be fine—you would not want to treat everyone exactly the same way. However, some of the differences may affect people's perception of whether you—and your Leadership OS—create fairness.

Unfortunately, people will not always judge you by what you do when you are at your best and creating a strong sense of fairness around you. They will judge you on how you are at your worst, when your natural bias slips through. They will judge you on the quality of your least effective relationships. So, identify them, focus on them and think about how you can use any of the techniques we have covered in the chapters on trust to build a more positive relationship with these people.

Doing it with Purposeful Authenticity

Some readers may look at these techniques and think back to a question we raised a few chapters ago when we explored creating a feeling of care. We asked how leaders can be systematic in building trust, and yet also be sincere and authentic. On the one hand, you need to be deliberate and thoughtful, because if you are not, you are effectively turning a blind eye to your impact. You are just acting, and hoping it has the effect you want. On the other hand, when you hear words like 'deliberate', they can sound mechanical and inauthentic.

For example, we once worked with a pacey, edgy, task-focused executive who had recently moved to a new firm. One of her challenges was that this new business was not as pacey or edgy and was far more relationship-based. Aware of this, she started using some simple techniques to help her be more attentive to relationships. One of these was making notes on the lives of her direct reports. She would make a note before each meeting to remind herself to ask them something about their personal lives; afterwards she would write down what she had learnt so she could remember to follow it up next time. She did this because she knew she needed to do more than she would naturally do to convey a sense of care for her people. But here's the thing: when one day her boss found out about this, he told her that she was being inauthentic. What do you think? Was she?

Strictly speaking, it was inauthentic because she was using an artificial process and projecting an image that was not her 'real' more task-focused self. However, we don't have a problem with that. Because this is another example of where focusing only on how we behave can be unhelpful. What was important in this situation was not whether she was authentic, but the impact she had on the people around her, and the Leadership OS she created.

Eventually, one of her direct reports figured out what she was doing. So she explained that she had a rotten memory and was not naturally good at attending to personal details, but that it was important to her that people knew she cared. They laughed about it, and it was fine. The employee now knew she cared enough to make an effort.

Moreover, the same applies to how you create a sense of fairness. Indeed, it is the same for every component of trust. You cannot leave them to chance, you need to be deliberate and systematic about them. With fairness, especially, it is most powerful when you become more deliberate, when you think more carefully about the nature of the psychological contract you have with the people around you. And when outcomes are not what people want, it is the combination of your *systematic* explanation of process and your ability to deliberately try to connect with your people's trust system that can enable you to create a sense of fairness. Being more purposeful about the impact you have empowers you to create a Leadership OS that simultaneously enables stronger performance *and* provides people with a better, more positive experience.

The Self-Replicating Contract

Fairness, then, is the fourth and final component of trust. It is the psychological contract between you and the people around you and it acts as a kind of wrapper for the other components, holding them in its many clauses and conditions. As such, it is critical to building an OS of trust.

This is why it is such a pity that so many leaders seem to struggle to create a sense of fairness. In survey after survey, employees say that violations of the psychological contract are not the exception but the norm. In fact, most people report that they feel that their bosses are not consistently fair [40].

There is an extra edge to this because studies show that you only have so many chances to build fairness. Once you are perceived to have broken psychological contracts with the people around you more than a couple of times, your reputation for fairness becomes stained and you have to work twice as hard to build it back up again [41].

Here's the good news, though. Fairness—like the other three components of trust—has a magical power. It replicates. Every time you act in a way that reinforces the fairness in your Leadership OS, the people in your system become more likely to follow your lead and act fairly themselves. In so doing, they further strengthen the sense of fairness in the OS and help create a reinforcing loop in which everyone's behaviour triggers reciprocal responses in others. This 'magic' is, of course, just the biological trust system at work, as people trigger positive reactions in each other. And it is why, although creating fairness may sound hard, it is a bit like toppling dominoes. You simply need to make a start.

Summary + Checklist

See Table 6.1.

Table 6.1 Summary of fairness

	OS function	Techniques
Fairness	• Encourages effort, initiative and innovation • Promotes cohesion • Prevents the negative impact of unfairness	• Explain the process • Use appraisals to create trust • Improve how you treat people you don't value

Table 6.2   Have you installed fairness in your leadership OS?

	✓	✗
Do your team believe you will reward them fairly?	☐	☐
Do people believe you *always* give credit where credit is due?	☐	☐
Do people believe that if they put in extra effort, you will notice and appreciate it?	☐	☐
Do people feel that being part of your team and what it is achieving is important to them?	☐	☐
Do people trust their peers on their team to always behave fairly?	☐	☐
Do people believe you are always objective and unbiased when giving them feedback and rating their performance?	☐	☐
Do people believe you explain the decisions you make about them and their performance?	☐	☐

Checklist

To help you think about whether you have successfully installed fairness in your OS, ask yourself how the people around you—your direct reports, peers and stakeholders—would respond to the following questions (Table 6.2).

References

1. J. Colquitt, C. P. Zapata-Phelan and Q. Roberson, "Justice in teams: A review of fairness effects in collective contexts," in *Research in personnel and human resources management*, Bingley, UK, Emerald Group Publishing Limited, 2005, pp. 53–94.
2. D. Knoch, A. Pascual-Leone, K. Meyer, V. Treyer and E. Fehr, "Diminishing reciprocal fairness by disrupting the right prefrontal cortex," *Science*, vol. 314, no. 5800, pp. 829–832, 2006.
3. M. Pillutla and J. Murnighan, "Unfairness, anger, and spite: Emotional rejections of ultimatum offers," *Organizational Behavior and Human Decision Processes*, vol. 68, pp. 208–224, 1996.
4. K. McAuliffe, P. Blake, N. Steinbeis and F. Warneken, "The developmental foundations of human fairness," *Nature Human Behaviour*, vol. 1, no. 2, p. 42, 2017.
5. C. Feng, Y. Luo and F. Krueger, "Neural signatures of fairness-related normative decision making in the ultimatum game: A coordinate-based meta-analysis," *Human Brain Mapping*, vol. 36, no. 2, pp. 591–602, 2015.
6. C. Beugré, "Exploring the neural basis of fairness: A model of neuro-organizational justice," *Organizational Behavior and Human Decision Processes*, vol. 110, no. 2, pp. 129–139, 2009.

7. J. Dulebohn, D. Conlon, I. Sarinopoulos, R. Davison and G. McNamara, "The biological bases of unfairness: Neuroimaging evidence for the distinctiveness of procedural and distributive justice," *Organizational Behavior and Human Processes*, vol. 110, no. 2, pp. 140–151, 2009.

8. T. Singer, B. Seymour, J. O'Doherty, K. Stephan, R. Dolan and C. Frith, "Empathic neural responses are modulated by the perceived fairness of others," *Nature*, vol. 439, no. 7075, p. 466, 2006.

9. S. Gupta, "Climate for innovation, procedural fairness and organizational commitment: An empirical study," *Management and Labour Studies*, vol. 34, no. 1, pp. 43–56, 2009.

10. O. Janssen, "Job demands, perceptions of effort-reward fairness and innovative work behaviour," *Journal of Occupational and Organizational Psychology*, vol. 73, no. 3, pp. 287–302, 2000.

11. M. Xerri, "Examining the relationship between organisational justice, job satisfaction and the innovative behaviour of nursing employees," *International Journal of Innovation Management*, vol. 18, no. 1, 2014.

12. A. Agarwal, "Linking justice, trust and innovative work behaviour to work engagement," *Personnel Review*, vol. 43, no. 1, pp. 41–73, 2014.

13. D. Shapiro and B. Kirkman, "Employees' reaction to the change to work teams: The influence of 'anticipatory' injustice," *Journal of Organizational Change Management*, vol. 12, no. 1, pp. 51–67, 1999.

14. W. Kim and R. Mauborgne, "Implementing global strategies: The role of procedural justice," *Strategic Management Journal*, vol. 12, no. S1, pp. 125–143, 1991.

15. D. De Cremer and T. Tyler, "The effects of trust in authority and procedural fairness on cooperation," *Journal of Applied Psychology*, vol. 92, no. 3, p. 639, 2007.

16. D. De Cremer, T. Tyler and N. Den Ouden, "Managing cooperation via procedural fairness: The mediating influence of self-other merging," *Journal of Economic Psychology*, vol. 26, no. 3, pp. 393–406, 2005.

17. M. Van Vugt and D. De Cremer, "Leadership in social dilemmas: The effects of group identification on collective actions to provide public goods," *Journal of Personality and Social Psychology*, vol. 76, pp. 587–599, 1999.

18. H. Li and E. Umphress, "Fairness from the top: Perceived procedural justice and collaborative problem solving in new product development," *Organization Science*, vol. 18, no. 2, pp. 200–216, 2007.

19. S. Yeşil and S. Dereli, "An empirical investigation of the organisational justice, knowledge sharing and innovation capability," *Procedia-Social and Behavioral Sciences*, vol. 75, pp. 199–208, 2013.

20. A. Li and R. Cropanzano, "Fairness at the group level: Justice climate and intraunit justice climate," *Journal of Management*, vol. 35, no. 3, pp. 564–599, 2009.

21. M. Elçi, M. Karabay and B. Akyüz, "Investigating the mediating effect of ethical climate on organizational justice and burnout: A study on financial sector," *Procedia-Social and Behavioral Sciences*, vol. 207, pp. 587–597, 2015.

22. H. Shih and E. Susanto, "Is innovative behavior really good for the firm? Innovative work behavior, conflict with coworkers and turnover intention: Moderating roles of perceived distributive fairness," *International Journal of Conflict Management*, vol. 22, no. 2, pp. 111–130, 2011.

23. P. Chansler, P. Swamidass and C. Cammann, "Self-managing work teams: An empirical study of group cohesiveness in 'natural work groups' at a Harley-Davidson Motor Company plant," *Small Group Research*, vol. 34, no. 1, pp. 101–120, 2003.

24. J. Georgalis, R. Samaratunge, N. Kimberley and Y. Lu, "Change process characteristics and resistance to organisational change: The role of employee perceptions of justice," *Australian Journal of Management*, vol. 40, no. 1, pp. 89–113, 2015.

25. J. Robbins, M. Ford and L. Tetrick, "Perceived unfairness and employee health: A meta-analytic integration," *Journal of Applied Psychology*, vol. 97, no. 2, p. 235, 2012.

26. A. Sert, M. Elci, T. Uslu and İ. Şener, "The effects of organizational justice and ethical climate on perceived work related stress," *Procedia-Social and Behavioral Sciences*, vol. 150, pp. 1187–1198, 2014.

27. W. Turnley and D. Feldman, "Re-examining the effects of psychological contract violations: Unmet expectations and job dissatisfaction as mediators," *Journal of Organizational Behavior*, vol. 21, no. 1, pp. 25–42, 2000.

28. Q. Roberson and J. Colquitt, "Shared and configural justice: A social network model of justice in teams," *Academy of Management Review*, vol. 30, no. 3, pp. 595–607, 2005.

29. T. Qiu, W. Qualls, J. Bohlmann and D. Rupp, "The effect of interactional fairness on the performance of cross-functional product development teams: A multilevel mediated model," *Journal of Product Innovation Management*, vol. 26, no. 2, pp. 173–187, 2009.

30. J. DeConinck, "The effect of organizational justice, perceived organizational support, and perceived supervisor support on marketing employees' level of trust," *Journal of Business Research*, vol. 63, no. 12, pp. 1349–1355, 2010.

31. J. Colquitt, D. Conlon, M. Wesson, C. Porter and K. Ng, "Justice at the millennium: A meta-analytic review of 25 years of organizational justice research," *Journal of Applied Psychology*, vol. 86, no. 3, p. 425, 2001.

32. J. Decety and K. Yoder, "The emerging social neuroscience of justice motivation," *Trends in Cognitive Sciences*, vol. 21, no. 1, pp. 6–14, 2017.

33. K. Mossholder, N. Bennett and C. Martin, "A multilevel analysis of procedural justice context," *Journal of Organizational Behavior*, vol. 19, pp. 131–141, 1998.

34. J. Greenberg, "Losing sleep over organizational injustice: Attenuating insomniac reactions to underpayment inequity with supervisory training in interactional justice," *Journal of Applied Psychology*, vol. 91, no. 1, pp. 58–69, 2006.
35. K. van den Bos, E. Lind, R. Vermunt and H. Wilke, "How do I judge my outcome when I do not know the outcome of others? The psychology of the fair process effect," *Journal of Personality and Social Psychology*, vol. 72, no. 5, pp. 1034–1046, 1997.
36. J. Brockner and B. Wiesenfeld, "An integrative framework for explaining reactions todecisions: The interactive effects of outcomes and procedures," *Psychological Bulletin*, vol. 120, pp. 189–208, 1996.
37. B. Güroğlu, W. van den Bos, S. Rombouts and E. Crone, "Unfair? It depends: neural correlates of fairness in social context," *Social Cognitive and Affective Neuroscience*, vol. 5, no. 4, pp. 414–423, 2010.
38. B. Erdogan, "Antecedents and consequences of justice perceptions in performance appraisals," *Human Resource Management Review*, vol. 12, no. 4, pp. 555–578, 2002.
39. R. Bies and D. Shapiro, "Voice and Justification: Their Influence on Procedural Fairness Judgments," *The Academy of Management Journal*, vol. 31, no. 3, pp. 676–685, 1988.
40. S. Robinson and D. Rousseau, "Violating the psychological contract: Not the exception but the norm," *Journal of Organizational Behavior*, vol. 15, no. 3, pp. 245–259, 1994.
41. S. Gilliland, L. Benson and D. Schepers, "A rejection threshold in justice evaluations: Effects on judgment and decision-making," *Organizational Behavior and Human Decision Processes*, vol. 76, no. 2, pp. 113–131, 1998.

Part II

Creating Clarity

7

Clarity

The Mental Map for Your OS

Cameron Mitchell is an American entrepreneur and the founder of a $300 million restaurant empire he started in his dining room in Columbus, Ohio. He built his business through hard work, the self-belief needed to make courageous decisions and the humility required to learn from his mistakes. That, and a single-minded focus on building a culture of great service. For him, that was what he and his restaurants were all about. Right up until the day, that is, he was caught out by a chocolate milkshake.

He was out with his family at a local diner when it happened. He had asked for a grilled cheese sandwich for his son, but the server politely informed him that it wasn't on the menu. Puzzled, Cameron pointed out that a club sandwich *was* on the menu, and asked if they couldn't just grill him one, leaving out all the ingredients except the cheese. Reluctantly, the server agreed.

Then Cameron asked if his son could have a chocolate milkshake, too. The server replied that they only had a huge Häagen-Dazs one that was too big for a young child. When Cameron pointed out that this was fine as his son could just have a bit of it, she apologised and said they couldn't do it, because it was for adults. So Cameron asked her to speak with her manager. She did, but returned saying that her manager agreed that they couldn't do it. Frustrated, Cameron spoke with the manager himself and, eventually, after a long discussion, his son got the milkshake.

© The Author(s) 2020
N. Kinley and S. Ben-Hur, *Leadership OS*,
https://doi.org/10.1007/978-3-030-27293-7_7

A week later, Cameron was on stage speaking at a conference and told the story of the grilled cheese and chocolate milkshake. He boasted that such a thing would never happen at one of his restaurants because of their emphasis on hospitality. By all accounts, the speech went well. Afterwards, however, an audience member approached him and told him that just a week before they had been in one of *his* restaurants and tried to order a chocolate milkshake. And they had been told no because it wasn't on the menu.

Years later, Cameron describes this moment as a 'gut punch'. He had worked to instil a culture of saying yes to customers throughout his restaurants. He prided himself on it. Clearly, the message wasn't getting through.

The following Monday, he called a senior executive meeting. He told the story and, for the next few hours, they debated what to do. Their solution was elegant. They would turn the evidence of their failure into the symbol of their success. They would make chocolate milkshakes the icon of the culture they wanted to create, one in which the answer was always yes and their staff were 'great people delivering genuine hospitality'. And not just *a* symbol, but *the* ever-present, everyday embodiment of what they wanted to be.

Today, everybody who starts working at one of their restaurants receives a chocolate milkshake and attends a workshop about what it means. Milkshakes are handed out at meetings and events. Great service is celebrated through a weekly Milkshake Award. Even the company logo has a milkshake on it. And every time staff gather to share a milkshake the toast is always the same, 'The answer is yes. What is the question?'

Clarity can be hard to create. Getting a disparate and dispersed group of people to have a shared common understanding of what is important and how things should be done is tough. However, when you do, when you get it right and it springs to life and has such an influence on how people act, day in, day out, it is the difference between good and brilliant performance.

Clarity Is You

The second of the three key elements of a Leadership OS is clarity. It is the understanding that exists about the strategy of the business, what is important, why it is important, what needs to be done, who is accountable for what, and how things should be done.

If trust is about keeping relationships and communication pathways open and positive, clarity is the messages sent and received through them.

It is what enables you to generate the focus, alignment, and unity that are essential for strategy implementation and business success [1].

So essential is clarity that it plays a central role in your Leadership OS, acting as a connecting lever between the other two elements. It reinforces trust and enables momentum, binding people together and serving as a foundation for action. Creating it is a critical part of any leader's job.

Moreover, as with trust, clarity seems to be becoming ever more critical as the business world becomes increasingly volatile, uncertain, complex and ambiguous. Studies show that as stress and uncertainty increase, so does the role that clarity plays [2]. The benefits of building it increase, and the penalties for not doing so grow sharper.

So, in this and the next four chapters, we are going to break clarity down. We are going to look at what it is, the role it plays in your Leadership OS, and at some of the things you can do to instal it in your OS. As with trust, however, our interest and focus are less about what you *do* and more about the *impact you have*—the environment you need to create and the experience you need to help others have.

What Clarity Is

Let's start by being clear about what clarity is. Working with a team of researchers, we have examined hundreds of research studies on clarity. We have also conducted our own research with thousands of leaders across the globe. In doing so, we discovered four distinct components of clarity (Fig. 7.1). Each of these must exist for clarity to emerge and, as such, each requires your attention. The four are:

1. Direction—the extent to which people have a shared understanding of what is important; in other words, the strategy and objectives of the business.
2. Accountability—the extent to which people feel responsible for what they do and have a clear sense of who is accountable for what.
3. Purpose—the extent to which people understand how what they do contributes to the business and feel that it matters.
4. Values—the extent to which people have a shared understanding of how things should be done.

Together, these four components combine to create a kind of mental map of your business, an understanding of the lie of the land, or what the firm

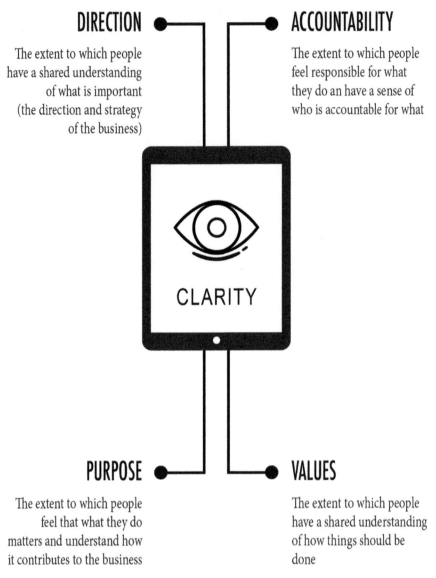

DIRECTION

The extent to which people have a shared understanding of what is important (the direction and strategy of the business)

ACCOUNTABILITY

The extent to which people feel responsible for what they do an have a sense of who is accountable for what

CLARITY

PURPOSE

The extent to which people feel that what they do matters and understand how it contributes to the business

VALUES

The extent to which people have a shared understanding of how things should be done

Fig. 7.1 The components of clarity

is about and what it is trying to do. It includes both task elements, such as what needs to happen, and people elements, such as how people will work together and should treat each other [3]. And like all maps, this one helps guide people and ensure they are heading in the right direction.

People Prefer Certainty

Studies show that most people, given a choice, will avoid uncertainty [4]. For example, when buying a house, many people choose a fixed-rate mortgage, where the interest rate is set in stone, over a variable-rate mortgage, where the rate can change. And this is the case even though variable mortgages have been shown to save money.

Another example is recent research looking at the use of URL shorteners. These are apps that can turn a long URL, such as https://leadershipos/blogposts/why-clarity-is-important into something shorter, such as https://goo.gl/PjwSmX. These apps became popular because of initial research showing that people liked shorter URLs. And they do. But what they do not like—even more than long URLs—is ambiguous ones. As a result, the study found that engagement rates were three times higher for websites with full-length descriptive URLs than for ambiguous shortened ones [5].

What Clarity Does

When we explored the role that the mental map created by clarity plays in an operating system, we discovered it serves four essential functions (Fig. 7.2).

A. Reduces Uncertainty

The first thing clarity does is to reduce uncertainty. It sounds obvious, but it is also crucial because studies show that the way people's brains process and respond to information or situations changes under uncertainty. And not always for the better.

For example, when faced with uncertainty, we might be expected to become more thoughtful. Yet we often don't. We do sometimes slow down and become more cautious. But studies show that we also start using less

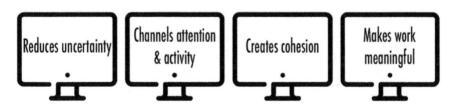

Fig. 7.2 The functions of clarity in a Leadership OS

conscious, logical and rational analysis, and we begin relying more on our experience, instincts and feelings. This is evident in studies of stock market asset pricing. In the absence of good quality information, investors become increasingly led by things like their inner, base levels of risk aversion and their general optimism or pessimism [6]. This shift in thinking has a big benefit, as it helps people to make quick and clear decisions and avoid the analysis-paralysis that ambiguity could lead to. But it also renders people far more prone to biases and errors in their decision-making. And this is why in our research we found that leaders who were viewed as creating high levels of clarity in their OSs, and thus as minimising the impact of uncertainty, were also seen as much better decision-makers.

Another thing uncertainty does is trigger similar neural threat detection pathways to the ones we saw when we looked at psychological safety in Section "The X-System" in Chapter 2. As uncertainty increases, activity in the amygdala also rises [7]. This sets off our trust system, with the social areas of the brain becoming less active and the task areas more active. As a result, we become more cautious, more likely to see the negative in things, and more prone to conflict. This explains why our research found that employees reported stress levels nearly 20% higher when working in OSs with lower levels of clarity. It also explains something called the *ambiguity effect*—the fact that people are less likely to act, take the initiative or respond to a call to action when they feel a situation is ambiguous.

Put this all together, and it is easy to see why reducing uncertainty is so vital: the cost of not doing it, of not creating clarity, is less effective decision-making, less trust and less action.

B. Channels Attention and Activity

The second thing that clarity does is to change what people pay attention to and do [8]. There are several ways it does this. The most obvious is that, as a leader, you can simply instruct or ask people to focus on and do certain things. Even if you do not directly ask people to do something, simply raising their awareness of a topic—like the importance of customer service—means they are more likely to see it and attend to it going forward. And, of course, by creating clarity about what is important to you and the business, you set down markers for reward and recognition—things for people to strive towards and try to attain and achieve. So clarity enables you to steer the ship, to make sure that attention and activity are focused on the right things.

C. Creates Cohesion

The third thing clarity does in your OS is to help align people. The shared mental map—and the mutual understanding, common purpose and shared objectives that go with it—helps bring people together and create cohesion. This is why studies show that OSs with higher levels of clarity tend to have stronger levels of teamwork [9]. As clarity rises, so do team communication [10] and coordination [11] levels. And this seems especially true under heavy workloads or in non-routine situations [12].

D. Makes Work Meaningful

The final thing clarity does is to help make work meaningful for people. In our research across the globe, we found that people working in OSs that have a high level of clarity are far more likely both to say that they have a strong sense of purpose at work and that they feel motivated.

There are a couple of reasons for this. First, and most simply, when people have a clear sense of why something is worth doing, it is more likely to be meaningful for them. Then, there is what is called the *progress principle*. This is the idea that people are more likely to view something as meaningful and motivating when they can see and feel that they are making progress with it. Clarity about objectives enables this, by giving people markers that help them see whether they are making progress or not. This is why people with clear goals consistently report higher levels of motivation than those with more ambiguous goals [13].

The Benefits of Clarity

Put these four functions together and you can see why clarity is a powerful lever for performance. Study after study has shown this, too. Consider these highlights from the research:

- Businesses in which there is a high degree of clarity and consensus among employees about what their strategy is tend to outperform those with less clarity and tend to have higher levels of profitability [14].
- Businesses whose external stakeholders have a greater degree of clarity about the firm's purpose and objectives are more likely to be high performing [15].

- Leadership teams that have a high degree of consensus about the strategy are more likely to execute it successfully [16].
- Firms in which there is a high degree of clarity about budget goals are more likely to be high performing [17].
- When teams have higher levels of clarity about their objectives and targets, they are more likely to reach them [18].
- Salespeople who have greater levels of clarity about their targets are more likely to achieve them [19].
- Research and development teams that report higher levels of clarity about their targets are more likely to innovate [20].

The list could go on. Little wonder, then, that in our research we discovered that leaders rated as high performing by their bosses and other senior stakeholders were also rated as creating OSs much higher in clarity by their direct reports. Compared with lower-performing leaders, the top performers created OSs that were 28% higher in direction, 19% higher in purpose, 24% higher in values and 15% higher in accountability. Across the board, high-performing leaders create OSs that have greater levels of clarity.

Creating Clarity: The Case of Zhang Xin and SOHO China

Zhang Xin's story is the quintessential rags-to-riches tale. When she was 19, she left the sweatshops of Hong Kong—where she had been working since the age of 14—and moved to London. She believed that England was a land of education and opportunity and that she needed to be there to secure the prosperous future she wanted (Fig 7.3).

Yet when she arrived, she had a sudden moment of doubt. After getting off the plane, she went into London and walked around for a while, before breaking down in tears. She didn't speak English. She didn't have a job or any money. She didn't know anyone in England. And she no longer had any idea what she was doing there or how she was going to make it work.

Despite the uncertainty facing her, Zhang Xin's personal pity party lasted less than an hour. She pulled herself together, got up and introduced herself to the first person she saw who might speak Chinese.

This attitude characterises Zhang Xin both as an individual and a professional. It also explains how she became the CEO of SOHO China, one of the largest real estate companies in the world.

Ask her employees to describe their boss, and they almost always remark on the speed at which she makes decisions. She has joked before that she

Fig. 7.3 Zhang Xin

doesn't do analysis, but dig deeper, and the truth is something else. Zhang's key traits are her vision and sense of direction. She is always looking ahead, doing the analysis *before* a decision needs to be made, not *when* it needs to be made. And she has a clear sense of direction—of what is important and what she wants to achieve.

These are the traits that led her to leave Hong Kong as a 19-year-old. They are the traits that led her to study the economics of privatisation for her Master's thesis at the University of Cambridge. They are the traits that helped her succeed in Goldman Sachs' investment banking group, advising Chinese companies on the process of privatisation during the 1990s. And they are the traits that helped her become 'The Woman Who Built Beijing' with SOHO China.

Zhang and her husband formed SOHO China in the 1990s as a real estate development company, with the vision of developing modern constructions for a modernising Beijing. And Zhang didn't want just to erect buildings: she wanted to erect beautiful buildings.

She was born in 1965 and grew up during the Chinese Cultural Revolution. To her eye, everything was grey: architecture, clothes, people, dreams. But her time in London and New York exposed her to how beautiful buildings could be and the impact they could have on their surroundings. So in the early days of SOHO China, Zhang brought in international architects to design her buildings. She didn't just want big edifices; she wanted iconic ones with beauty, personality and identity that could help transform communities and society. Today, this clear vision runs through all of SOHO China. It is a core principle that Zhang both lives herself and ensures is embedded deep in the culture of the business.

Zhang's capacity for clarity extends beyond her architectural vision. She has made sure that her role in running the company she co-founded is clear, with her and her husband having clear delegation of responsibilities. And she is similarly clear in her people leadership. She talks of how she believes everyone has a unique talent and how her role is to help people identify it, develop it and maximise its potential. Wherever she goes, whatever she does, creating clarity is part of her job. And it has reaped its rewards.

Since the mid-1990s, SOHO China has constructed more square footage than any Chinese emperor ever did. Zhang's focus on bringing art and beauty to her edifices has created some of the most unique buildings in China. And she has helped redefine how people and society connect through the spaces they live and work in.

SOHO China eventually transitioned from a property developer to a property owner and landlord; later, it focused on opportunities inside buildings, including entering the co-working space market. These changes don't happen by luck or instinct; they happen because of Zhang and her team's proactive analysis that perform and the clear vision they create for the company, its future and the future of Chinese society. Her clarity, direction and decision-making helped her begin her life in London in the 1980s, and it is still helping her company shape the skylines across China today.

A Crisis of Clarity

Given how central creating clarity is to what leaders do, and that it delivers such benefits, we could be expected to have it down to an art form by now. Instead, we seem to find it tough. Study after study has shown this, and in our research nearly 60 per cent of firms believed their employees did *not* have a clear and common understanding of the business strategy.

And looking at the research carried out across the globe over the past 30 years, it is clear that clarity seems to be becoming less and less common.

The reasons for this are probably less to do with the capabilities of leaders and more to do with the nature of the context they work in and the challenges they face. Simply put, the context and challenges are becoming harder and more complex.

Markets are becoming more changeable and the environment less predictable, and when change occurs, it seems to happen faster. Then there is big data. The access to far greater data sets and the analytics they enable are undoubtedly both a driving force of much of the change around us and a fantastic opportunity for businesses. But they are also a threat and a source of uncertainty, since the quantity of data available is currently outpacing growth in the quality of the data. So big data may be providing a bigger picture, but for the moment it's not clear that it is always a better one.

These factors increase the need for leaders to create clarity. But several factors make the impact of what leaders do to create this clarity far less certain. Probably the most significant of these is globalisation. As business becomes more multinational, leaders are increasingly coming face to face with national cultural differences in people's desire for clarity [21]. So, people from countries like the US, the United Kingdom, India, China and Singapore tend to have a lower need for clarity than people from Italy, Korea, Mexico, Belgium and Russia. And these differences mean there is a greater requirement for leaders to be aware of their impact and be able to adjust their approach [22].

Forces like these are rendering one-size-fits-all, do-this, behavioural and competency-based approaches to leadership increasingly unreliable. They underscore the importance of leaders focusing more on the actual impact they have and the Leadership OSs they create. So over the next four chapters, we are going to focus on just this, paying particular attention to how the changing business world is making the task of creating clarity ever trickier.

As before, we will offer practical techniques for what you can do. But also as before, we are not suggesting a specific solution, but rather offering a range of options to choose from. We recommend you try a few, watch your impact and adjust and hone your approach to your work context.

We will be suggesting techniques for each of the four components of clarity. But to get you started, there is one quick but crucial tip that applies to every aspect of creating clarity. It speaks to a fundamental tension that is part of every component of a Leadership OS. Because just as with every aspect of trust, and as we will see later with every aspect of momentum, too much of a good thing can quickly become a bad thing.

How to Be an Uncertainty Regulator

The core function clarity plays in your Leadership OS is reducing uncertainty. One step you can take in this regard is to become more conscious, deliberate and systematic about focusing on uncertainty and—where useful—minimising it.

A simple way to get started is to ask your team where the ambiguity lies. Ask them what they are not clear about that they would like to be. Ask them which things make them pause and be more cautious.

But there is a tension to be aware of here: in almost all modern businesses, there is a need for speed. And since uncertainty tends to cause people to pause, there is a natural urge for leaders to want to eradicate uncertainty wherever it exists. To be clear, this is *not* what we advocate. Sometimes, pauses are good. Moments that force people to stop and think—and, in doing so, perhaps change what they think and how they react—are important drivers of growth and progress. It is from them that reflection, improvement and innovation come.

Therefore, when you identify uncertainty, you need to decide whether it is useful and whether it is having a negative effect. Unfortunately, because people differ in how they respond to uncertainty, and because uncertainty can have different effects in different situations, there are no hard and fast rules about how to work this out.

As a broad guide, signs of too little uncertainty could include people not questioning or debating issues, inhibited creativity or people being inflexible in how they work and collaborate. Signs of too much uncertainty, by contrast, could include lack of activity or planning, or a lack of team cohesion and focus.

However, all of these could be signs of other things, unrelated to uncertainty. For example, a lack of debate could be down to insufficient psychological safety. So, to understand what is really going on, you have to speak to your people. When you find an uncertainty, you need to ask them what impact it is having on them. And, specifically, how it changes what they do and how they do it.

In this sense, over the coming chapters we are urging you not to become an uncertainty eradicator or hunter, not to become a leader who is all about clarity and nothing else. We are urging you to become an *uncertainty regulator*. Someone who uses clarity like a specialist tool. Who sometimes heightens clarity in their Leadership OS to drive activity forwards and sometimes lowers it, to slow things down and force people to stop and think. Clarity is your accelerator and brake pedal rolled into one.

References

1. R. Stagner, "Corporate decision making: An empirical study," *Journal of Applied Psychology*, vol. 53, no. 1, pt. 1, pp. 1–13, 1969.
2. S. Hannah, M. Uhl-Bien, B. Avolio and F. Cavarretta, "A framework for examining leadership in extreme contexts," University of Nebraska Management Department Faculty Publications. Paper 39, 2009.
3. Y. Reuveni and D. Vashdi, "Innovation in multidisciplinary teams: The moderating role of transformational leadership in the relationship between professional heterogeneity and shared mental models," *European Journal of Work and Organizational Psychology*, vol. 24, no. 5, pp. 678–692, 2015.
4. C. Camerer and M. Weber, "Recent developments in modeling preferences— Uncertainty and ambiguity," *Journal of Risk Uncertainty*, vol. 5, pp. 325–370, 1992.
5. J. Constine, "Shorter is better, but avoid url shorteners," *AdWeek*, 6 April 2011.
6. L. Epstein and M. Schneider, "Ambiguity, information quality, and asset pricing," *The Journal of Finance*, vol. 63, no. 1, pp. 197–228, 2008.
7. M. Hsu, M. Bhatt, R. Adolphs, D. Tranel and C. Camerer, "Neural systems responding to degrees of uncertainty in human decision-making," *Science*, vol. 310, no. 5754, pp. 1680–1683, 2005.
8. K. Weick, *The social psychology of organizing* (2nd ed.), London: McGraw-Hill, 1979.
9. K. Dale and M. L. Fox, "Leadership style and organizational commitment: Mediating effect of role stress," *Journal of Managerial Issues*, pp. 109–130, 2008.
10. M. Waller, N. Gupta and R. Giambatista, "Effects of adaptive behaviors and shared mental models on control crew performance," *Management Science*, vol. 50, no. 11, pp. 1463–1613, 2004.
11. R. Stout, J. Cannon-Bowers, E. Salas and D. Milanovich, "Planning, shared mental models, and coordinated performance: An empirical link is established," *Human Factors*, vol. 41, no. 1, pp. 61–71, 1999.
12. M. Marks, S. Zaccaro and J. Mathieu, "Performance implications of leader briefings and team-interaction training for team adaptation to novel environments," *Journal of Applied Psychology*, vol. 85, no. 6, pp. 971–986, 2000.
13. T. Amabile and M. Pratt, "The dynamic componential model of creativity and innovation in organizations: Making progress, making meaning," *Research in Organizational Behavior*, vol. 36, pp. 157–183, 2016.
14. J. Parnell, "Strategic clarity, business strategy and performance," *Journal of Strategy and Management*, vol. 3, no. 4, pp. 303–324, 2010.
15. F. Buytendijk, "The five keys to building a high performance organization," *Business Performance Management Magazine*, vol. 4, no. 1, pp. 24–47, 2006.
16. L. Hrebiniak and C. Snow, "Top-management agreement and organizational performance," *Human Relations*, vol. 35, no. 12, pp. 1139–1157, 1982.

17. I. Kennis, "Effects of budgetary goal characteristics on attitudes and performance," *The Accounting Review*, vol. 54, no. 4, p. 707, 1979.
18. J. Hu and R. Liden, "Antecedents of team potency and team effectiveness: An examination of goal and process clarity and servant leadership," *Journal of Applied Psychology*, vol. 96, no. 4, pp. 851–862, 2011.
19. "The effect of comprehensive performance measurement systems on role clarity, psychological empowerment and managerial performance," *Accounting, Organizations and Society*, vol. 33, no. 2, pp. 141–163, 2008.
20. C. Peralta, P. Lopes, L. Glison, P. Lourenço and L. Pais, "Innovation processes and team effectiveness: The role of goal clarity and commitment, and team affective tone," *Journal of Occupational and Organisational Psychology*, vol. 88, no. 1, pp. 80–107, 2015.
21. G. Hofstede, *Culture's Consequences: comparing values, behaviors, institutions, and organizations across nations* (2nd ed.), Thousand Oaks, CA: Sage, 2001.
22. R. Arvey, H. Dewhirst and J. Boling, "Relationships between goal clarity, participation in goal setting, and personality characteristics on job satisfaction in a scientific organization," *Journal of Applied Psychology*, vol. 61, no. 1, pp. 103–105, 1976.

8

Direction

Imagine yourself in this situation.

Every year, we run a leadership development programme with leaders from around the world. In one session, we give the participants 5 minutes to prepare a 60-second speech—*the* speech that they would give to their team back at work—entitled, 'What is important'. The things they would tell their team about the direction they and the business are heading in, and what they want them to focus on, do or achieve. Some leaders concentrate on broad strategic objectives, others home in on particular key performance indicators (KPIs), and still others talk about how they want people to work together.

We only give people five minutes to prepare because—as we say to them—it is something they probably already do and certainly should already know. Once prepared, each person in the group takes it in turns to stand up and speak. At the end of each speech, we ask the others in the group to provide feedback. How clear it was, how memorable or how inspiring. How it was structured, how it was delivered and what the speaker could do to improve it. In this way, it is a typical presentation-skills exercise. Except it comes with a twist. Because after the feedback, we ask the rest of the group a simple question: 'What can you remember?'

The results are remarkably consistent. For over 95% of speeches, the audience can remember surprisingly little of what was said. Just the odd word or phrase, usually. Amazingly, this is true even after they realise we will be asking them what they can remember at the end of the speech. Even with this set-up, ready to be asked, they remember staggeringly little of it—a speech just 60-seconds long.

© The Author(s) 2020
N. Kinley and S. Ben-Hur, *Leadership OS*,
https://doi.org/10.1007/978-3-030-27293-7_8

So how much do you think your team remember about what you tell them is important?

When we check this, when we ask teams, peers and stakeholders whether a leader does indeed create a clear sense of what is important, the results are startling. Over 98% of leaders believe they create a clear sense of direction. Yet only 30% of peers agree with the leaders' rating of themselves, only 27% of direct reports agree and only 24% of key stakeholders agree.

Moreover, this is without checking whether *what* these people believe the leader has said is similar—whether the leader has managed to create a unified, shared understanding. On the odd occasion we do check that, the numbers fall even lower.

When we talk about clarity, most people think of strategic goals, tactical objectives and KPIs. They think of mission statements, inspiring visions and goal setting. Yet this chapter is about none of those things.

The reason for this is that these are all *inputs*—things leaders do. What we are interested in are the *outputs*: the extent to which your Leadership OS and the people operating within it have a clear and shared sense of direction. This could be your board, your investors, your peers or your direct reports and their extended teams. Do they have a common understanding of the strategy and objectives of the business? And do they understand what you and the business need from them—what their team needs to achieve, or what their own individual goals are?

If you think about our metaphor of clarity as being a mental map of your business, direction is the landmarks on it, the coordinates or focal points that let people know where they are and how they are progressing.

So, how good are you at creating a shared sense of direction in your Leadership OS?

The Power of Clear Direction: The Case of Carlsberg and Cees 't Hart

When Cees 't Hart was appointed CEO of Carlsberg Breweries in June 2015, the company was in a mess (Fig. 8.1). Literally. Confusion and dysfunction reigned as the firm's 30 different operating companies—spread all over the world—each moved forward with varying degrees of success, and there was no unifying sense of direction of where the company was headed.

't Hart was committed to changing this. Within months of starting, he convened Carlsberg's top 60 leaders on a large yacht outside Amsterdam. As a leader, he loves to work through metaphors, in both words and actions,

Cees 't Hart

Fig. 8.1 Cees 't Hart

and the yacht served just this purpose for him. He called the trip *Sail '22* and announced that the purpose was to make sure everyone was 'on the boat and in the boat'—working together to develop a strategy and committed to implementing it. Moreover, by referencing 2022, he was saying that this would be a long-term—seven-year—voyage that relied on everyone contributing.

This initial meeting launched a series of follow-up sessions, to refine priorities and establish the culture that 't Hart wanted to cultivate for the future. Throughout this fine-tuning, however, he was clear and consistent about which indicators he wanted tracked and why. This gave his message focal points. And to make sure people committed to them, 't Hart introduced his AAA principles: Alignment, Accountability and Action. The idea was simple. With the direction set, people needed to follow it, and there was no room to pursue other things. Not all could commit to the new direction, of course. And those who did not were asked to leave, no matter how good their prior record of delivering performance.

't Hart wasn't done yet, though. Having introduced the *Sail '22* plan and the AAA principles, he added a final element to his message. As before, he used a metaphor. He told first his leaders and then all his employees to imagine they were a football (soccer) team. He said that due to the previous, decentralised culture, they were essentially playing on 30 different pitches around the world. They were only concerned about winning on their pitch and didn't think or care enough about the other 29 pitches. He wanted them to play as one team on one pitch.

To encourage this, he asked them to think about the role they played on the pitch, in the team. Operations, country experts and delivery professionals would be the attackers—on the front end of the company's efforts. Supply chain would be the midfielders, controlling the process and connecting the different parts of the firm. And legal, finance and risk management would be the defence, making sure nothing bad happened, so that the company could benefit from the midfielders and attackers doing their job.

Time will tell whether 't Hart succeeds. But the first four years of his seven-year journey have yielded steadily improving financial results. At the time of writing, the share price was up 73% compared to the day he joined. All sorts of contributory factors have helped with this, not least the culture 't Hart has created. However, the starting point and the centrepiece of it all has been the *Sail '22* plan and the clear and shared sense of direction it created.

What Direction Does

Like any component of clarity, direction helps reduce uncertainty [1]. As such, it stops the triggering of the neural threat-detection pathways that make people less social, less trusting and more cautious and negative. On that basis alone, clear direction is worth it. However, direction also performs four other functions in your Leadership OS (Fig. 8.2).

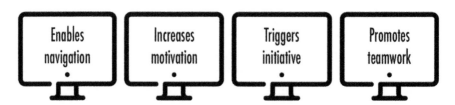

Fig. 8.2 The functions of direction in a Leadership OS

A. Enables Navigation

Direction is more than just a point on a map, something people passively follow. It is something people can use to help navigate for themselves. It allows them to make sense of where they are and what they need to do, without you—as their leader—standing over them, holding the map all the time.

In recent years, scientists have been able to use new brain imaging techniques to see the neurological basis for this. When we come into contact with new information, events and situations, we use two different pathways in our brains to process and understand what is happening [2]. One is a bottom-up pathway, driven by what we see. If it detects potentially important sensory information—such as loud alarms or sudden movement—it activates and sends signals through the brain to get us to pay attention. This is why some things will *always* grab our attention, no matter what we are doing.

The second pathway is a top-down one, and we use it to look for things. Whereas the bottom-up channel is essentially passive, receiving information with the occasional alarm bell going off, the second pathway is far more active. It is as if we have a list of things we are interested in, and the brain is constantly using this second pathway to check every piece of sensory data against the list [3].

For example, imagine arriving in a city in a country you have never visited before. Taking a taxi to your hotel, you would look out of the window and … see things. And what is most likely to attract your attention are the things that interest you, the things that are on the list held by your top-down attention system. If it is architecture, your brain would be checking for interesting-looking buildings and homing in on them when it detected them. Or if it is fashion, your brain might focus on people more.

So, when you create direction in your Leadership OS, when you do something to clarify what is important, you change how people process information. You don't just give them a goal; you effectively add something to the list that their second neural pathway uses to control their attention. And as a result, they pay more attention to anything they encounter that is related to the direction you have set [4].

Just as with the biological trust system, this processing happens so quickly that people are not even aware of it. Afterwards, once they have paid attention to something and thought about it, they can explain why something is relevant. But the actual act of first noticing it, of whether they pay attention to it, is all automatic processing.

So this mechanism means that when your Leadership OS provides a sense of direction for people, they are more able to navigate for themselves.

It makes people more able to make sense of new information and events, to make their own decision about whether it is relevant and useful to help them get where you and they need them to go. Clear direction turns people's brains into a compass.

B. Increases Motivation

The second thing direction does in your Leadership OS is to provide a lever for motivation, and it does this in a couple of ways. First, some people find direction in and of itself to be motivational. They like having a map and knowing where they are going, having something to aim for. The stereotype of this is traders or salespeople—those motivated by the challenge of a target.

The second way direction motivates people is by enabling them to identify when they make progress. Without a sense of direction—a map of where you are and where you are heading—it is almost impossible to know if you are moving forwards or backwards. But direction enables people to establish that what they are doing is positive and value adding. Without it, and thus without a way of showing progress, you could not reward or recognise anyone, and they would not be able to recognise and feel motivated by what they have accomplished. And as such, direction is a required foundation for motivation.

The role that direction plays in motivating people is evident in the research findings, too. Just having clear direction has been found to reduce staff turnover [5] and to improve employee morale [6], satisfaction [7] and engagement [8].

C. Triggers Initiative

Combine navigation with motivation, and you have a recipe for initiative. When people can read their own map, when they can use what they know about what is important and desirable to work out which way is forward, this enables them to take the initiative.

We saw in the previous chapter that one consequence of uncertainty is that the benefits of taking action are not always clear. Direction, by removing this uncertainty, frees people up for action. It also boosts their confidence to take such action. Our own research shows that people working in Leadership OSs with high levels of direction report on average being 13% more confident, a finding replicated in other studies [9]. And this combination of reduced uncertainty and increased confidence is why having a sense of clear direction has been shown to improve levels of commitment, initiative taking and creativity [10].

D. Promotes Teamwork

One final thing that direction does in your Leadership OS is improving communication [11] and teamwork [12]. It does this in four simple ways. First, it creates a shared understanding of things. When an OS provides a clear sense of direction, people are more likely to see things the same way, since they are working from the same map [13].

Second, direction creates points of collaboration. When people understand both their own and other people's roles, it makes it clearer where they need to cooperate to succeed. And as a result of knowing this, they are more likely to work together effectively in these moments.

Third, by creating a shared map and a common understanding of which way is forward, direction reduces fault lines. It lessens the negative impact of natural differences between people. Things like gender, tenure and functional background are all far less likely to create tensions and difficulties when people have something common to focus on [14].

Finally, when conflict does arrive, direction makes resolving it easier [15]. Teams working in a Leadership OS with clear direction have been found to have lower levels of defensiveness and anxiety [16], to discuss opposing views more openly and to resolve them more quickly [17].

Add these four functions of direction together, and the result is improved performance at every level [18]. Clear business strategic direction has been found to improve overall firm performance across a number of different financial metrics [19]. This is true at a business unit level [20], at a project level in terms of project success [21] and at an individual level, in terms of both worker productivity [22]. And in our own research, leaders with OSs high in direction were rated 24% higher for performance by their bosses. So direction is a powerful and essential force in any effective Leadership OS.

How Direction Is Created

In 2012, a team of researchers conducted a study across 99 businesses in the US, Europe and Asia. Their focus was how a sense of direction is created and, specifically, whether it is produced more by central, CEO-led strategy pronouncements, or by individual leaders working with their teams. The results were consistent, regardless of the national culture of the business. Local, individual leaders have a far stronger impact on people's sense of direction than top-down, headquarter-led declarations [23].

For example, if we take the earlier case of Cees 't Hart at Carlsberg, he clearly led the way. It was his strategy, his direction. But he made it work through the top 60 leaders he invited to the yacht. And *they* then made it work through the leaders in their teams. So, direction is created locally— business by business, team by team—by each individual leader.

When we look at *how* to do this, we find the same issues as before. Because leaders are operating in different situations with different demands and different people, there are no hard-and-fast rules that will always work.

What About Mission Statements?

Over the past 20 years, mission statements have been incredibly popular tools. They are declarations of why an organisation exists and what its overall goal is. And whole libraries have been written about how to do them well. Yet when you check the independent research on whether they have a positive impact on business performance, the evidence is mixed at best. The answer seems to be 'maybe, sometimes, in some situations'—and with varying advice about what types of scenarios they do work in. So, just like capabilities, mission statements are unreliable drivers of performance.

There are some *general* rules that will work in many cases, of course. For example, we know that in most scenarios, any message about what is important tends to be more effective if it is brief, simple and repeated [24]. We know that developing a sense of psychological safety is essential, since without it people can hold back from voicing concerns about direction and so remain uncertain [25]. And we know that effective planning processes can also increase clarity of direction [26]. Beyond this, however, what you need to do to create a sense of direction varies.

For you as a leader, this means that to create a sense of direction—as with the other components of a Leadership OS—you need to be careful and deliberate in what you do, curious about and sensitive to your impact and ready to adjust your approach to optimise your impact. With that in mind, here are three techniques that we have repeatedly seen to be effective with leaders around the world (Fig. 8.3).

Fig. 8.3 Three techniques to create a sense direction

Make People Feel Informed

To have a clear sense of direction, people need to know things. They need information. When they don't feel informed, the top-down attention pathway in their brains doesn't know what to look for. When that happens, they are more likely to feel uncertain. And when they feel uncertain, their neural threat-detection pathways are triggered in ways that reduce trust and increase caution and anxiety.

So, a simple way to reinforce how clear people feel about their direction is to think about the amount of information you share. Too much can be overload. But too little can undermine direction. Finding the sweet spot between the two is a matter of trial and error but, as a rule, try to expand what you share. Think about what information you do not share now but could. There will always be something. For example, regularly releasing as much information on your company's financial performance as you appropriately can. Or making sure that you have a routine section in team meetings during which you share some of what you know is going on in the company.

This is all separate to whatever you do to articulate the direction you want to set. It is background activity, to support and reinforce the sense of direction you are trying to establish. The extra information you are open with does not even have to be closely related to the direction. You are trying to make people feel informed in general.

Choose Your Words Carefully

The late Steve de Shazer, a famous psychotherapist of his generation, wrote the wonderfully titled book *Words Were Originally Magic* [27]. His key point was that the words and phrases we use can do things to the people who hear them—they can evoke a reaction in people, or change how to think and feel about things. And, as a leader, the words and phrases you choose to use have the same power—they can do something to the people who hear them.

The second technique to try, then, is to be more conscious and deliberate with the language you use. If you think back to the 'what is important' exercise described at the start of the chapter, this is about perfecting it.

To start, get some feedback on the way you communicate now. Then, as you prepare your message, try using different words and phrases. We know leaders who look like naturals at conveying a clear message, but in reality, they are careful and deliberate. They will use A/B testing before announcements and speeches, asking the people around them whether they prefer phrase A or phrase B.

Some researchers also suggest that providing examples can help people connect with what is said [28]. Similarly, talking about people and telling a story about them related to what you are trying to convey can be useful [29]. Finally, describing the desired future may allow people to better connect with what you are trying to convey [30].

Check Understanding and Impact

The final technique is simple but critical. You need to check how your message about what is important and the direction you want people to follow is received. The reason this is so crucial is that every time you say something about direction, you need to strike a careful balance. On the one hand, you need to be clear enough that you are understood. On the other hand, if you are too clear, you can inadvertently have a negative impact, appearing overly rigid and undermining confidence, initiative and creativity [31].

There is no special trick to this, you just need to take the time to check and ask, or get someone to do it for you. Either way, to be sure you have got the balance right, you need to be deliberate and systematic in checking.

A Sense of Direction

Creating a sense of direction is a critical foundation for any effective Leadership OS. In our research, direction is consistently the highest-rated component of clarity found in the Leadership OSs of top-performing leaders. It is something the best leaders get right.

When delivering a message, people naturally tend to focus most on what they want to say, on what they want to communicate. However, our research, and that of others, shows that what is most important is *not* the content of what you say, but two other factors. It is the way, the manner, in which you communicate your message. And it is what other people understand—the clarity, or lack therefore of, that they take from what you say. As the leaders in the development exercise described at the start of this chapter found out, communicating direction *to* a group of people is one thing; creating a sense of direction *in* others requires something more. You need to look beyond what you want to say and what you are doing, and focus more on what other people need to hear.

Summary + Checklist

See Table 8.1.

Table 8.1 Summary of direction

	OS function	Techniques
Direction	• Enables navigation • Increases motivation • Triggers initiative • Promotes teamwork	• Make people feel informed • Choose your words carefully • Check understanding and impact

Checklist

To help you think about whether you have successfully installed direction in your Leadership OS, ask yourself how the people around you—your direct reports, peers and stakeholders—would respond to the following questions (Table 8.2).

Table 8.2 Have you installed direction in your OS?

	✓	✗
Would people say that you make it easy for them to understand what you want and expect from them?	☐	☐
Do people believe that you help them to understand the overall direction and strategy of the business?	☐	☐
Do people understand what you believe is important?	☐	☐
Do people believe that you share information and keep them informed?	☐	☐

References

1. J. Hirsch, J. Peterson and R. Mar, "Psychological entropy: A framework for understanding uncertainty-related anxiety," *Psychological Review*, vol. 119, no. 2, pp. 304–320, 2012.
2. M. Corbetta and G. Shulman, "Control of goal-directed and stimulus-driven attention in the brain," *Nature Reviews Neuroscience*, vol. 3, pp. 201–215, 2002.
3. E. Miller, "The prefrontal cortex and cognitive control," *Nature Reviews Neuroscience*, vol. 1, pp. 59–65, 2000.
4. H. Aarts, "On the emergence of human goal pursuit: The nonconscious regulation and motivation of goals," *Social and Personality Psychology Compass*, vol. 1, pp. 183–201, 2007.
5. S. Jung, "Why are goals important in the public sector? Exploring the benefits of goal clarity for reducing turnover intention," *Journal of Public Administration Research and Theory*, vol. 24, no. 1, pp. 209–234, 2014.
6. S. Rahman and P. Bullock, "Soft TQM, hard TQM, and organisational performance relationships: an empirical investigation," *Omega*, vol. 33, no. 1, pp. 73–83, 2055.
7. R. Arvey, H. Dewhirst and J. Boling, "Relationships between goal clarity, participation in goal setting, and personality characteristics on job satisfaction in a scientific organization," *Journal of Applied Psychology*, vol. 61, no. 1, pp. 103–106, 1976.
8. E. Mahon, S. Taylor and R. Boyatiz, "Antecedents of organizational engagement: Exploring vision, mood and perceived organizational support with emotional intelligence as a moderator," *Frontiers in Psychology*, vol. 5, p. 1322, 2014.
9. C. Pearce and M. Ensley, "A reciprocal and longitudinal investigation of the innovation process: The central role of shared vision in product and process innovation teams (PPITs)," *Journal of Organizational Behavior*, vol. 25, no. 2, pp. 259–278, 2004.
10. K. Dale and M. L. Fox, "Leadership style and organizational commitment: Mediating effect of role stress," *Journal of Managerial Issues*, pp. 109–130, 2008.
11. M. Marks, S. Zaccaro and J. Mathieu, "Performance implications of leader briefings and team-interaction training for team adaptation to novel environments," *Journal of Applied Psychology*, vol. 85, no. 6, p. 971, 2000.
12. P. Hong, A. Nahm and W. Doll, "The role of project target clarity in an uncertain project environment," *International Journal of Operations & Production Management*, vol. 24, no. 12, pp. 1269–1291, 2004.
13. S. Mohammed, L. Ferzandi and K. Hamilton, "Metaphor no more: A 15-year review of the team mental model construct," *Journal of Management*, vol. 36, no. 4, pp. 876–910, 2010.

14. D. Van Knippenberg, J. Dawson, M. West and A. Homan, "Diversity fault-lines, shared objectives, and top management team performance," *Human Relations*, vol. 64, no. 3, pp. 307–336, 2011.

15. H. Bateman, P. Bailey and H. McLellan, "Of rocks and safe channels: Learning to navigate as an interprofessional team," *Journal of Interprofessional Care*, vol. 17, no. 2, pp. 141–150, 2003.

16. S. Sims, G. Hewitt and R. Harris, "Evidence of a shared purpose, critical reflection, innovation and leadership in interprofessional healthcare teams: A realist synthesis," *Journal of Interprofessional Care*, vol. 29, no. 3, pp. 209–215, 2015.

17. S. Alper, D. Tjosvold and K. Law, "Interdependence and controversy in group decision making: Antecedents to effective self-managing teams," *Organizational Behavior and Human Decision Processes*, vol. 74, no. 1, pp. 33–52, 1998.

18. S. McComb, S. Green and W. Compton, "Project Goals, Team Performance, and Shared Understanding," *Engineering Management Journal*, vol. 11, no. 3, pp. 7–12, 1999.

19. F. Kellermanns, J. Walter, S. Floyd, C. Lechner and J. Shaw, "To agree or not to agree? A meta-analytical review of strategic consensus and organizational performance," *Journal of Business Research*, vol. 64, no. 2, pp. 126–133, 2011.

20. F. Jing, G. Avery and H. Bergsteiner, "Enhancing performance in small professional firms through vision communication and sharing," *Asia Pacific Journal of Management*, vol. 31, no. 2, pp. 599–620, 2014.

21. D. Aga, "Transactional leadership and project success: The moderating role of goal clarity," *Procedia Computer Science*, vol. 100, pp. 517–525, 2016.

22. J. Purcell, N. Kinnie, S. Hutchinson, B. Rayton and J. Swart, *People management and performance*, London and New York: Routledge, 2009.

23. S. Colakoglu, "Shared vision in MNE subsidiaries: The role of formal, personal, and social control in its development and its impact on subsidiary learning," *Thunderbird International Business Review*, vol. 54, no. 5, pp. 639–652, 2012.

24. S. Kantabutra, "What do we know about vision," *The Journal of Applied Business Research*, vol. 24, no. 2, 2008.

25. P. Flood, E. Hannan, K. Smith, T. Turner, M. West and J. Dawson, "Chief executive leadership style, consensus decision making, and top management team effectiveness," *European Journal of Work and Organizational Psychology*, vol. 9, no. 3, pp. 401–420, 2000.

26. R. Stout, J. Cannon-Bowers, E. Salas and D. Milanovich, "Planning, shared mental models, and coordinated performance: An empirical link is established," *Human Factors*, vol. 41, no. 1, pp. 61–71, 1999.

27. S. de Shazer, *Words were originally magic*, London, UK: W.W. Norton, 1994.

28. R. Allen and J. Allen, "A sense of community, a shared vision and a positive culture: Core enabling factors in successful culture based health promotion," *American Journal of Health Promotion*, vol. 1, no. 3, pp. 40–47, 1986.

29. Y. Yuan, J. Major-Girardin and S. Brown, "Storytelling is intrinsically mentalistic: A functional magnetic resonance imaging study of narrative production across modalities," *Journal of Cognitive Neuroscience*, vol. 30, no. 9, pp. 1298–1314, 2018.

30. A. Carton, C. Murphy and J. Clark, "A (blurry) vision of the future: How leader rhetoric about ultimate goals influences performance," *Academy of Management Journal*, vol. 57, no. 6, pp. 1544–1570, 2014.

31. R. Reiter-Palmon, B. Wigert and T. de Vreede, "Team creativity and innovation: The effect of group composition, social processes, and cognition," in *Handbook of Organizational Creativity*, Cambridge, MA, Academic Press, 2012, pp. 295–326.

9

Accountability

This chapter is twinned with fairness.

In Chapter 6, we described fairness as the psychological contract that underpins trust and binds people to both your Leadership OS and the wider business. Accountability is the other side of that contract. For fairness to prevail, people must be held accountable for what they do, and accountability can only work if it is perceived to be fair. In this sense, accountability is part of the glue that holds not only your OS but also the whole social fabric of your organisation together [1].

People are said to be accountable when three things happen: when some aspect of what they do is monitored or measured; when there is an evaluation of whether what they do is good or bad; and when there is a consequence to this. This last point is particularly important. Accountability only really exists when there are consequences for what people do.

Imagine a kid taking a cookie she shouldn't. Her parents hold her accountable if they see the cookie is gone (monitoring); tell her she shouldn't have taken it (evaluation); and then tell her she cannot have gaming time, say, for that day as punishment (consequence). All three things need to happen, but it is the consequence that makes us say the child has been held accountable.

With these steps in mind, organisations invest large amounts of time and money in processes such as performance management systems and pay-for-performance incentive schemes. And although debate may rage over the effectiveness of some of the mechanisms used—in particular the

© The Author(s) 2020
N. Kinley and S. Ben-Hur, *Leadership OS*,
https://doi.org/10.1007/978-3-030-27293-7_9

incentive schemes—the importance and benefits of accountability itself are more or less universally accepted.

This is not just a belief or hope, either. Substantial research supports it, from all over the world. When people are held accountable in a fair manner, their performance levels go up. Stop holding them accountable, and the opposite happens. So, done well, accountability can produce better performance.

Even the people on the receiving end of accountability—employees—tend to like it, or at least prefer it to *not* having accountability. Neuroscience supports this, too. You might expect people not to like accountability, since it introduces an element of risk—the possibility that they might fail. However, we saw in the chapter on clarity that people's brains are highly sensitive to uncertainty. And as it turns out, they are more sensitive to uncertainty than to risk [2]. So most people are less sensitive to—and thus prefer—the risk of being set targets, and being held accountable for them, than the uncertainty of not having accountability.

The Dark Side of Accountability

Just because accountability *can* work, however, does not mean that it always *does*. Back in the 1980s, accountability was mostly about outcomes—the objectives set and results achieved. But people started worrying that focusing only on outcomes could inadvertently lead to business cultures ripe for reckless shortcuts and unethical behaviours. They also became concerned that short-term objectives might be prioritised over sustainable success. So, a focus on process—on *how* results are achieved—was introduced to accountability, most famously in the guise of balanced scorecards.

This more balanced approach, looking at both *what* people achieve and *how* they achieve it, has undoubtedly helped. But it hasn't solved the problem. Over the years, there has been a continuous trickle of research all pointing to one thing. Even with a balanced approach, accountability can still have a negative effect. Some studies have shown it can reduce cooperation [3], knowledge sharing [4] and teamwork [5]. Others have revealed it can increase politicking [6] and stress [7], and lower levels of flexibility and openness to change [8]. And still others have pointed to territoriality and failure to delegate effectively. Once you line it all up, it is a long list. So, it is not merely a case that accountability is good, because it has a dark side.

The reason these negative side effects persist, and the solution to 'doing' accountability right without creating these adverse effects, lies in a simple but fundamental issue. Our approach to accountability has been all wrong.

Creating Accountability: The Case of René 'the Doberman' at Deutsche Telekom

Being appointed CEO of one of the world's premier companies at the age of 43 sounds like a dream come true for most young executives (Fig. 9.1). But when that dream comes with a flat stock price, flatter revenues, declining profits, 32% state ownership, a bloated unionised workforce, a culture of entitlement and distrust, and an industry that is constantly changing, that dream might seem more like a nightmare.

But not for René Obermann, who in his previous roles had earned the nicknames 'The Bulldozer' and 'The Doberman'.

Fig. 9.1 René Obermann

When he was appointed CEO of Deutsche Telekom (DT) in November 2006, he knew the challenges. He had been CEO of T-Mobile, DT's largest and fastest-growing division, since 2002. While revenues for T-Com, DT's fixed landline and broadband group, had decreased 11% from 2003 to 2005, revenues for Obermann's T-Mobile had increased by 29%.

When he took over DT, he quickly held a series of one-day workshops with a new handpicked leadership team and soon after launched a simple strategy: Focus, Fix and Grow. Focus on getting the right people and culture in place. Fix the broken operational structures. Grow with new initiatives and opportunities.

Obermann knew that a solid foundation was the first step. At DT, he saw a conflict within the company's culture that he believed was fundamentally holding the firm back. On the one side, he saw entrenched and entitled stakeholders looking to hold on to the past, and on the other side, entrepreneurial stakeholders looking to change for the future. And through it all, there was a lack of accountability. In a culture that emphasised seniority, tenure and stability, poor performance was not consistently penalised, and initiative, entrepreneurship and innovation were not sufficiently encouraged and rewarded. As a result, productivity, innovation and customer service at DT were all inferior to those of its competitors.

Obermann saw DT's hierarchical corporate structure and failing performance management processes as part of the problem. But he did not make significant changes to them. Instead, he focused on the people in this system. He believed that if he had the right people in place, whatever changes were necessary would happen organically. As he put it, they needed to 'get the right people on the bus and the wrong people off the bus'.

What Obermann was looking for in people, more than anything else, was *ownership*. People who would not walk past problems. People who would take responsibility for fixing things. People who would take it personally if the business did not do well.

Getting the right people on the bus involved converting the top leadership from a cadre of diplomats to a group of entrepreneurs focused on changing both the culture and performance of the company. Obermann appointed Tim Höttges as CEO of T-Home, the newly restructured T-Com, where the biggest problems lay. Höttges had been Obermann's number two at T-Mobile and was blunt in his assessment of the new division and its culture: 'Our service sucked, our response times sucked, and our productivity sucked'.

Such directness was uncommon at DT but was vital to changing the culture. So was what happened next. Within a few months, Höttges did two things. He replaced over half of the senior management in T-Home. And he hit the road to meet frontline employees face to face, spending a week at each of dozens of local operations around Germany. He listened to them. He learnt from them. He connected with them. And in return, they began to believe in him.

In addition to Höttges, Obermann made many other senior leadership changes. Most of the appointments were internal promotions, select members of Obermann's inner circle whom he knew had the qualities he wanted. They were young, in their early to mid-forties. Most had experience working outside of DT. And they all shared the same quality Höttges had shown: an attitude of owning issues and acting on them, a willingness to name problems and then do something about them. Armed with this sense of accountability, Obermann's team would instil a new focus on performance.

It was just the first step of many that Obermann took, but it was the one that enabled everything that followed. For the next six years, he pursued his strategy of Focus, Fix and Grow, before leaving DT at the end of 2013. During this time, he led the company through the huge telecoms market transformation of the mid-2000s and shepherded it through the 2008 financial crisis. Moreover, he did this while reducing employee headcount by 20,000 and fundamentally changing the culture of the business. This achievement was built on his platform of getting the right people with the right attitude on the bus, and on his insistence that these leaders *own* what they do.

How to Think About Accountability

The problem with accountability is how we think about it. We tend to think of it as something given to people (you are accountable) or as something done to them using performance review processes (you will be held accountable).

The reason for this is the association in our minds between accountability and consequences. Between a child taking a cookie she shouldn't and being punished for it, or someone at work missing targets and receiving a reduced bonus as a result. Because of this link, there is a tendency to think of accountability as something that is applied to people from outside of them.

Obermann understood that this is just one kind of accountability—and it is not the self-sustaining kind. It needs to be continually reinforced from outside; businesses and leaders have to follow up by rewarding or punishing people. He made sure that people who did not deliver were developed or moved. But he also knew that real, self-sustaining, performance-driving accountability is *not* something imposed from outside. It is something that comes from inside people. It is something they feel, an inner sense of ownership and responsibility for what they do.

This type of accountability is an inner drive. It does not depend on external consequences. And, critically, it is a powerful driver of how people behave. In fact, if you can build a Leadership OS that helps people to feel this way, it can change their behaviour in three crucial ways (Fig. 9.2).

A. Focuses Attention and Increases Effort

When people feel they own something, they are more likely to focus on it and take care of it. This is why company directors tend to take a more active role in organisational decision-making when they have a personal financial stake in a company [9]. It is why workers in businesses with share-ownership schemes for employees tend to show higher levels of commitment—especially in small firms where the impact of doing so is more visible [10]. And it is why individuals who feel a strong sense of accountability for the work they do show higher levels of motivation [11], commitment [12], competitiveness [13], work intensity [14] and thoroughness [15]. So, when your Leadership OS evokes feelings of ownership and accountability in people, they are more likely to focus on and invest time and effort in what they do.

B. Makes Shared Responsibility Work

The second thing accountability does is to lay an essential foundation for teamwork. When groups of people work together, there is often some shared responsibility. In the corporate world, this has become increasingly common with the rise of so-called agile teams, which form for specific project-based purposes. One challenge in making such teams as effective as possible is a psychological phenomenon known as *social loafing* [16]. This is the fact that people tend to work harder when they are on their own than when part of a

Fig. 9.2 The functions of accountability in a Leadership OS

group. When responsibility is shared, there is a natural tendency for people to sit back a bit, to push a little less hard, to invest a little less effort. To let others do their thing.

When people feel a sense of ownership and personal accountability, however, this naturally occurring effect completely disappears. In fact, when a sense of personal accountability is combined with shared responsibility, people work better in groups than alone, with higher levels of productivity [17].

C. Promotes Ethical Behaviour

The final thing that a sense of accountability does is to promote ethical behaviour. Specifically, studies have shown that when people feel a sense of ownership, responsibility and accountability for what they do, they are far less likely to engage in self-serving behaviours [18]. Instead, they are more likely to do what is right for the business and their colleagues. This is why people with a strong sense of accountability are more likely to be good corporate citizens and invest more time helping colleagues and in activities beyond the immediate remit of their role [19].

This inner-driver type of accountability, then, fulfils a vital role in any effective Leadership OS. How though, can you, as a leader, help ensure people feel this way?

Creating a Sense of Accountability

Setting and communicating objectives and then holding people accountable for meeting them is an essential part of any leader's role. But an inner feeling of responsibility and ownership is not something that you can simply give to people. It has to be evoked, aroused and inspired within people. And this requires a different approach because it brings a different challenge.

Since this inner accountability occurs within the black box of people's minds, a lot depends upon what people bring with them. For example, we know that some people seem to hold themselves more accountable than others, demonstrating self-criticism without any external prompting [20]. Others, such as those from more hierarchical national cultures, are more likely to automatically accept and respond to set objectives with an inner feeling of accountability for them [21]. We also know that people differ in the degree to which they see set accountabilities as a threat or an opportunity [14]. And some people, such as those low in confidence, can react negatively to being given extra accountability [22].

To evoke an inner feeling of accountability in people, then, you need a Leadership OS that touches on and affects what goes on inside people's minds. You effectively need to 'reach inside' people and change how they feel about themselves and the world. The good news is that you, as a leader, are ideally placed to do this because, just as with the other components of a Leadership OS, your relationships with people are crucial for determining whether they develop a sense of psychological ownership and accountability for what they do [23].

As before, there are no simple 1–2–3 steps to follow because different people will react differently to what you do. But there are three techniques you can use to try to evoke a sense of accountability in people (Fig. 9.3).

Enable Autonomy

For people to feel a sense of psychological ownership and accountability for something, they need to feel that they have some measure of control over it [24]. That they can affect it, influence it or make a difference to it.

The most obvious way to achieve this with your direct team is to give them actual control. You can involve them in target setting, give them responsibility for planning how to reach objectives, and—most importantly—make sure you don't micromanage them. In other words, delegate effectively.

There is, however, a subtler yet more powerful way of giving people a feeling of control over what they do. Rather than giving them control over a specific accountability, you can try to build a more generalised feeling of control within them—the belief that they are free and able to act to influence what goes on around them in general. The word psychologists use to describe this is *autonomy*. And there is consistent research showing that

Fig. 9.3 Three techniques to create accountability

if your Leadership OS helps people to feel a sense of autonomy, they will demonstrate much higher levels of psychological ownership and personal accountability for what they do [25].

We will look at how to create a sense of autonomy in more depth in the later chapters on motivation and empowerment. But for now, there are five simple tips you can try to help people feel a sense of autonomy, and you can adapt them to use with anybody, be they your team, your board or other key stakeholders.

- Ask yourself what decisions the person or team in question have control over. Then ask what additional decisions or choices you could give them some control over that they do not currently have. They do not have to be big decisions. The point is that decisions are a measure of autonomy. If there is nothing about their work that they are free to make decisions about, then they have no autonomy. Conversely, if they work in a Leadership OS that asks them to make decisions, no matter how big or small, they will have a greater sense of autonomy.
- Keep people informed. Give them information about how the business is doing, what other teams are doing, what you are doing. This will help build autonomy because when people feel informed, they feel more able to make decisions and act.
- Ask people for their opinions. Continually. Repeatedly. Make sure they feel that you think their views are valuable and worth listening to. Again, this works because it helps people feel more capable.
- Praise people when they do things well. It may not sound related, but research shows that praise boosts people's confidence levels, and when people feel confident they feel more able to act. This is why people with high levels of confidence usually report feeling a higher level of ownership for what they do [26].
- One final tip to try is to ask people how much structure they like. As a leader, you may be incredibly detail-oriented, planned and ordered in the way you do things. Alternatively, you may be freer-flowing and more spontaneous. Either way, there is a tendency to be the same with everyone, providing the same level of structure for across the board. The issue with this is that other people's preferences for the amount of structure they like will differ, and if they get either too much or too little, it can affect their sense of autonomy and ability to influence. The simplest way to resolve this is to ask people how much structure they prefer, and then try—as far as possible—to adapt how much structure you provide for them. So, ask, discuss and adapt.

Promote Identity

The second technique you have available to help build a sense of accountability in others is to help them feel that what they do and the objectives they have are part of their identity, of who they are. When people believe something is part of them, it drives a sense of ownership in them.

The best way to promote this feeling of identity is by developing people's sense of their expertise. The feeling of being an expert grounds people in a subject; it becomes part of how they define themselves. This could be as simple as saying to them, 'You're the expert on this.' It could be investing in extra training for them. If they have a task to do that is new to them, it could be asking them to go and read and make themselves an expert and then report back to you on what they find. However you do it—and it needs to be different with each person—the key is to make people feel an expert in what they do, that doing a particular thing well is part of who they are. Be that serving customers, managing people or giving you advice.

Encourage Investment

The final technique at your disposal is to give people opportunities to invest in what they do. This works because when they invest in things, they are more likely to value them and feel a sense of ownership. This is why—with some people—incentive schemes involving shares in a business can help boost their sense of ownership and accountability. But actual financial investment is not required. Simply investing time and energy in something can also lead to feelings of accountability for it [27].

So, if you see people investing time and energy in aspects of their work, say so. Notice it and, in doing so, help them to notice it. And if people show an interest in something, encourage small side projects on the topic. As long as mini side projects do not detract from core objectives and work, they will automatically add value in terms of how they help to strengthen people's sense of ownership and accountability.

The Other Way to Accountability

These, then, are some of the techniques available to help ensure that your Leadership OS builds psychological ownership in people. They are not the first tools people usually reach for. There is the temptation—and even a tendency—to focus on the external and more visible processes that seem to embody accountability: budgeting, setting targets and annual performance reviews.

But these formal processes risk distracting you from the real task at hand [28]. All too often, when businesses and leaders think they are creating accountability with these processes, all they are doing is focusing people on a particular set of targets. To create a real, inner, self-sustaining sense of accountability in people, you need to balance all the target setting and progress monitoring—which are undoubtedly necessary—with an equally strong emphasis on building psychological ownership.

It is an essential foundation for people's sense of clarity about what matters to them and what they do, and thus what they need to do next. Indeed, by creating clarity for people about what is important to them, you even touch on their sense of identity—who they are as a professional. And it is this connection between having clarity about what needs doing and people's sense of identity that we will explore in more depth in the next chapter as we look at purpose.

Summary + Checklist

See Table 9.1.

Table 9.1 Summary of accountability

	OS function	Techniques
Accountability	• Focuses attention and increases effort • Makes shared responsibility work • Promotes ethical behaviour	• Enable autonomy • Promote identity • Encourage investment

Table 9.2 Have you installed accountability in your Leadership OS?

	✓	✗
Would people say that you make them feel accountable for what they do?	☐	☐
Would people say you make sure they feel a sense of ownership for what they do?	☐	☐
Do people believe that you regularly ask them for their opinion?	☐	☐
Do you people feel that you involve them in decision-making?	☐	☐
Do people believe that you would help them to get involved in things they find interesting?	☐	☐
Do people believe that you share information readily and keep them feeling informed?	☐	☐

Checklist

To help you think about whether you have successfully installed account-ability in your Leadership OS, ask yourself how the people around you—your direct reports, peers and stakeholders—would respond to the following questions (Table 9.2).

References

1. P. Tetlock, "The impact of accountability on judgment and choice: Toward a social contingency model," *Advances in Experimental Social Psychology*, vol. 25, pp. 331–376, 1992.
2. D. Bach, B. Seymour and R. Dolan, "Neural activity associated with the passive prediction of ambiguity and risk for aversive events," *Journal of Neuroscience*, vol. 29, no. 6, pp. 1648–1656, 2009.
3. S. Adelberg and C. Batson, "Accountability and helping: When needs exceed resources," *Journal of Personality and Social Psychology*, vol. 36, pp. 343–350, 1978.
4. H. Peng, "Why and when do people hide knowledge?," *Journal of Knowledge Management*, vol. 17, no. 3, pp. 398–415, 2013.
5. H. Campbell-Pickford, G. Joy and K. Roll, "Mutuality in business," Said Business School, Oxford, UK, 2016.
6. P. Fandt and G. Ferris, "The management of information and impressions: When employees behave opportunistically," *Organizational Behavior and Human Decision Processes*, vol. 45, pp. 140–158, 1990.
7. G. Ferris, T. Mitchell, P. Canavan, D. Frink and H. Hopper, "Accountability in human resource systems," in G. R. Ferris, S. D. Rosen and D. T. Barnum (Eds.), *Handbook of human resource management*, Oxford, UK, Blackwell, 1995, pp. 175–196.
8. M. Baer and G. Brown, "Blind in one eye: How psychological ownership of ideas affects the types of suggestions people adopt," *Organizational Behavior and Human Decision Processes*, vol. 118, no. 1, pp. 60–71, 2012.
9. R. Long, "The effects of employee ownership on organizational identification, employee job attitudes, and organizational performance: A tentative framework and empirical findings," *Human Relations*, vol. 31, no. 1, pp. 29–48, 1978.
10. J. Harrisdon, P. Singh and S. Frawley, "What does employee ownership effectiveness look like? The case of a Canadian-based firm," *Canadian Journal of Administrative Sciences*, vol. 35, no. 1, pp. 5–19, 2016.
11. M. Enzele and S. Anderson, "Surveillant intentions and intrinsic motivation," *Journal of Personal and Social Psychology*, vol. 64, pp. 257–266, 1993.

12. M. Mayhew, N. Ashkanasy, T. Bramble and J. Gardner, "A study of the antecedents and consequences of psychological ownership in organizational settings," *The Journal of Social Psychology*, vol. 147, no. 5, pp. 477–500, 2007.

13. A. Hall, D. Frink and M. Buckley, "An accountability account: A review and synthesis of the theoretical and empirical research on felt accountability," *Journal of Organizational Behavior*, vol. 38, no. 2, pp. 204–224, 2017.

14. S. Lanivich, J. Brees, W. Hochwarter and G. Ferris, "PE Fit as moderator of the accountability–employee reactions relationships: Convergent results across two samples," *Journal of Vocational Behavior*, vol. 77, no. 3, pp. 425–436, 2010.

15. K. Siegel-Jacobs and J. Yates, "Effects of procedural and outcome accountability on judgment quality," *Organizational Behavior and Human Decision Processes*, vol. 65, pp. 1–17, 1996.

16. E. Weldon and G. Gargano, "Cognitive loafing: The effects of accountability and shared responsibility on cognitive effort," *Personnel Social Psychology Bulletin*, vol. 14, no. 1, pp. 159–171, 1988.

17. R. Slavin and A. Tanner, "Effects of cooperative reward structures and individual accountability on productivity and learning," *The Journal of Educational Research*, vol. 72, no. 5, pp. 294–298, 2014.

18. D. Rus, D. van Knippenberg and B. Wisse, "Leader power and self-serving behavior: The moderating role of accountability," *The Leadership Quarterly*, vol. 23, no. 1, pp. 13–26, 2012.

19. L. van Dyne and J. Pierce, "Psychological ownership and feelings of possession: Three field studies predicting employee attitudes and organizational citizenship behavior," *Journal of Organizational Behaviour*, vol. 25, no. 4, pp. 439–459, 2004.

20. P. Yarnold, K. Mueser and J. Lyons, "Type A behavior, accountability, and work rate in small groups," *Journal of Research in Personality*, vol. 22, no. 3, pp. 353–360, 1988.

21. E. Snape, D. Thompson, F. Yan and T. Redman, "Performance appraisal and culture: Practice and attitudes in Hong Kong and Great Britain," *The International Journal of Human Resource Management*, vol. 9, no. 5, pp. 841–861, 2011.

22. M. Royle, A. Hall, W. Hochwarter, P. Perrewé and G. Ferris, "The interactive effects of accountability and job self-efficacy on organizational citizenship behavior and political behavior," *Organizational Analysis*, vol. 13, no. 1, pp. 53–71, 2005.

23. B. Erdogan, R. Sparrowe, R. Liden and K. Dunegan, "Implications of organizational exchanges for accountability theory," *Human Resource Management Review*, vol. 14, no. 1, pp. 19–45, 2004.

24. N. McLntyre, A. Srivastava and J. Fuller, "The relationship of locus of control and motives with psychological ownership in organizations," *Journal of Managerial Issues*, vol. 21, pp. 383–401, 2009.

25. S. Dawkins, A. Tian, A. Newman and A. Martin, "Psychological ownership: A review and research agenda," *Journal of Organizational Behavior*, vol. 38, no. 2, pp. 163–183, 2017.

26. J. Avey, B. Avolio, C. Crossley and F. Luthans, "Psychological ownership: Theoretical extensions, measurement, and relation to work outcomes," *Journal of Organizational Behavior*, vol. 30, pp. 173–191, 2009.

27. J. Pierce, T. Kostova and K. Dirks, "Toward a theory of psychological ownership in organizations," *The Academy of Management Review*, vol. 26, no. 2, pp. 298–310, 2001.

28. S. Kim and J. Lee, "Impact of competing accountability requirements on perceived work performance," *The American Review of Public Administration*, vol. 40, no. 1, pp. 100–118, 2010.

10

Purpose

Right now, sitting in the corner of an art gallery somewhere in the world is an exhibit that tells you all you need to know about why purpose at work is important.

At first glance, it looks like a simple box, set on tall legs to bring it to eye height. The bottom half is made of wood, and the top half is made of clear plexiglass, revealing a large pile of one cent coins inside. There is a hand crank on one side and a small hole in the front of the box, with a little shelf inside, to collect the cents the box releases. Designed by the American artist Blake Fall-Conroy, the exhibit is called Minimum Wage Machine. The idea is this: if you turn the hand crank, the machine will drop a cent every 4.5 seconds. If you turn it for an hour, you will earn $8, the same as New York State's minimum wage when the exhibit was first shown on December 2014.

Turning the hand crank will earn you as much money as many jobs pay, but apart from the task of turning the hand crank—which has no purpose other than dispensing cents—it is about as meaningless as it could get. And that's the point. The exhibit is designed to show people what it is like to have a job that has no purpose, except for earning cents.

Watching people encounter this machine is fascinating. Not so much their reactions to it when they first see it, but what happens after they start turning the hand crank. How quickly their smiles turn to something else, first as they become bored of turning the crank, and then as they realise what the implications are for people who feel this way about their work. Having no purpose is no joke.

We're here to put some purpose into purpose.

© The Author(s) 2020
N. Kinley and S. Ben-Hur, *Leadership OS*,
https://doi.org/10.1007/978-3-030-27293-7_10

A lot has been written about the subject over the last decade. A lot of headlines and hype, all hailing the need for organisations and leaders to create a purpose for their people. Some of this has been fascinating and genuinely useful, but a larger amount hasn't been.

Some of it has been more aspirational than practical. There has been a tendency to focus on organisational purpose, with less emphasis on what steps individual leaders need to take. There has also been a drift towards more nebulous takes on purpose, which talk about it in almost spiritual terms.

Other bits have evoked cynicism. There has been a lurking perception that some businesses create and use purpose statements inauthentically, that they use the rhetoric of service to some higher ideal—like making the world a better place—to hide the real societal value of the organisation and what it can offer its employees. Cynicism has also resulted because there is often a disconnect between what firms say about their purpose and what they actually do about it. One recent survey found that only 37% of employees think their firm's operations are aligned with its stated purpose [1].

Creating purpose, then, is not easy for organisations or leaders to do well. As a result, there is a pervading scepticism about the idea of purpose, a feeling that it may have no purpose itself.

Reading this, you as a leader will fall into one of three groups. Your organisation or business unit may have a stated company-wide purpose. You may have created a purpose for your business or team. Or your firm, unit or team may have no stated purpose. Whichever group you fall into, the core challenge with creating purpose is the same: it is not something you can just give to people. They can *take* a sense of purpose from their jobs and what the business does. But you cannot just hand it to them because what counts as purposeful differs between people. What we find purposeful, you may not. So, stating a purpose does not guarantee that other people will feel this way.

The fact that people's reactions vary makes your role as a leader so pivotal because that reaction—that connection between people and purpose—is made within your Leadership OS. And your OS will either help or hinder it from happening. It is the mechanism that enables or prevents people from linking what they do to a purpose, whether that purpose is stated by the business, by their boss or a personal one they may have themselves.

Getting this connection to work is not easy. It is worth getting right, though, because all the evidence shows that when people *do* feel a sense of purpose, the impact can be powerful.

Creating Purpose: The Case of Indra Nooyi at PepsiCo

In a business world obsessed with short-term profits—all eyes on the next quarter's results—how on earth do you create a balance with building a sense of purpose? (Figure 10.1).

It was this question that characterised Indra Nooyi's tenure as CEO of PepsiCo from 2006 to 2018. She spent 12 years finding a balance between her long-term vision for the company and the demand for continual short-term success. It wasn't easy.

In her first Letter to Shareholders, she boldly introduced her idea: Performance with Purpose. She wrote, 'We believe Performance – achieving financial results – matters most when it is combined with Purpose – improving people's lives'. This may sound strange for a soft-drinks company, but Nooyi meant it. Her vision was a company that both delivered shareholder returns *and* nudged society towards healthier choices, more inclusive behaviour and more environmentally friendly practices. She was determined, too.

Fig. 10.1 Indra Nooyi

For the rest of her tenure, Performance with Purpose was the theme of every letter she wrote to shareholders.

Shortly after this letter, PepsiCo positioned its products into three categories: Fun for You, Better for You and Good for You. There was both acceptance and purpose in this. Nooyi was quick to remind people: 'I didn't create Pepsi Cola. I didn't create Doritos. I'm just trying to take the products and make them healthier' [2].

Nooyi steered her team to rethink PepsiCo's classic products—Doritos, Cheetos, Lay's chips—to be less greasy, less salty and more appealing to a health-conscious consumer. And the acquisitions Pepsi made under her leadership show that she was trying to nudge the company towards more Better for You and Good for You options: Sabra Hummus, Naked Juices, Bare Foods, Kevita beverages and others.

Soon after, PepsiCo launched a new global marketing campaign under the banner 'Every generation refreshes the world. Now it's your turn'. The campaign included grants for consumers to change—or refresh—their communities and won accolades for its innovative approach.

Not everything Nooyi did worked. In a shock move, PepsiCo decided in 2010 not to advertise during the Super Bowl championship game for the National Football League, for the first time in 23 years. Instead, it announced it would spend money on the Pepsi Refresh Project—a scheme awarding $20 million in grants to community projects in the US. Despite high awareness levels and positive consumer feedback, the scheme was pulled two years later—mainly, it is believed, because it failed to lift drinks sales.

Yet Nooyi continued making bold moves. Around the same time, PepsiCo became the first major publicly traded company to formally state that access to clean water is a human right. Since then, water usage and safe water access have become core pillars of PepsiCo's commitments, with targets around water use reduction, supporting community water initiatives in India and the funding of municipal water treatment in Jordan. These schemes have been lauded for their impact, with the company's potato farmers reducing water consumption by 50%.

Importantly, Nooyi's Performance with Purpose was not just words. It represented real, substantial corporate actions that had a positive impact on people's lives. It was something people could believe in. And, critically, although the vision was very much hers, she made sure the purpose was shared. Performance with Purpose became *the* focus of the company. The language of it was built into processes and conversations. It became how people talked about what they did. And managers and leaders at every level were asked to find ways to help employees connect with it.

This was achieved in three ways. Employees were encouraged to get involved in sustainability-related activities. They were given more voice by being asked for their input on projects and encouraged to take the initiative by finding ways to improve products and add to the good work being done. Finally, to reinforce this involvement, Nooyi pushed a culture of recognition (most famously, writing letters of thanks to the parents of her executives). Systematically, she worked to ensure the whole company, from top to bottom, had an opportunity to connect with her vision.

The impact of this—of creating a shared purpose that the company believed in, connected to and got behind—can be seen in the results Nooyi delivered. From 2006 to 2017, PepsiCo's revenue grew from $35 billion to $63.5 billion, and by the end of her tenure, the total shareholder return was 162%.

Nooyi's biggest legacy, however, is not the numbers, but the broader business culture she left behind her, infused with and energised by the shared purpose she created. There is an old saying that 'leadership is what is left in the room after you have gone'. If that is so, Nooyi's legacy will be how she still affects the attitudes and behaviour of the people in the company today. It is an impact that will likely live on for many years. And in the meantime, it will have made people's lives better.

What Purpose Is

What Nooyi did at PepsiCo is a great example of a big societal purpose created by the C-suite, brought to life by leaders and managers, and believed in by employees. Yet although this kind of big societal purpose is the one that grabs the most headlines, it is just one type of purpose, not the most common and not always the most powerful, either.

Purpose is the extent to which people feel and understand how what they do makes a difference *and* feel that it matters. It is the answer to the question of why work is worth doing. In this sense, it is like accountability in that the end result is that people care more about what they do. But whereas accountability is more about ownership and responsibility ('I need to take care of this because it is part of me and because I ought to'), purpose is more about the qualities of the task ('I need to take care of this because it is an important and good thing to do').

After reviewing decades of research on purpose, we have found that there are three key types.

Contributing to a Broader, Societal Purpose

This is PepsiCo's type of purpose: a significant contribution to wider society, making the world or people's lives better in some way. It is probably the most difficult type of purpose to get right. But when companies *do* get it right, it can significantly enhance both individual and business performance levels, as employees show higher levels of commitment and invest themselves in pursuing the goals of the purpose [3].

Doing Something Valuable for Others

This is believing that you are doing something that adds value for others and so has significance. A good example here is the difference in performance levels between retail-store shelf stackers who simply stack the shelves because it is what they are told to do and those who understand how what they do makes a difference to customers' experience and thus the store's performance. Research shows that when work has a clear goal and a clear value, people feel a greater sense of purpose in it [4] and tend to work harder at it and perform better at it [5].

Doing Something Valuable for Oneself

Finally, there is the purpose that is about believing your work adds value to you personally. This may be because you need the money to support your family or send your children to the right school. It may be because it allows you to do something you enjoy doing. Or it may be because you get a sense of pride from your expertise at what you do. Either way, when people feel that work helps them fulfil a particular need in their life, it has greater meaning for them [6].

What Purpose Does

People can have more than one purpose at work, of course. And whichever type(s) of purpose they have, the impact is broadly the same. When your Leadership OS enables and supports people to connect what they do at work with a purpose, three things tend to happen (Fig. 10.2).

Fig. 10.2   The functions of purpose in a Leadership OS

A. Enhances Motivation

The first thing purpose does is to boost motivation [7]. Research shows that when people report feeling that their work has a sense of purpose, they demonstrate higher levels of engagement [8], commitment [9] and dedication [5]. As a result, they are more likely to show initiative in their work [10] and to have higher levels of performance [11].

B. Increases Happiness, Resilience and Confidence

The second thing purpose does is to make people feel good about themselves and what they do [12]. People who say their work has purpose simply report being happier. And that's just the start of it. They also report sleeping better [13] and appear to be healthier and live longer. Studies show that they have lower levels of heart-related health problems [14], lower risks of dementia and age-related cognitive decline [15] and lower mortality rates [16]. In fact, purpose appears to have a bigger impact on longevity than happiness does [17].

This positive impact on how good people feel has useful knock-on effects on how they work, too. Most obviously, it appears to lower stress levels or at least help protect from the impact of stress [18], reducing absenteeism [19] and turnover [20]. It has also been shown to improve how confident people feel about themselves and what they do. And this, in turn, has been shown to increase people's willingness and ability to show initiative and be proactive [21].

C. Improves Teamwork, Cohesion and Collaboration

The final thing purpose does is to bind people together, in particular when they have a shared purpose. Neuroscientists have shown that when people feel purpose, it triggers the release of oxytocin—the brain chemical at the heart of their trust system [22]. This primes them to be more trusting, social and collaborative (and this applies even when their purpose is unique to them). And when a team or business has a shared purpose, the effect of everyone feeling this way is better teamwork and increased levels of cohesion and cooperation [23].

How Purpose Is Created

Having explored what purpose is and does, your role as a leader is to ensure your Leadership OS helps people connect what they do at work to a particular purpose. It could be a grand societal purpose, a team purpose you have articulated or something personal to them.

This is fundamentally different from the traditional view of the leader's role in creating purpose, which has tended to emphasise the need for leaders to create and articulate an inspiring vision that people can follow. There is no doubt that strategies and visions can be inspiring, but the words themselves do not create a sense of purpose. That only happens when people see or understand a personal connection to it.

There are, of course, all sorts of factors that contribute to whether people make such a connection. For many years, national culture was thought to play a significant role. The idea was that some cultures might make people more open to feeling a sense of purpose. Yet recent large-scale studies have found that there are far more similarities than differences between countries in how people feel purpose at work, and the differences that *do* exist are not large [24].

A more significant factor is individual differences—the fact that people can experience and interpret things differently. For example, people's personality [5] and beliefs about their career can play a role [25], in that not everyone has the same level of need to feel a sense of purpose at work. Then there are personal finances, as—unsurprisingly—research has found that people are more likely to find earning money purposeful if they have less of it and a greater need for it [26]. Factors such as these explain why two people can hear the same objective or speech and react differently to it—one finding purpose in it, the other not.

So, there are many factors beyond your control that can affect whether people find purpose in particular things. Yet there are also factors that are within your control and can make a big difference. Researchers have found that the environment people work in, the OS leaders create, is one of the key factors—if not the major one—in determining whether people feel a sense of purpose.

Fig. 10.3   Three techniques to create purpose

Our focus here is on what you can do to ensure that, when people see or hear a particular objective, they can feel a sense of connection to it and so find it purposeful. Or, if your business and team have either no stated strategic vision or an uninspiringly bland one, we outline what you can do to help people connect what they do every day at work with a personal objective.

There are three techniques, or devices, that research has shown that you, as a leader, can use to help people make a connection and feel a sense of purpose (Fig. 10.3). They are the same whether you are a CEO talking to investors or the board, a business unit leader talking to your leadership team or a frontline manager talking to your people. As with all the techniques in this book, however, *how* you approach them should vary slightly according to the audience. And, as before, this is not a series of steps to be followed in order; context will dictate which ones are most likely to be successful.

Emphasise Task Significance

In our review of the last 50 years of research on what helps people feel a sense of purpose, the factor for which there was by far the most evidence was task significance [6]. It is the degree to which people believe or understand how what they do adds value and makes a difference. It is important because if they don't feel they are having an impact on anything, it is hard to feel that there is any purpose in what they do.

As a leader, there are several things you can do to help people understand the significance of what they do. They should not be reserved for when you are talking about purpose with people; they are things you can—and should—do every day, whenever possible. Probably the most important one is to comment continually on how people's work benefits others. This could be the impact it has on customers ('That's great – when you do that, the customer feels you understand them'), on colleagues ('The marketing team are going to love this') or bottom-line metrics ('This is really going to help the team meet its numbers').

A larger-scale example of this is the highly popular midnight event for staff that Disney Parks holds every year. Employees are given a series of clues and asked to solve a puzzle that takes them through the various areas of the park. The event is partly about bonding and simply having a good time. But it is also about giving staff the same experience—the same feeling of fun and happiness—that they are asked to provide their customers. It is thus an exercise in helping people to understand and connect with the value of what they do.

Other things you can try to help people understand the significance of what they do include:

- When talking to people about what they do, ask them how they think it adds value to and supports the company's broader goals. And if they don't have a clear answer, help them understand. In fact, this is a conversation that you should have systematically with all your direct reports—and ensure they do the same with their reports, too.
- When talking about objectives, set the scene by discussing overall, big-picture goals first, followed by the specific details of tasks or objectives. This makes it easier for people to connect the two.
- When talking about achievements, be sure to mention how they add value to others.
- When talking with functional teams, be sure to connect their contribution to bottom-line metrics.
- Never minimise the importance of routine or small work tasks. Always talk them up as important and explain why they are.
- Highlight the complexity of tasks—the suggestion that what people do is difficult can help them to feel that doing it is important.

Build Task–Self Fit

The second biggest factor we found affecting whether people feel a sense of purpose is the degree to which they feel there is a good fit between their job and what they enjoy doing and are good at [27]. Simply praising people for what they do can help them to feel a sense of good fit. There are also several conversations you can have with people—questions you can use in your meetings with them—that can help them to reflect on—and hopefully to feel—this sense of fit. The idea here is to help people realise that they add value to what they do and, thus, that there is some purpose in it.

- Ask people what it is about the business that they feel most fits them—how they feel that the culture of the business and they are similar (e.g., 'If the culture of the business were a person, what would the similarities between you be?').
- Ask them what they enjoy about their role.
- Enquire about the strengths and expertise that people bring to the role and how these help them succeed in it.

Create Shared Practices

The final technique you can use to help build a Leadership OS that supports people in feeling a sense of purpose is to create shared practices. These include regular routines such as team meetings or shared approaches such as a focus on quality or pace. The important aspect is that it is something done with or shared with other people. Research shows that when you do this, people are more likely to feel that they are part of something bigger than themselves. And when they feel this, it appears to reinforce the sense that they are doing something significant. So, whenever you can, bring people together as a group, emphasise the things they have in common and talk about the shared goals and approaches you have.

The Foundations of Purpose

Whether you are handed a stated organisational purpose chosen by your company, whether you are a CEO who needs to create one, or—as is far more common—whether you are a leader in a business without a compellingly articulated purpose, the challenge you face is the same. How can you evoke a feeling of purpose in people?

The traditional approach has been to focus on creating and articulating an inspiring vision. This is undoubtedly important, but it is also insufficient because purpose is not something that you can merely announce, give or assign to people. They must feel or understand a sense of connection to it. And this is where your Leadership OS comes into play. It is the ground in which this connection grows. You and your OS are what determines whether this connection flourishes or fails.

There is no doubt that the hype and hyperbole surrounding purpose have evoked a degree of cynicism in some people. This is unfortunate because, in our research with thousands of leaders across the globe, the Leadership

OS component that most differentiates high-performing leaders from low-performing ones is purpose. Our findings are supported by organisational level research, too. Companies that are rated by their employees as having a clear and strong purpose have been shown to have stronger financial performance [22]. So when purpose is done right, it is one of the most powerful drivers of performance at your disposal.

There is also evidence that it is becoming even more vital, since having a clear sense of purpose appears to be more important to younger generations than older ones. In a survey of millennials, 71% ranked finding work that is meaningful as one of the top three factors determining their choice, and 30% ranked it as the most important factor. Millennials are also willing to make less money and work longer, non-traditional hours, as long as they feel their work has purpose [28].

The headlines in the media may go to inspiring-sounding strategic visions. But a purpose does not need to be big to be powerful. What really matters is the degree to which people can connect what they do—day in, day out—with some objective or benefit. If organisations are to make this happen more often, the solution lies in the OSs that leaders create. Because it is there, within these environments, that these connections grow, and purpose is created.

And as we will now turn to see, it is also there that purpose can be strengthened—or undermined—by the power of values.

Summary + Checklist

See Table 10.1.

Table 10.1 Summary of purpose

	OS function	Techniques to build it
Purpose	• Enhances motivation • Increases happiness, resilience and confidence • Improves teamwork, cohesion and collaboration	• Emphasise task significance • Build task–self fit • Create shared practices

Checklist

To help you think about whether you have successfully installed purpose in your Leadership OS, ask yourself how the people around you—your direct reports, peers and stakeholders—would respond to the following questions (Table 10.2).

Table 10.2 Have you installed purpose in your Leadership OS?

	✓	✗
Would people say that you help them feel that what they do matters?	☐	☐
Do people feel you help them understand how what they do benefits others?	☐	☐
Do people believe you help them understand how what they do fits into the company's overall strategy?	☐	☐
Do people feel you help them see that there is a good fit between their strengths and expertise and what they do in their roles?	☐	☐
Do people feel you help them see the links between what they want to achieve from working and what they do?	☐	☐

References

1. V. Keller, *The business case for purpose*, Brighton, MA: Harvard Business School Publishing, 2015.
2. J. Glotz, "Indra Nooyi: 12 key moments of her tenure as PepsiCo CEO," *The Grocer*, 8 August 2018.
3. J. Milliman, A. Czaplewski and J. Ferguson, "Workplace spirituality and employee work attitudes: An exploratory empirical assessment," *Journal of Organizational Change Management*, vol. 16, no. 4, pp. 426–447, 2003.
4. M. Ghadi, M. Fernando and P. Caputi, "Describing work as meaningful: Towards a conceptual clarification," *Journal of Organizational Effectiveness: People and Performance*, vol. 2, no. 3, pp. 202–223, 2015.
5. A. Grant, "The significance of task significance: Job performance effects, relational mechanisms, and boundary conditions," *Journal of Applied Psychology*, vol. 93, no. 1, p. 108, 2008.
6. T. Schnell, T. Höge and E. Pollet, "Predicting meaning in work: Theory, data, implications," *The Journal of Positive Psychology*, vol. 8, no. 6, pp. 543–554, 2013.
7. B. Rosso, K. Dekas and A. Wrzesniewski, "On the meaning of work: A theoretical integration and review," *Research in Organizational Behavior*, vol. 30, pp. 91–127, 2010.
8. D. May, R. Gilson and L. Harter, "The psychological conditions of meaningfulness, safety and availability and the engagement of the human spirit at work," *Journal of Occupational and Organizational Psychology*, vol. 77, no. 1, pp. 11–37, 2004.
9. M. Geldenhuys, K. Laba and C. Venter, "Meaningful work, work engagement and organisational commitment," *SA Journal of Industrial Psychology*, vol. 40, no. 1, pp. 1–10, 2013.
10. Y. Akgunduz, C. Alkan and Ö. Gök, "Perceived organizational support, employee creativity and proactive personality: The mediating effect of meaning

of work," *Journal of Hospitality and Tourism Management*, vol. 34, pp. 105–114, 2018.

11. A. Wrzesniewski, "Finding positive meaning in work," in K. S. Cameron, J. E. Dutton and R. E. Quinn (Eds.), *Positive organizational scholarship: Foundations of a new discipline*, San Francisco: Berrett-Koehler Publishers, 2003, pp. 296–308.

12. E. Deci and R. Ryan, "Facilitating optimal motivation and psychological well-being across life's domains," *Canadian Psychology*, vol. 49, no. 1, pp. 14–23, 2008.

13. E. Kim, S. Hershner and V. Strecher, "Purpose in life and incidence of sleep disturbances," *Journal of Behavioral Medicine*, vol. 38, no. 3, pp. 590–597, 2015.

14. S. Ward and L. King, "Work and the good life: How work contributes to meaning in life," *Research in Organizational Behavior*, vol. 37, pp. 59–82, 2017.

15. P. Boyle, A. Buchman, L. Barnes and D. Bennett, "Effect of a purpose in life on risk of incident Alzheimer disease and mild cognitive impairment in community-dwelling older persons," *Archives of General Psychiatry*, vol. 67, no. 3, pp. 304–310, 2010.

16. M. Koizumi, H. Ito, Y. Kaneko and Y. Motohashi, "Effect of having a sense of purpose in life on the risk of death from cardiovascular diseases," *Journal of Epidemiology*, vol. 18, no. 5, pp. 191–196, 2008.

17. J. Forgas and R. Baumeister, *The social psychology of living well*, London: Routledge, 2018.

18. B. Allan, C. Dexter, R. Kinsey and S. Parker, "Meaningful work and mental health: job satisfaction as a moderator," *Journal of Mental Health*, vol. 27, no. 1, pp. 38–44, 2018.

19. M. Steger, B. Dik and R. Duffy, "Measuring meaningful work: The work and meaning inventory (WAMI)," *Journal of Career Assessment*, vol. 20, no. 3, pp. 322–337, 2012.

20. C. Arnoux-Nicolas, L. Sovet, L. Lhotellier, A. Di Fabio and J. Bernaud, "Perceived work conditions and turnover intentions: The mediating role of meaning of work," *Frontiers in Psychology*, vol. 7, p. 704, 2016.

21. S. Raub and H. Liao, "Doing the right thing without being told: Joint effects of initiative climate and general self-efficacy on employee proactive customer service performance," *Journal of Applied Psychology*, vol. 97, no. 3, pp. 651–667, 2012.

22. P. Zak, *Trust factor: The science of creating high-performance companies*, New York, NY: AMACOM, 2017.

23. Z. Zhang, D. Waldman and Z. Wang, "A multilevel investigation of leader—Member exchange, informal leader emergence, and individual and team performance," *Personnel Psychology*, vol. 65, no. 1, pp. 49–78, 2012.

24. R. Vecchio, "The meaning of working, MOW international research team," *Journal of Organizational Behavior*, vol. 10, no. 1, pp. 1–100, 1987.

25. A. Wrzesniewski, C. McCauley, P. Rozin and B. Schwartz, "Jobs, careers, and callings: People's relations to their work," *Journal of Research in Personality*, vol. 31, pp. 21–33, 1997.
26. K. Vohs, N. Mead and M. Goode, "The psychological consequences of money," *Science*, vol. 314, no. 5802, pp. 1154–1156, 2006.
27. R. Duffy, K. Autin and E. Bott, "Work volition and job satisfaction: Examining the role of work meaning and person–environment fit," *The Career Development Quarterly*, vol. 63, no. 2, pp. 126–140, 2015.
28. A. Levit and S. Licina, *How the recession shaped millennial and hiring manager attitudes about millennials' future careers*, Downers Grove, IL: Career Advisory Board, 2011.

11

Values

Talking about values without using the word 'integrity' is hard. We're going to try. This chapter is not about which values are best or most desirable, or which will lead to higher performance, because although there are constants, these things also change slightly according to the situation. Instead, it is about what values do to the way people work, how they help create clarity, and how you and your Leadership OS can help create them, whatever you choose them to be.

Every company, every leader, every person has values. They may not be written down, they may not be formally stated, but they are there. They can affect almost every aspect of how people think, feel and behave at work. They are the feelings and beliefs that people have about what is right and wrong, how people should behave and how things should be done. And whether you are a CEO, divisional director or first-line leader, the challenge with values is the same: how do you turn feelings and beliefs into actions, into something real and sustained?

Living Values: The Case of Daniel Birnbaum at SodaStream

In 2007, 45-year-old Daniel Birnbaum was secure in his job as president of Nike's business in Israel. Then, his friend Yuval Cohen purchased SodaStream for $6 million and asked Birnbaum to be its CEO. His friends and family thought he was crazy to consider it, but to Birnbaum, it felt like a challenge, and it did not take him long to accept (Fig. 11.1).

© The Author(s) 2020
N. Kinley and S. Ben-Hur, *Leadership OS*,
https://doi.org/10.1007/978-3-030-27293-7_11

Daniel Birnaum

Fig. 11.1 Daniel Birnbaum

The challenge he saw was for SodaStream, the maker of a system that allowed consumers to make fizzy drinks at home, to compete in the global carbonated drinks business. And it was a big challenge. In 2007, SodaStream had revenues of $90 million, compared with Coca-Cola's $29 billion and PepsiCo's $39 billion. But Birnbaum relished the fight, and fights like this would define much of his tenure as SodaStream's CEO.

One of the first came with 'The Cage', one of SodaStream's marketing initiatives. It was a minivan-sized box filled with the number of discarded cans and bottles of soda a family throws away in a year. The first cage appeared in Belgium, but others soon popped up in high-profile locations in 25 markets around the world. When a Coke executive saw the company's trashed cans and bottles on display, a cease and desist letter was immediately sent to SodaStream. But Birnbaum won, and people loved the rebellious attitude that he and SodaStream showed in standing up to Coke.

Then in 2013, SodaStream paid for a TV commercial for the 2013 Super Bowl on CBS. The company created an edgy ad showing Coke and Pepsi bottles exploding, a metaphor for all the bottles that could be eliminated by switching to SodaStream's products. When CBS rejected the ad, Birnbaum posted the ad online, where it received more views and public relations impressions than the much tamer revised ad that aired during the game. A similar scene occurred in 2014, this time when Fox rejected SodaStream's edgy ad.

Birnbaum believed he was taking the moral high ground, promoting a healthier and more environmentally friendly product, while refusing to be bullied by much larger competitors. In doing so, he positioned SodaStream as a brand through which customers could express their own values. And he used this connection to values to engage with broader social issues.

By 2013, most of the company's products were produced at the Mishor Adumim plant in the disputed zone between Israel and the West Bank, where more than 500 Palestinian employees worked alongside 1000 Israeli employees. Hiring Palestinian workers was one of Birnbaum's first initiatives when he joined SodaStream. He made sure the Palestinian workers were paid the same wages and benefits as the Jewish ones, and many were managers, overseeing mixed teams of Palestinian and Jewish workers. The move attracted criticism, with some suggesting that it was helping perpetuate the political situation there. Again, though, Birnbaum stuck to his position. His view was that providing economic opportunity could only help and he was proud that SodaStream was showing that Palestinians and Jews could coexist productively and peacefully.

However, the pressure built, and when in 2015 SodaStream tried to relocate its operations and employees to a new facility in Israel's Negev Desert, the Israeli government only granted 74 of the 500 Palestinian employees permits to work there. Then, in early 2016, Prime Minister Benjamin Netanyahu allowed those permits to expire. Birnbaum was furious.

He argued that providing economic opportunities for Palestinians promoted a less violent, more secure situation for Israel. Moreover, he compared what SodaStream was doing to the Judaic concept of *tikkun olam* ('repairing the world'), which enjoins individuals to promote the welfare of society at large. By now, clearly, he was fighting for more than just beverages. After a year of public argument with Netanyahu, SodaStream was granted permits for the 74 Palestinian workers. Birnbaum is on record as saying this was one of the happiest days of his life.

Then, on 20 August 2018, PepsiCo announced that it was acquiring SodaStream for $3.2 billion. PepsiCo CEO Indra Nooyi had disclosed her plans to retire just two weeks earlier, but it was clear she was heavily involved in the deal, as it would continue her mission to create Performance with Purpose at the company. Nonetheless, the implementation of the acquisition has fallen to her successor, Ramon Laguarta, and it will be a while before the impact of the deal is known.

The early signs are that PepsiCo understands how important Birnbaum's fighting spirit and values are to the culture, mission and success of the business. When the acquisition closed, all of SodaStream's 3000 employees received a bonus—up to $5000—as a thank you for their contribution to the company's success. And, just two weeks later, Birnbaum announced that the company would build a manufacturing facility in the Gaza Strip.

There is no doubt that Birnbaum is an excellent example of a leader who has inspired his company through the way he has lived and acted on his values. However, although it is his big strategic and political decisions that have captured the headlines, the real power of his impact lies elsewhere—because Birnbaum's values are not just his anymore, they are SodaStream's.

Speak to employees, and they talk of a dynamic environment, in which creativity, risk-taking and freedom to express ideas are all encouraged and valued. He has changed the culture of the business, as the values and behaviours he so embodies have become mirrored in the way the people around him work.

Birnbaum, then, has not just lived his values, he has brought them to life in the day-to-day activity of people. And it is that, more than any strategic decision, that gives hope that Birnbaum's legacy and SodaStream's future will be sustained. A person with strong values is one thing—a whole company with shared values is quite another.

What Values Are

Values are a core part of the fabric of your Leadership OS. Mention the word 'values', and the tendency is to think of whether someone is ethical and honest. But values extend beyond this, permeating everything people do at work.

Many of them revolve around how you treat and work with other people, such as how you handle disagreements and challenge ideas. Yet they can also be about punctuality—for example, whether it is okay for meetings to start five minutes late. They can be an emphasis on quality or a focus on deadlines. Or they can be unspoken standards about how long or short a presentation slide deck should be. As with purpose, values do not have to be big to be powerful. Slight differences in how people do things can have a significant effect.

The key here is that values are not just what you believe or feel. They are what you do, how you behave. For all practical purposes, a value believed but never acted on is not a value at all. And when it comes to thinking about how Leadership OSs help create values, and how they then affect what people do and how they act, this is the crucial shift in thinking we need to make. To stop thinking of values as ideas in our heads, and to start thinking of them as things that we do.

How to identify your values

So how can people identify what their values are? One useful technique is to turn the question on its head. Ask yourself: what are the things you would not do? And what are the things you see others do that provoke a reaction in you—that make you irritated, impatient or angry? In other words, what are the things that evoke a visceral, emotional response in you? Find these, and you will find your values.

How Your Leadership OS Helps Create Values

Mark Carney, the Governor of the Bank of England, was once asked what he thought about the fact that banks seemed to be going through a period in which they were blaming individual employees—whom they referred to as 'bad apples'—for repeated run-ins with industry regulators. 'If you get enough bad apples', he replied, 'then after a while you have to wonder if there is something wrong with the barrel'.

In this analogy, your Leadership OS is the barrel, helping create good or bad apples Broader national and organisational cultures clearly also have an impact on the values people hold. Every individual's personal history can play a part, as can events in a company's or team's history. And some roles will tend to attract people with a particular set of values [1]. But the most influential force driving the way people work is the operating system they work within—the Leadership OS you create.

It was for this reason that we once declined a request to design a process for selecting trainee traders with high integrity. We knew that selecting people for integrity is technically tough, since it is easy to fake. But more than that, we knew that the key lever for ensuring those trainees had the values the company wanted was to make sure that the business had the leaders and culture that would encourage and support those values. So, instead, we designed a programme to develop the OSs of their leaders.

This does not mean that setting values is straightforward. Values are not like orders you can give or force on people. Research shows that if you impose values, people may follow them for a while, but the values are unlikely to be reliably sustained [2]. Like purpose, values need to be accepted and adopted.

The good news here, though, is that people generally *will* take on the values of those around them. Research shows that when people move to a new team, they tend to adopt the ways of working, standards and values of this new group. And the longer someone stays in a group, the more likely they are to adhere to its values [3].

This is what happened in SodaStream. Birnbaum did not order everyone to be more open, creative and risk-taking. He behaved this way himself, and the operating environment he created around him then encouraged other people to behave the same way, too. After a while, they adopted his way of working and, eventually, these other people started influencing the behaviour of the people around them, as well. And so it spread.

When it comes to how values form, Leadership OSs do two things. Through the behaviour that leaders role-model, they communicate something about which values and ways of working are desirable. And through the ways in which leaders behave towards and react to others, they encourage or discourage the adoption of certain values. If your boss thanks you when you (rightly) challenge a decision of theirs, you are more likely to do it again. If they react badly, you are less likely to.

Of course, what is role-modelled by leaders and what is encouraged by their Leadership OSs may not always be the same. There is no shortage of examples of leaders who behave one way but expect something different from other people. Do as I say, not as I do. And there is no shortage either of leaders who explicitly state they want people to behave in a certain way ('I want people to challenge me'), but then unconsciously—through their body language or tone of voice—discourage people from doing just that.

Yet when leaders can align what they do with what their Leadership OS encourages, this alignment can be a powerful force for change, influencing the values and behaviour of the people around them. And when other people start aligning their values and behaviour with that of the leader, this alignment can become a powerful force for performance. The key for turning values into performance, then, is alignment: making sure that the values your OS encourages are aligned with the way you behave, so that the values of the people around you are aligned with yours.

How Aligned Values Affect What People Do

Researchers have shown that when a leader creates a Leadership OS in which people's values and ways of working align, it tends to have three significant impacts (Fig. 11.2).

A. Promotes teamwork and trust

By far the biggest and most common impact that aligning values has is on people's relationships with each other [4], how they treat each other and work together. The reason this effect is so powerful is that it operates at a biological level. When people share work values, they have a shared set of rules for how to behave towards each other. These shared expectations reduce uncertainty [5], which in turn both lessens the chances that the brain's threat detection system will be triggered and increases the chances that their trust system will be activated [6]. This is why teams with shared values also tend to have higher levels of trust [7].

As a result, all the benefits that come with higher levels of trust come with shared values. People tend to be more collaborative, open-minded and positive. Conflict is therefore reduced [8], successful interactions made more likely [9], and teamwork and team performance improved [10]. Add it all together, and this explains why people in teams with strongly aligned values tend to report greater levels of satisfaction at work [11] and reduced levels of stress [12].

Moreover, this improvement in people's relationships extends beyond the immediate team. When individuals' values align with those of the people around them, they become more oriented to other people in general. Employees with strongly aligned values thus show far greater concern for shareholders, owners and customers than workers whose values are not aligned with those of their colleagues [12].

Fig. 11.2 The functions of aligned values in a Leadership OS

B. Reinforces effort and commitment

The second way aligned values affect people comes as a result of this increased teamwork and trust. Because they feel a greater sense of connection with the team, people tend to work harder. Specifically, research shows that having aligned values boosts people's commitment and effort levels. For example, in a study of Silicon Valley tech firms, companies with strongly aligned values were found to have significantly higher levels of cohesiveness and willingness to work hard [13]. Similarly, teams with more strongly aligned values have been shown to demonstrate higher levels of work effort and persistence [14]. And as a result, businesses [15] and teams [16] with aligned values consistently show higher performance levels.

C. Drives better and quicker decisions

The final way that having aligned values can drive performance is by improving problem-solving [17] and decision-making [18]. The increased trust that alignment breeds, plus the increased collaboration and information flow that follow, produce more informed and better-discussed decisions. Moreover, since studies show that individuals are more likely to focus on shared, team or organisational goals when their values are aligned [12], the teams they form tend to be more cohesive in their focus, quicker to make decisions and thus faster to act [19].

These three effects, then, are the core mechanisms through which a Leadership OS that promotes aligned values can influence people's behaviour and drive better performance. The challenge is: how do you ensure that your OS creates this alignment?

How to Align Values

To a certain extent, if you put a group of people in a room for long enough, their values will align. Maybe not entirely, but at least partially. Especially if you give them a shared goal, like company performance.

One of the reasons this gradual alignment happens lies in the fact that most people generally share the same values. Studies show that although meeting someone who has values that directly contradict yours may be memorable, it is also relatively rare. Instead, what most commonly seems to separate people is not what values they hold, but which order they prioritise them in [20]. For example, quality may be *the* single most important thing for your colleague. For you, however, it may be more crucial that things get done on time. This does not mean that quality is not important for you, just that it is not the main priority. So, aligning values is usually more about shifting priorities than fundamentally changing what people believe.

The good news, then, is that it is not always as difficult as it may sound. So much so, that some alignment tends to happen spontaneously, without you doing anything. The not so good news, however, is that you cannot rely on this spontaneous process.

For starters, some people are more open to aligning values than others [21]. So with some people, teams and businesses, it can take considerable effort to create alignment. Then, there is the fact that today's more global and dispersed teams make aligning values both more difficult and more important. It is more difficult because teams tend to be more diverse and to spend less time all in the same room together. This means that spontaneous alignment happens more slowly and to a lesser extent. And it is more important because under these conditions, the opposite of values alignment—where people's approaches fragment and teamwork and trust break down—is more likely to happen [22].

Moreover, if you are proactive, deliberate and systematic in ensuring your Leadership OS promotes aligned values, then you are more likely to succeed in aligning them, thereby gaining all the associated benefits. And when we look at the research on what you can do that is most likely to help this alignment happen, four key techniques stand out (Fig. 11.3).

Discuss and Define

Studies from around the world have repeatedly found that no matter what national culture you live in, discussing, agreeing and stating values can be a powerful device for aligning them. In fact, studies show that doing

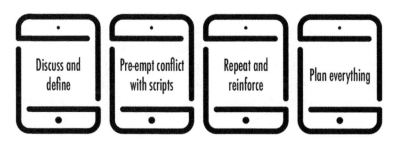

Fig. 11.3 Four techniques to create aligned values

this is more likely to align the way and degree to which people enact their values than giving them feedback or incentivising them to behave in a certain way.

The evidence is so solid that it has become common practice in many businesses. The standard approach is to set time aside for the team to discuss their values and ways of working during a team meeting or off-site. At the end of the discussion, a list of the most important values is agreed, and the mere exercise of having discussed these values can help align people around them.

However, although this is a commonly undertaken practice, often it is not done well. And in our experience, there are a few things you can do that can make the difference between whether this exercise adds just a little value or has real impact:

- Be sure to discuss what a value or way of working looks like in action, in terms of what specific behaviours it involves. Otherwise, people can end up talking about something, such as customer service, while having quite different behaviours in mind.
- Be sure to discuss how the value or way of working will make a difference. By discussing its impact, you emphasise and reinforce the importance of enacting it.
- If you, as the leader, have a value you want others to align with, you are more likely to succeed if you state it as an objective, rather than a value. For example, say you have a value that focusing on customer needs is your company's raison d'être and the source of its success. You could simply state this, and then lead by example. But research shows that people are more likely to align with it if, rather than stating it as a value or belief, you name an objective it would produce, such as higher customer satisfaction scores. You can then ask your team to identify what ways of working are most likely to deliver this. And by doing this, they are more likely to adopt the value, since you are allowing them to generate it rather than giving it to them.
- Make sure to follow up and have a continuing conversation about these ways of working. Having a one-off discussion can help to some degree, but referring to what has been agreed at regular intervals is far more powerful. It reinforces the agreed values. It allows you and others to check and discuss whether the values are really being lived. And perhaps most importantly, it communicates that living by your values is important to you.

Pre-empt Conflict

The second technique at your disposal to help align values is an off-shoot of the first. But it is so important that it is worth saying separately. One of the things about values is that they are often invisible, and you tend to notice them most when things go wrong or times are tough. This is because these moments—when you are under pressure or stress—are when values are most likely to drive your behaviour. And so, in these challenging times, values become most influential in determining whether you are successful or not.

If you are trying to align people's values, it is therefore crucial that you include the way people manage tough moments: how they disagree, how they challenge and how they support each other under pressure.

One useful way to do this is to ask your team to reflect on what psychologists refer to as the *scripts* people often use in these situations. Scripts are what people tend to say and do in a particular scenario. For example, think about your script for disapproval. What do you usually say when you disapprove of what someone has done because the quality is not good enough? How do you tend to say it? If you reflect on past occasions when you have done this, you will probably be able to spot a pattern. Something about the way in which you generally do it that is very 'you'. And you can use this technique with your team to help them think about and discuss their values in highly charged and demanding situations. It is useful because if you ask your team to identify the team script for how they tend to respond in these circumstances, it can depersonalise the situation and prevent them from assigning blame.

So, first describe a scene to them, one involving something going wrong or people disagreeing. Next, ask them to discuss and identify how the team typically responds. And finally, ask them to agree how they would like to respond going forward. What their values are about how to react and support each other in these moments.

Repeat and Reinforce

This one is simple. Once you have defined some values, repeat them, repeat them, repeat them. A lot. Although it is possible to overdo it, in our experience most leaders overestimate the degree to which they refer back to values. Yet when you talk about them, you remind people of them, and they are more likely to align with them. Even referring to events or behaviours with simple phrases like 'That's what we're about' can help.

Then, when you see someone enacting a value in an exemplary way, publicly comment on it and praise it. Since early 2000, the CEO of JetBlue has sent an email to the entire company every Sunday to share a story about an employee who lives the company's values through their actions at work. At the time of writing, that is nearly a thousand emails. And that is a lot of repetition and reinforcement.

Plan Everything

Well, not *everything*. But research has shown that teams who put more time and effort into planning tend to have more aligned values [23]. There is something about the process of discussing what and how things need to happen that helps align people's ways of working. So, the fourth technique is to encourage *joint* planning. The key here is that some discussion needs to be had. And in teams where people tend to operate in distinct areas and do not have to create joint plans with their peers, one approach you can use is to suggest—as a matter of good practice—that people present and ask for feedback on their plans for their areas with their peers.

Building Critical Mass

It is good for a leader to enact their values; people tend to like leaders who 'walk the talk'. But one thing that stands out from the research is that it is not enough. Most people do not just copy or align with their leaders, they tend to align with what the majority of others say and do [3]. So, if you have one set of values, but your team has another, someone new in the team is more likely to adopt the team's values over time than yours—unless you have deliberately brought them in to change people's ways of working.

As a leader, your views are, of course, particularly influential in steering people's values. But you need to work at it, you need to be proactive, deliberate and systematic. And you need to build a critical mass of people whose values are all aligned in the way you believe most helpful.

The way to do this is through your Leadership OS, by making sure that the values it encourages and promotes are aligned with the values you enact and want others to adopt.

Like the other components of clarity—direction (people's shared sense of what is important), accountability (their sense of ownership) and purpose (their sense that what they do matters)—the power of values, people's understanding of how things should be done, lies in their ability to make things predictable. To reduce uncertainty and friction, and focus and coordinate activity. If trust is the beating heart of your operating system, values and the other components of clarity are the mind and brain of it.—the compass that helps people know where they are heading, why they are heading there and how they should do it.

So, your Leadership OS has a heart and a mind. Now, let's turn to the spirit of it. To the drive and energy of your OS, to momentum.

Summary + Checklist

See Table 11.1.

Table 11.1 Summary of values

	OS Function	Techniques to build it
Values	• Promotes teamwork and trust • Reinforces effort and commitment • Drives better and quicker decisions	• Discuss and define • Pre-empt conflict with scripts • Repeat and reinforce • Plan everything

Checklist

To help you think about whether you have successfully installed values in your Leadership OS, ask yourself how the people around you—your direct reports, peers and stakeholders—would respond to the following questions (Table 11.2).

Table 11.2 Have you installed values in your Leadership OS?

	✓	✗
Would people say you act in a way that reflects the values of the business?	□	□
Do people believe you label and state what your values are?	□	□
Do people feel that you encourage them to behave in the same way—with the same values—as you do?	□	□
Do people believe you help them think about how their values fit in with those of the people around them?	□	□
Do people believe you regularly praise or reward them for enacting the company's values?	□	□

References

1. D. Feldman, "The development and enforcement of group norms," *Academy of Management Review*, vol. 9, no. 1, pp. 47–53, 1984.
2. S. Cha and A. Edmondson, "When values backfire: Leadership, attribution, and disenchantment in a values-driven organization," *The Leadership Quarterly*, vol. 17, pp. 57–78, 2008.
3. M. Gruys, S. Stewart, J. Goodstein, M. Bing and A. Wicks, "Values enactment in organizations: A multi-level examination," *Journal of Management*, vol. 34, no. 4, pp. 806–843, 2008.
4. S. Markham, F. Yammarino, W. Murry and M. Palanski, "Leader–member exchange, shared values, and performance: Agreement and levels of analysis do matter," *The Leadership Quarterly*, vol. 21, no. 3, pp. 469–480, 2010.
5. E. Schein, *Organizational culture and leadership*, San Francisco, CA, Jossey-Bass, 1985.
6. D. Goleman and R. Boyatzis, "Social intelligence and the biology of leadership," *Harvard Business Review*, vol. 86, no. 9, pp. 74–81, 2008.
7. N. Gillespie and L. Mann, "Transformational leadership and shared values: The building blocks of trust," *Journal of Managerial Psychology*, vol. 19, no. 6, pp. 588–607, 2004.
8. C. Fisher and R. Gitelson, "A meta-analysis of the correlates of role conflict and ambiguity," *Journal of Applied Psychology*, vol. 68, no. 2, pp. 320–333, 1983.
9. B. Meglino, E. Ravlin and C. Adkins, "A work values approach to corporate culture: A field test of the value congruence process and its relationship to individual outcomes," *Journal of Applied Psychology*, vol. 74, no. 3, pp. 424–432, 1989.
10. R. Fitzpatrick, "A literature review exploring values alignment as a proactive approach to conflict management," *International Journal of Conflict Management*, vol. 18, no. 3, pp. 280–305, 2007.
11. Z. Onağ and M. Tepeci, "Team effectiveness in sport teams: The effects of team cohesion, intra team communication and team norms on team member satisfaction and intent to remain," *Procedia-Social and Behavioral Sciences*, vol. 150, pp. 420–428, 2014.
12. B. Posner, J. Kouzes and W. Schmidt, "Shared values make a difference: An empirical test of corporate culture," *Human Resource Management*, vol. 24, no. 3, pp. 293–309, 1985.
13. C. O'Reilly and D. Caldwell, "The impact of normative social influence and cohesiveness on task perceptions and attitudes: A social information processing approach," *Journal of Occupational Psychology*, vol. 58, no. 3, pp. 193–206, 1985.
14. M. Patterson, A. Carron and T. Loughead, "The influence of team norms on the cohesion–self-reported performance relationship: A multi-level analysis," *Psychology of Sport and Exercise*, vol. 6, no. 4, pp. 479–493, 2005.

15. J. Kotter and J. Heskett, *Corporate culture and performance*, New York, NY, The Free Press, 1992.

16. J. Chatman and F. Flynn, "The influence of demographic heterogeneity on the emergence and consequences of cooperative norms in work teams," *Academy of Management Journal*, vol. 44, no. 5, pp. 956–974, 2001.

17. S. Taggar and R. Ellis, "The role of leaders in shaping formal team norms," *The Leadership Quarterly*, vol. 18, no. 2, pp. 105–120, 2007.

18. F. Kellermanns, S. Floyd, A. Pearson and B. Spencer, "The contingent effect of constructive confrontation on the relationship between shared mental models and decision quality," *Journal of Organizational Behavior*, vol. 29, no. 1, pp. 119–137, 2008.

19. [19] D. Caldwell and C. O'Reilly III, "The determinants of team-based innovation in organizations: The role of social influence," *Small Group Research*, vol. 34, no. 4, pp. 497–517, 2003.

20. S. Schwartz, "Universals in the content and structure of values: Theoretical advances and empirical tests in 20 countries," *Advances in Experimental Psychology*, vol. 25, pp. 1–65, 1992.

21. S. Livi, A. Kruglanski, A. Pierro, L. Mannetti and D. Kenny, "Epistemic motivation and perpetuation of group culture: Effects of need for cognitive closure on trans-generational norm transmission," *Organizational Behavior and Human Decision Processes*, vol. 129, pp. 105–112, 2015.

22. K. Moser and C. Axtell, "The role of norms in virtual work: A review and agenda for future research," *Journal of Personnel Psychology*, vol. 12, no. 1, pp. 1–6, 2013.

23. G. Janicik and C. Bartel, "Talking about time: Effects of temporal planning and time awareness norms on group coordination and performance," *Group Dynamics: Theory, Research, and Practice*, vol. 7, no. 2, p. 122, 2003.

Part III

Generating Momentum

12

Momentum

The Drive and Spirit of an Effective OS

Trust and clarity are both critical for a high-performing Leadership OS, but on their own, they are not enough. There is a third key element: momentum.

It is not a term you will have often heard applied to leadership, but it is no less vital for that. In our review of over 1000 studies, searching for the core aspects of OSs, we found a small cluster of deeply interconnected components. Together, they form momentum—the capacity for action, the drive to get things moving and make things happen. And without it, you and your OS are going nowhere.

What Momentum Is

You know momentum when you see it. There is a dynamic quality to the way people operate. They act with pace and focus. They invest themselves in what they do, commit themselves to it, become absorbed by it. They seem to do a little extra, try a little harder, and they seem to enjoy doing it [1]. If your business or team had an 'on' switch or power button, momentum would be it.

Like all 'on' switches, this one is important. In fact, from our research with thousands of leaders around the world, momentum emerged as the Leadership OS element that most distinguishes high-performing leaders

© The Author(s) 2020
N. Kinley and S. Ben-Hur, *Leadership OS*,
https://doi.org/10.1007/978-3-030-27293-7_12

from low-performing ones. On average, when leaders' OSs have strong levels of momentum, their performance is rated over 17% higher by their bosses compared with leaders whose OSs are low in momentum.

Why and how momentum is so vital is the story of this chapter. It begins with the four components that together create momentum (Fig. 12.1). They are:

1. Motivation—the extent to which people feel motivated by what they are doing and trying to achieve.
2. Confidence—the extent to which people feel confidence in both themselves and the organisation.
3. Empowerment—the extent to which people feel empowered to do their jobs.
4. Connection—the extent to which people feel a sense of community and relatedness—that they are all 'in it together'.

Motivation

Every two years the top 24 national football (soccer) teams in Europe gather to compete under the gaze of millions of fans. In 2016, someone else was watching, too: a group of researchers from the UK's University of Staffordshire [2]. Looking at 51 games in the competition, they were interested in how players sang their national anthems before each match. They recorded whether players sang and, if so, with what intensity. They also watched facial expressions and body language, such as whether the players stood closely together or put their arms around each other. They then compared how teams sang their national anthems with how well they did in the subsequent match.

They found that the level of passion displayed by players during the anthems predicted their team's subsequent success or failure. Teams that sang with greater passion went on to concede fewer goals and win more matches. As spectators, we generally find the national anthems the least interesting part of the game. But we should have been paying more attention. Because our passion for what we do matters.

Such passion is the embodiment of motivation, the best-known component of momentum. Motivation is the desire to do something, the extent to which people feel impassioned and energised. It is the foundation of momentum because in order for people to commit themselves to what they are doing, they need to want to do it [3].

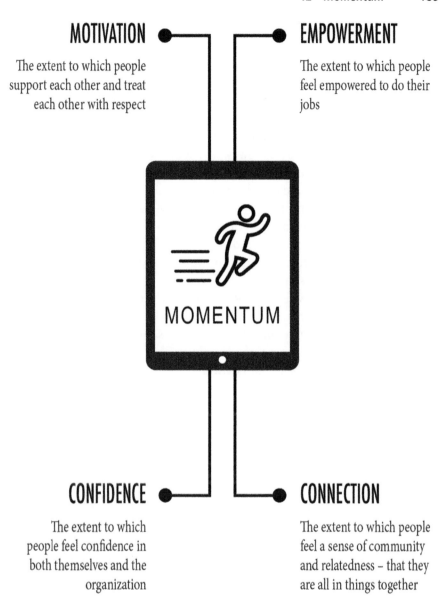

MOTIVATION

The extent to which people support each other and treat each other with respect

EMPOWERMENT

The extent to which people feel empowered to do their jobs

CONFIDENCE

The extent to which people feel confidence in both themselves and the organization

CONNECTION

The extent to which people feel a sense of community and relatedness – that they are all in things together

Fig. 12.1 The components of momentum

Unsurprisingly, motivation is a critical driver of high performance. Some of this is because of the obvious—that highly motivated people put more effort into their work. But as we will see in the next chapter, some of the uplift in performance is due to a more surprising consequence of motivation—that it can improve people's judgement and decision-making.

Confidence

Sports psychology is a booming business these days. The reason is that professional teams and trainers know something that businesses would do well to remember: for people to perform their best—at the highest level they can—they need to feel confident about what they are doing [4].

A recent review of 45 studies showed that, on average, confidence accounts for almost 15% of how well people do at sports [5]. That may not sound like a lot, but if you think of the huge number of different factors involved, 15% is massive. It is certainly big enough to be the difference between success and failure, or good and great. And our own research into the impact of different OS components on the performance of a leader's team confirms this finding, too. Just over 15% of performance was due to confidence—that's more than motivation, or indeed any other individual component of a Leadership OS.

As we will see in Chapter 14, confidence has this effect because it enhances people's expectations of themselves and makes them more likely to show initiative, be creative and demonstrate resilience. So, motivation may be the best-known component of momentum, but it is not the most important. That honour belongs to confidence.

Empowerment

The British Army's Leadership Code makes interesting reading [6]. Military units are renowned for being some of the most hierarchical, command-and-control, do-as-you-are-told environments there are. Yet in his brief introduction to the Code, General Sir Nicholas Carter uses the word 'empowerment' four times. Read on, and it becomes clear that empowering people is a constant refrain running through the Code. Time and again, it talks of the importance of empowering and supporting platoon sergeants and squad leaders to think for themselves and make decisions. If you want people to act, they need to be empowered to do so.

What works in the army works in businesses, too [7]. Our research shows that Leadership OSs high in empowerment produce stronger levels of performance. As we will see in Chapter 15, when people feel empowered, they put in more effort and are more collaborative and more agile in the way they respond to changing circumstances. They also feel more confident and motivated, so empowerment is a crucial aspect and reinforcer of momentum.

Connection

The final component of momentum is perhaps the least expected one. Connection is the extent to which people feel a sense of community and team. It is the feeling of being part of something, that 'we're all in it together'. It is thus a good thing in general because it creates a sense of social cohesion, binding people into a unit. But it is also important for momentum because when we feel connected to someone or something, we try harder.

Thus, connection not only improves trust and collaboration but also increases people's commitment to what they do. When Leadership OSs help people feel a sense of connection, those people tend to show higher levels of engagement and more discretionary effort—the energy they put into their work over and above what they are required to [8].

As we will see in Chapter 16, connection is a kind of social glue that reinforces and binds together the other components of momentum. When people feel connected, they are more likely to feel motivated, confident and empowered. And when they feel these things, connection is what ensures that people act in a cohesive and coordinated fashion.

Generating Momentum: The Case of Tony Hsieh at Zappos

We don't normally associate the words *cult* and *culture*, but they have the same roots. The dictionary definition of the word 'cult' is 'a great devotion to a person, idea, object, movement or work'. Corporate culture, meanwhile, is created by instilling a particular way of doing things and a certain devotion to products, the company mission, or the work people do. An effective culture thereby joins people together in a way that makes the company greater than the sum of its parts. So successful leadership thus often involves walking a fine line between creating culture and creating a cult. And few corporate leaders have spent as much time walking this fine line as Tony Hsieh, the CEO of Zappos (Fig. 12.2).

Hsieh has long referred to his inner circle as his 'tribe' and Zappos' employees are referred to as 'members' or 'Zapponians'. They don't log into their computers with a personal password; they have to pass an 'identify-a-fellow-Zapponian' quiz, which changes daily. They frequently show up to meetings dressed as bunny rabbits or superheroes…just because they feel like it. And new employees are given a 'culture book', written by current employees, highlighting their favourite aspects of working at Zappos.

Fig. 12.2 Tony Hsieh

By most accounts, Zappos employees love working for Zappos. And this all comes from Hsieh—who proudly claims that company culture is the firm's main business strategy. Relationships have always been a huge part of Hsieh's approach to business. These relationships—both between people and with the company—provide the momentum that propels Zappos towards its mission goal of delivering happiness. This is not just some PR-line or cliché that Zappos uses to connect with customers, either. It is an attitude that is fundamental to Zappos' DNA and Hsieh's approach to leadership. Perhaps the best example of this is the way that Hsieh talks about employees' relationships with their jobs. He says that while other companies talk about work–life separation and balance, Zappos strives for work–life integration. The result is a completely unique corporate culture.

It's certainly not for everyone. In fact, new employees are offered a thousand dollars to quit if they determine that the Zappos culture is not for them. Fewer than two per cent of new employees take the cash; the rest commit to the Zappos mission.

Some casual observers have suggested that Zappos is more like a cult than a company with a unique culture. That it is all about Hsieh. Yet look closer and it becomes clear that while he guides and facilitates Zappos' unique culture, there are many aspects of the firm that were established by the employees and for the employees. For instance, the company officially has 10 values. None of these are about profits or financial performance, and instead they are all about individual attitudes and a sense of family. And all were created—crowdsourced—by Zappos' employees. So when they claim to believe in the same things and share the same core values, it's true.

What Hsieh has done at Zappos, then, is to motivate, connect and empower people in order to generate a unique passion for the firm and its work—a momentum that ultimately not only delivers employee happiness, but also customer happiness. It may be an extreme example, but the company's profits are also proof that investing in momentum makes good business sense.

What Momentum Does

As with trust and clarity, the importance of momentum lies in what it does to people. As you might expect from something that is all about actuating people and harnessing their energy, momentum is strongly based in the neurological workings of people's brains. And as the following chapters show, individuals' reward and threat detection systems are both heavily involved. The objective for you, as a leader, is to create an OS that puts these two systems into a positive state of activation. When you achieve this, momentum is created, and it fulfils two main functions in your Leadership OS. One of them you can probably guess, but the other is more surprising (Fig. 12.3).

A. Generates Drive

The first and most predictable thing that momentum does is to generate drive. When you have a Leadership OS that is high in momentum, and when people feel it, they work harder [9] and are more productive [10]. How much more productive they are has been a matter of debate among academics, but estimates vary between 2 and 12 times more productive [11].

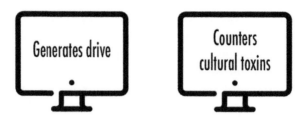

Fig. 12.3 The functions of momentum in a Leadership OS

Employees high in momentum are also more likely to take the initiative, drive creativity and innovation, and show higher levels of entrepreneurship [12]. When they encounter difficulties, they persist for longer [9] and experience less stress and fatigue [13]. They also report higher levels of job satisfaction and are more likely to show loyalty to their organisation and less likely to leave it [10]. And because of this, employees high in momentum consistently perform better, especially in complex roles [14].

B. Counters Cultural Toxins

For many businesses, these are testing times, with low economic growth and high uncertainty being persistent challenges. The responses required—innovation, efficiency and adaptability—are well understood, if not always easy to implement. Yet the further challenge is that tough times make the solutions harder to achieve because hardship and uncertainty also change the way people behave—and all too often, not in a good way.

For example, the most obvious impact of tough times is stress, and although stress can have a multitude of effects on people, few people are made better by it. Then there are gossip and political behaviours. Both have been found to increase with higher degrees of uncertainty and lower business optimism, and both undermine trust. Teams can also become more siloed, and leaders under pressure tend to delegate less, becoming more drawn into the detail of delivery as they seek to ensure delivery.

These cultural changes are usually less noticeable than the commercial issues, and as such, can become like cultural toxins, lurking beneath the surface of day-to-day operations and poisoning a company's ability to respond effectively.

One of the surprising things about momentum, however, is that it protects against and counters these cultural toxins through its four components. *Motivation* and *confidence* have been found to shield people against stress. *Empowerment* can guard leaders against descending too far into the detail of delivery. And *connection* can protect against siloed operation.

Creating Momentum

Employee engagement is not the same as momentum—it is a narrower concept, more akin to motivation—but it is an interesting indicator. And what stands out most from surveys about engagement is just how low levels tend to be. For example, a 2018 study of over 8 million employees in over 1000 companies found that 35% of people were not engaged, with an additional 38% only moderately engaged [15]. This means that only about a quarter of employees feel strongly engaged in what they do. That is—or should be—deeply worrying, especially when it is considered in light of our research, which shows that leaders tend to overrate their ability to create a Leadership OS high in momentum.

It is also, however, a source of opportunity, since an increase in momentum is—as we have seen—likely to produce an increase in performance. Unfortunately, creating an OS high in momentum is not straightforward. It requires you to activate people's motivation, confidence, empowerment and connection, and all four must be activated to create momentum—it is not enough to focus on only one or two of them. This is easier said than done, too, since what makes people feel these things varies between individuals and situations. A whole host of factors are involved, with one recent study finding 24 separate causes involved in motivation alone [16], things like job design, personality differences and compensation [17].

Leaders therefore need to be ready with a range of techniques and be prepared to use a degree of trial and error to see which works best in each scenario and with each team member. Over the next 4 chapters, we will introduce 16 such techniques you can try.

Momentum can also be tricky to build because it tends to be quite unstable, with people's momentum levels often going up and down several times a day [18]. It thus needs repeated attention. The good news, though, is that with a systematic focus, you as a leader are ideally placed to build and support momentum through your OS. Moreover, once you start to give it more attention, the daily volatility in momentum tends to decrease. So not only can you build momentum but you can also make it more sustainable [19].

If trust is the heart of your Leadership OS, the foundation that breaks down barriers and enables collaboration; if clarity is the head and mind of your OS that brings focus, alignment and ownership; then momentum is the spirit of your OS that drives activity. You are pressing the power button on your OS, activating the people around you. You are helping people give their best and be their best. You are helping people thrive.

References

1. J. Halbesleben and A. Wheeler, "The relative roles of engagement and embeddedness in predicting job performance and intention to leave," *Work & Stress*, vol. 22, no. 3, pp. 242–256, 2008.
2. M. Slater, S. Haslam and N. Steffens, "Singing it for 'us': Team passion displayed during national anthems is associated with subsequent success," *European Journal of Sport Science*, vol. 18, no. 4, pp. 541–549, 2018.
3. P. Green Jr., E. Finkel, G. Fitzsimons and F. Gino, "The energizing nature of work engagement: Toward a new need-based theory of work motivation," *Research in Organizational Behavior*, vol. 37, pp. 1–18, 2017.
4. K. Hays, O. Thomas, I. Maynard and M. Bawden, "The role of confidence in world-class sport performance," *Journal of Sports Sciences*, vol. 27, no. 11, pp. 1185–1199, 2009.
5. S. Moritz, D. Feltz, K. Fahrbach and D. Mack, "The relation of self-efficacy measures to sport performance: A meta-analytic review," *Research Quarterly for Exercise and Sport*, vol. 71, no. 3, pp. 280–294, 2000.
6. The Centre for Army Leadership, "The army leadership code" [Online]. Available: https://www.army.mod.uk/media/2698/ac72021_the_army_leadership_code_an_introductory_guide.pdf. Accessed 27 May 2019.
7. F. Mendes and M. Stander, "Positive organisation: The role of leader behaviour in work engagement and retention," *South African Journal of Industrial Psychology*, vol. 37, no. 1, pp. 1–13, 2011.
8. J. Xu and H. Cooper Thomas, "How can leaders achieve high employee engagement?" *Leadership & Organization Development Journal*, vol. 32, no. 4, pp. 399–416, 2011.
9. D. Schunk and P. Ertmer, "Self-regulation and academic learning: Self-efficacy enhancing interventions," in M. Boekaerts, P. R. Pintrich and M. Zeidner (Eds.), *Handbook of self-regulation*, San Diego, CA: Academic Press, 2000, pp. 631–649.
10. J. Harter, F. Schmidt and T. Hayes, "Business-unit-level relationship between employee satisfaction, employee engagement, and business outcomes: A meta-analysis," *Journal of Applied Psychology*, vol. 87, no. 2, p. 268, 2002.
11. J. Pfeffer and R. Sutton, "Profiting from evidence-based management," *Strategy & Leadership*, vol. 34, no. 2, pp. 35–42, 2006.
12. F. Walumbwa, B. Avolio and W. Zhu, "How transformational leadership weaves its influence on individual job performance: The role of identification and efficacy beliefs," *Personnel Psychology*, vol. 61, no. 4, p. 793–825, 2008.
13. T. Britt, C. Castro and A. Adler, "Self-engagement, stressors, and health: A longitudinal study," *Personality and Social Psychology Bulletin*, vol. 31, no. 11, pp. 1475–1486, 2005.

14. M. Christian, A. Garza and J. Slaughter, "Work engagement: A quantitative review and test of its relations with task and contextual performance," *Personnel Psychology*, vol. 64, no. 1, pp. 89–136, 2011.
15. AON, "2018 trends in global employee engagement," New York, NY: AON Plc., 2018.
16. K. Wollard and B. Shuck, "Antecedents to employee engagement: A structured review of the literature," *Advances in Developing Human Resources*, vol. 13, no. 4, pp. 429–446, 2011.
17. C. Bailey, A. Madden, K. Alfes and L. Fletcher, "The meaning, antecedents and outcomes of employee engagement: A narrative synthesis," *International Journal of Management Reviews*, vol. 19, no. 1, pp. 31–53, 2017.
18. A. Bakker, "Daily fluctuations in work engagement: An overview and current directions," *European Psychologist*, vol. 19, no. 4, pp. 227–236, 2014.
19. K. Breevaart, A. Bakker, J. Hetland, E. Demerouti, O. Olsen and R. Espevik, "Daily transactional and transformational leadership and daily employee engagement," *Journal of Occupational and Organizational Psychology*, vol. 87, no. 1, p. 138, 2014.

13

Motivation

Motivation is possibly the most written about aspect of leadership. It is probably the one element that everyone agrees is important. And it is something that leaders are believed to affect directly. As such, it is thought to be one of the key levers that leaders have at their disposal to drive performance. If there is a poster child of the traditional 'behave-like-this-and-you'll-get-that-great-outcome' approach to leadership, this is it.

Yet motivation is also something about which views have changed substantially and are changing still. Over the past 20 years, newly developed statistical techniques have enabled much larger research studies. These have yielded new insights, which have in turn led to significant shifts in the advice given about how best to approach this part of leadership. Now that guidance is evolving again, as new scanning technologies have enabled advancements in neuroscience in the past few years.

What this developing understanding reveals more than anything is that even though the topic may feel familiar, we know a lot less than is generally assumed. Perhaps that is why, despite all the advice available, only 28% of leaders say they feel confident in their ability to motivate people to get the best from them [1]. For something so universally believed to be critical for performance, that is low. Fortunately, in Leadership OSs, we have a solution.

© The Author(s) 2020
N. Kinley and S. Ben-Hur, *Leadership OS*,
https://doi.org/10.1007/978-3-030-27293-7_13

Why Motivating People Is Difficult

Motivation is all about desire. It is the extent to which people feel driven or moved to act. In fact, the word derives from the Latin for 'to move' (*movere*). How much has been written about it? Well, a quick Google search returns almost two *billion* results. We must confess we haven't read them all yet. We have, however, reviewed every major economic, psychological and neuroscientific study on motivation over the last 50 years. And what stands out most clearly from this research is just how oversimplified most of the advice about motivation given to leaders is.

For example, we tend to talk of motivation simply in terms of whether people are motivated or not. But motivation is not like a light switch with just an 'on' or 'off' setting. There are levels of motivation. These levels are hugely variable, too, changing on a daily and even hourly basis [2]. There are different types of motivation, as well, which can affect people in different ways.

Although we tend to think of motivation as being a positive thing, it can have a negative effect in some situations. It can lead individuals to act in ways that would normally be seen to be unacceptable [3]. And it can sometimes reduce performance by interfering with elements of people's capability, such as complex decision-making [4]. Moreover, running through all of this is the fact that leaders—and the vast majority of research—tend only to focus on how they motivate their direct reports. Their impact on the motivation levels of peers and stakeholders receives far less attention.

There is, then, a vast gap between the simple picture commonly presented about motivation and what we know from the research. There are two main reasons for this. The first is that motivation is driven by neurological processes deep within us, and the neurology is extraordinarily complex. The second is that motivation is also one of the aspects of leadership most influenced by context. It is affected by the cultures people come from and operate in; by the business situations and challenges facing them; and by their personal histories, personalities and preferences. All of these things have been shown to affect how motivated people feel by something in any given moment. And this adds even more complexity.

There are certainly some things we can do that, generally speaking, will help to motivate people. But a particular person, on a specific day, regarding their motivation for a certain thing? This is so riddled with context that there can be no fixed rules. Even though motivation is presented as an area in which leaders can have a direct impact on people ('just follow these simple steps to boost motivation levels'), it is, in reality, a shining example of how unpredictable and unreliable that impact is. And *that* is why so many leaders find motivating people difficult: it is complex and unpredictable.

It is also why focusing on Leadership OSs can help. When we think about the impact we want to have, rather than simply following pre-set rules of what to do, we are more able to take context into account. To understand how to do this, to set up our Leadership OSs so that people feel more motivated within them, we need first to understand some of the complexity that all the research has revealed. In particular, we need to understand the two main perspectives that have emerged on what motivation is and how it works.

How Motivation Works

Many of the first studies of motivation focused on trying to identify what triggers it. The idea was that different things motivate us in different ways. So researchers decided to categorise different types of motivators, and this approach has stuck. Today, our understanding is driven by two main theories, each of which presents a different way to categorise what motivates us and how it does so. The first distinguishes between *intrinsic* and *extrinsic* motivation; the second, between *approach* and *avoidance* motivation.

Intrinsic vs. Extrinsic Motivation

Intrinsic motivation is fuelled by *internal* desires and fears rather than external rewards. It is the motivation to act simply because we find something pleasurable or fulfilling—for example, listening to music, having responsibility or mastering a particular skill. Extrinsic motivation, by contrast, is that driven by *external* rewards and punishments—things like praise, bonuses and criticism. So, objectives that emphasise growing expertise or beating a personal best tap into intrinsic motivation, whereas goals that are all about achieving commission levels or bonuses are extrinsic motivators.

Early research mostly focused on how to use extrinsic rewards and punishments to get people to do more or less of certain things [5]. It tried to put some science behind the carrot-and-stick approach that parents and pet owners alike have used for centuries. The basic principle is that if you reward certain behaviours, you will get more of them; if you punish behaviours, you will get less of them. And today, thanks to this research, there is a whole science behind how to make things like prizes, bonuses and feedback work effectively. In the workplace, this led to the pay-for-performance approach that most organisations now use, and the 1990s saw a whole raft of management books focused on goal setting and feedback—using external motivators to drive performance levels.

Then, in the 2000s, things changed. First, research emerged showing that extrinsic motivators—and money in particular—do not always motivate. They appear to be less motivating for complex tasks and at high pay levels [6], are better at driving effort and quantity of work than improving quality [7], and some people just seem less responsive to external rewards [8].

The financial crisis of 2008 reinforced growing doubts, calling massive bonuses into question. Soon after, popular management books came out proclaiming that extrinsic motivators could lead to unhelpful and unethical behaviour [9], and that people's inner, intrinsic motivation to be successful or happy was more powerful and more sustainable for driving performance [10]. Furthermore, the real danger, they noted, was that extrinsic rewards could actually undermine and reduce people's intrinsic motivation [11]. It was quite some message: that rewards can undermine your inner love of doing something.

Recent neurological studies have reinforced this message, too. They have found that some people are indeed less driven—on a biological level—by external rewards [12]. They have revealed that goals driven by intrinsic motivation (such as a desire for recognition) are represented in different parts of the brain than goals driven by external motivators (such as targets to meet sales goals) [13]. And they have shown how, on a biological level, rewards can indeed reduce intrinsic motivation [14]. As a result, the advice given to leaders over the last decade has mostly focused on how to build people's intrinsic motivation.

In the past few years, however, the pendulum has begun to swing again. New neurological studies have revealed that although extrinsic rewards can undermine intrinsic motivation in certain circumstances, they don't always and can at times even enhance it [15]. Today, then, the advice for leaders is both to build people's intrinsic motivation and use extrinsic motivators such as spot bonuses, praise and feedback.

Approach vs. Avoidance Motivation

The second theory to explain motivation looks at it in terms of *approach* and *avoidance* (sometimes also referred to as *promotion* and *prevention*).

Approach motivation is all about pursuing things we like or want—things like food, money and success. Avoidance motivation is all about escaping things we fear or do not like—things like pain, criticism and dangerous animals. So, while intrinsic/extrinsic motivation is about whether motivators are internal or external, approach/avoidance motivation is about whether things are positive or negative.

What is particularly interesting about the approach/avoidance distinction is the neuroscience behind it. This has shown that it is based on two distinct neural systems—one involved in how we respond to reward, the other in how we respond to threat [16].

Approach motivation is based on the brain's reward system. This system is so fundamental to our functioning that it exists in all but the simplest life forms. It is there for a simple purpose: to ensure that we are more likely to repeat behaviour that produces positive outcomes. When something positive happens, a chemical called dopamine is released in the brain, and one of its major effects is to make us feel good. We feel it, the brain registers it and, as a result, we want more of whatever triggered it.

We appear to be born with some of the triggers of this reaction, such as our liking for sweet tastes. Most triggers, though, are learnt. These can be things like what colours we prefer and which hobbies we enjoy; at work they can include aspects like networking [17], money [18] and having our curiosity satisfied [19].

Avoidance motivation, meanwhile, is based in the same threat-detection system we described in the previous chapters on trust and its components. There, we showed how danger and uncertainty can trigger this system. But it can be triggered by anything we want to avoid, including things like criticism and failure. Whereas our reward system makes us feel more positive about things, our threat-detection system has the opposite effect when triggered, making us more anxious and cautious, and more motivated to act to avoid something.

So, from all the research into motivation over the past 50 years, two main approaches have emerged. Together, they describe four types of motivation (Table 13.1).

Each of these types of motivation affects people in a different way. Which of them is driving a person's behaviour at any particular moment, or which would be the most effective lever to drive performance, depends on a host of contextual factors, most notably, the situation and the people involved. But the ultimate impact they have on people's performance, and thus the role they play in your Leadership OS, is broadly the same.

Table 13.1 Four types of motivation

Internal and external motivators		Positive and negative motivators	
Intrinsic	Extrinsic	Approach	Avoidance
Internal drive to do something	Externally applied reward or punishment	Seeking out rewarding things	Acting to avoid unpleasant or threatening things
Growing expertise	Praise	Money	Criticism
Beating personal best	Criticism	Success	Losing face/respect
Responsibility	Bonuses	Recognition	Failure

What Motivation Does

Whichever type is involved, people's performance is impacted in two main ways (Fig. 13.1).

A. Increases Effort

The main effect motivation has is to increase the effort people put into things and thereby also their performance. In fact, in almost every situation studied, motivated people perform better than unmotivated people. They work harder and persist longer when they encounter difficulties [20]. They are more likely to take the initiative and they show higher levels of entrepreneurialism [21]. There are some caveats, though, some situations in which higher motivation can undermine performance, such as if there is an over-reliance on extrinsic rewards only. But in general, high motivation equals high effort.

B. Improves Judgement

The other main effect motivation has is to improve people's judgement. High levels of positive motivation elevate people's mood, and when that happens, they become more open, creative and able to integrate new

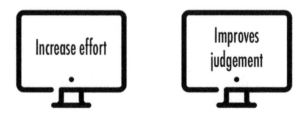

Fig. 13.1 The functions of motivation in a Leadership OS

information [2]. High levels of negative motivation (criticism or concern), meanwhile, improve people's focus, memory and decisiveness. As a result, regardless of whether motivation is positive or negative, people who have higher levels show an enhanced ability to learn [22] and improved performance on complex thinking tasks [23]. So, although we tend to associate motivation with action, it also has an impact on thinking.

There is, however, one crucial 'but' to these findings. Most of the time, motivation has positive effects on judgement. However, if levels of motivation get too high, it can end up having a *negative* effect on things like complex problem-solving and creativity, since people become too focused on outcomes [4]. Studies also show that extreme levels of avoidance motivation can impair people's ability to concentrate. And there is some evidence that the neural mechanism involved here may be the same as in ADHD (attention deficit hyperactivity disorder) [24]. So, in most situations motivation improves judgement, but there are limits, and extreme levels can be a bad thing.

Leading Through Motivation: The Case of Yvon Chouinard at Patagonia

Yvon Chouinard (Fig. 13.2), the founder and chairman of Patagonia, a maker of high-end outdoor clothing and equipment, called his first book *Let My People Go Surfing*. This book title could just as easily be the company's mission. Indeed, at the company's headquarters in California, each day's surf conditions are displayed on boards throughout the office, and employees do take time off to enjoy them. When they get to the beach, they are likely to see Chouinard already out in the water.

Chouinard founded Patagonia in the late 1970s. Since then, the company's actual mission statement has incorporated three core values: 'To build the best product, cause no unnecessary harm, and use business to inspire and implement solutions to the environmental crisis'.

These are not just words, either. Take Chouinard's commitment to sustainability. In 2002, Chouinard and friend Craig Mathews of Blue Ribbon Flies founded '1% for the Planet', a consortium of companies committed to donating 1% of company revenue to environmental causes. By the end of 2018, more than 1800 companies in 45 countries had joined. In addition, after Patagonia switched to using only organic cotton in its products in the mid-1990s, other companies such as Nike, Target, Marks & Spencer and Gap increased their use of organic cotton. Levi Strauss, another privately held California-based apparel maker, has worked with Chouinard and Patagonia both on how it can bring more social responsibility into its

Fig. 13.2 Yvon Chouinard

supply chain and on how it can pursue an impactful social mission without compromising its pursuit of profits. Even Walmart has sought advice from Patagonia on how it can integrate more environmental sustainability into its corporate strategy.

Patagonia's mission statement does not say anything, directly, about employees or people. But it does completely revolve around them. When making hiring decisions, Chouinard has long believed that finding people who live the company's mission—who are genuinely motivated by it—is far more important than their education or other measurable accomplishments.

Chouinard believes this because living the mission is what he is all about. He refers to himself as a reluctant businessman, who became an entrepreneur only because he wanted to develop mountain climbing equipment that was less environmentally damaging. Today, he sees himself as the entrepreneur who comes up with wild and crazy ideas, then leaves it to others to figure these ideas out and bring them to life. This is why hiring for motivation as well as capability is so important for Chouinard, so he can then step back and give his people the freedom to do what they do best.

When Chouinard speaks of freedom for his people, he is really sincere. It means letting them do their jobs in whatever way works best for them. It means letting them go surfing when conditions are right. It means being among the first companies in the US to offer an on-site day-care facility for employees' children (subsidised), and one of the first to offer both maternity and paternity leave for employees. It means holding meetings at off-site climbing and surfing locations and providing paid sabbaticals for employees to volunteer for environmental organisations. So, having hired for motivation, Chouinard makes sure that the company's culture sustains it, too. And the result? Massively motivated employees who would run through walls for the business.

To be fair, Patagonia is different from many other companies: it is privately held (by Yvon and his wife, Malinda), its annual turnover is only about $550 million, and it has fewer than 1500 employees. It thus has flexibility that other companies may not have. However, Chouinard is evidence that focusing on employee motivation can make good business sense. The reluctant businessman is now a billionaire.

Priming Your OS for Motivation

The relationship between motivation and performance, then, is far more complicated than commonly presented. There are different types of motivation, different parts of the brain involved, and people and situations can differ so much that there simply is no straightforward recipe for motivating them. For example, some people appear biologically more predisposed to feeling intrinsic motivation, whereas others are more likely to respond to extrinsic motivators [25]. And without putting all your team through expensive medical brain scans, there is no easy way to tell which group someone falls into.

This means two things for you as leader. First, since there are no reliable ways to *make* people feel motivated, you need to think more in terms of how to create an environment—a Leadership OS—that promotes motivation, an environment in which people are more likely to feel that way. Second, this requires a degree of trial and error in how you do this. As with the other components of your Leadership OS, then, you will need to try different techniques, watch to see which work with whom, and then adjust your approach accordingly.

Based on our review of the past 50 years of research on this, we have identified four plus one techniques you can try. We say four *plus* one, because four of them are each designed to affect a different type of motivation, and one of them touches every type. They will not always work with everyone, but each has been shown to work in a wide range of situations and with a variety of people from different cultures and backgrounds.

To help you choose which to use, and what to try next if your first attempt does not work, we have created a simple model that shows what type of motivation each technique affects (Fig. 13.3). We recommend that, at a minimum, you try the 'plus one' technique and two of the others. If possible, try all five. The more you try, the greater your chances of success.

The 'Plus One': Set Goals

The 'plus one', setting goals, is something you always need to think about. Done well, the mere act of setting goals can motivate people. But because goals at work usually involve targets, they also set people up for reward or punishment (in terms of perceived failure or a lack of bonus) later.

There are whole libraries' worth of guidance on how to set good goals, and we do not want to repeat it here. If you are unsure, google it. There are, however, five findings from the research into the relationship between goals and motivation that are worth knowing about, so that when you set goals you can be more aware of how you might be impacting people's motivation:

- **Involve people**. People are more likely to be motivated by goals they feel they were involved in setting. So, wherever possible, discuss goals with people before assigning them.
- **Use proximal goals**. With people whose confidence is not rock-solid, a series of small goals or steps towards a bigger objective tend to be more motivating than big goals [26].

Fig. 13.3 Four plus one techniques to improve motivation

- **Create a challenge**. Just setting goals has been shown to trigger many people's reward system [14]. Describing how an individual's goals contribute to the wider team and overall business increases this effect on the reward system [27]. And setting challenging goals can increase motivation more than less challenging goals, as long as the individual believes they can achieve them [28]. So, set challenging goals, but talk with people about how achievable they think they are, and remind people you believe they can succeed.
- **Adapt the way you describe the challenge**. If you think someone is particularly sensitive to approach motivators, such as achievement and reward, emphasise the opportunities in a challenge. If you believe they are more sensitive to avoidance motivators—to not making mistakes—emphasise the importance of the task and the risks of not getting things right.
- **Emphasise expertise**. With complex or broad tasks, emphasising someone's expertise can increase their motivation for it [29]. So, tell people you think they are the right person for the job, and why you think they can do it.

Increase Autonomy (Intrinsic and Approach Motivators)

Research into intrinsic motivation shows that by far the most powerful influence on it is people's sense of autonomy. Their sense of being in control and having a choice. People with high levels of autonomy have been found to be more intrinsically motivated and thus more able to sustain effort, perform well and achieve their goals [30]. Moreover, in the last few years, autonomy has also been shown to enhance the motivating impact of extrinsic rewards [31]. So, all round, autonomy is a critical ingredient for motivation.

As someone's leader, you have a crucial role to play in ensuring they feel a sense of autonomy. Your role is particularly important when you need people to do something because you have to let them know in a way that still leaves them feeling they have a choice. So, if possible, involve people in setting targets. And if you cannot do that, make sure you emphasise that how they reach those targets is up to them.

People always have a degree of choice in what they do. There is always some element, no matter how small, that they have control over. Even if it is just the attitude they bring and the effort they apply. Your role is to find that element and remind them of it.

Give Recognition (Extrinsic and Approach Motivators)

The obvious way to boost a person's approach motivation—their desire for something they find rewarding—is with an extrinsic reward. And the easiest type of reward to give is recognition. This could be a spot bonus, but more often is simply praise. It works because every time you give someone recognition, you are triggering their reward system.

If it is a spot bonus, it does not have to be big to have an impact. The food retailer Prêt à Manger, for example, gives leaders a set number of 'Wow' cards to use each year. These are scratch cards with small rewards, such as £10 or a restaurant voucher, which leaders can hand out to employees whom they see acting in ways they want to reinforce.

Praise, meanwhile, is possibly the cheapest, easiest and most underused form of reward there is. It is especially effective with people who are new to a task or relatively junior. Its impact is also heightened in more collectivist cultures, where face and public pride are especially important. And in every situation, the basic rule with praise is to do it in public wherever possible, in order to increase its impact.

Seal Against Leaks (Intrinsic and Avoidance Motivators)

Your inner fears can sometimes have powerful positive effects. We know many a successful leader for whom the main motivating force in their careers was a fear of failure. But there are also smaller, more hidden inner concerns that can harm your motivation, causing it to leak away from you. And stopping these potential leaks is often the best way to help people's motivation through intrinsic and avoidance motivators. Three stand out:

- **Stop free-riding**. When people work in groups, if they believe that other people are not contributing as much as they could, their motivation tends to suffer as well [32]. So, to stop motivation leaking, it is important that everyone in a team is seen to be giving their best and you, as a leader, need to make sure everyone does. The two best ways to accomplish this are by building accountability and giving feedback.
- **Do not let setbacks fester**. Setbacks have been shown to reduce motivation, especially when they are left unaddressed or undiscussed [2]. So, to stop motivation leaking, if someone suffers a setback, make sure to discuss it with them and help them think about how to respond.
- **Stop silo-isation**. The more siloed people become in their work, the less sense of responsibility they feel to the team, which in turn can lower their

motivation [33]. To stop this leakage, make sure you emphasise how everyone contributes to the overall team strategy and connect people as much as possible. (We will look at this in more depth in Chapter 16 on connection).

Give Constructive Criticism (Extrinsic and Avoidance Motivators)

Criticism can be a dangerous thing. Delivered poorly, it can lower confidence, trust and motivation. Sometimes, however, it is necessary and if it is done well, it can even enhance motivation. A few rules can help here. Most of them focus on protecting people's sense of self-confidence, which makes it easier for them to respond positively to the criticism and helps maintain their motivation:

- **Be balanced**. Do not mention only the negative; be sure also to mention a few positives.
- **Emphasise what they can still achieve**. Do not just criticise—also describe how changing what they do may help them to reach an objective.
- **Criticise in private**. Wherever possible, do not add to the shame of receiving criticism by doing it publicly. This is vital in collectivist cultures, where face and public respect are highly valued.
- **Depersonalise it**. Wherever possible, depersonalise the criticism. You can do this by talking about the issues involved in terms of challenges that many people face. Or you can say things like, '*We* have an issue here. How can we make *this* work better?';
- rather than 'You did this wrong—next time do it this way'. Again, this is especially important in collectivist cultures.
- **Choose your moment**. If someone is extremely busy, stressed or in a bad mood, it is probably not the best time to offer constructive criticism. So, where possible, find a psychologically safe setting for the feedback.

Nourishing Motivation

There is no doubt that leaders can have a huge impact on how motivated people feel. But the impact they have is not direct and it is rarely straightforward. Creating a Leadership OS that is full of highly motivated people is therefore not about pulling levers to make people feel motivated about certain things. It is about creating an environment that enables and encourages motivation, an environment that nourishes it.

Despite the promises of the 'follow-these-simple-steps' articles, creating such an OS is more often than not a case of trial and error. And our experience as leaders, and as people researching and working with leaders, is that for most people this is what leadership often feels like: we try things and then try our best to make them work. In this chapter, we have presented a way to approach motivation in a more informed, structured and systematic trial-and-error way. Not only will it yield better results but, somehow, it feels like a more honest approach, too.

We will use this same approach in the next chapter, too, when we turn to look at confidence, the second component of momentum.

Summary + Checklist

See Table 13.2.

Table 13.2 Summary of motivation

	OS function	Techniques to build it
Motivation	• Increases effort • Improves judgement	• Set goals • Increase autonomy • Give recognition • Seal against leaks • Give constructive criticism

Checklist

To help you think about whether you have successfully installed motivation in your Leadership OS, ask yourself how the people around you—your direct reports, peers and stakeholders—would respond to the following questions (Table 13.3).

Table 13.3 Have you installed motivation in your Leadership OS?

	✓	✗
Do people feel that the goals you set are motivating?	☐	☐
Do people believe that you emphasise the choices they have in their work?	☐	☐
Do people feel that you regularly recognise them for what they do?	☐	☐
Do people believe that you will act if you see someone in your team repeatedly not giving their best?	☐	☐
Do people believe that you give constructive criticism in a way that helps them improve their performance?	☐	☐

References

1. N. Kinley and S. Ben-Hur, *Changing employee behavior*, London: Palgrave MacMillan, 2015.
2. T. Amabile and M. Pratt, "The dynamic componential model of creativity and innovation in organizations: Making progress, making meaning," *Research in Organizational Behavior*, vol. 36, pp. 157–183, 2016.
3. S. Rick and G. Loewenstein, "Hypermotivation: Commentary on 'the dishonesty of honest people'," *Journal of Marketing Research*, vol. 45, no. 6, pp. 645–648, 2008.
4. B. Pelham and E. Neter, "The effect of motivation of judgment depends on the difficulty of the judgment," *Journal of Personality and Social Psychology*, vol. 68, no. 4, pp. 581–594, 1995.
5. S. Di Domenico and R. Ryan, "The emerging neuroscience of intrinsic motivation: A new frontier in self-determination research," *Frontiers in Human Neuroscience*, vol. 11, p. 145, 2017.
6. D. Ariely, U. Gneezy, G. Loewenstein and N. Mazar, "Large stakes and big mistakes," *The Review of Economic Studies*, vol. 76, no. 2, pp. 451–469, 2009.
7. G. Jenkins Jr., A. Mitra, N. Gupta and J. Shaw, "Are financial incentives related to performance? A meta-analytic review of empirical research," *Journal of Applied Psychology*, vol. 83, no. 5, pp. 777–787, 1998.
8. G. L. Stewart, "Reward structure as a moderator of the relationship between extraversion and sales performance," *Journal of Applied Psychology*, vol. 81, no. 6, pp. 619–627, 1996.
9. D. Welsh and L. Ordóñez, "The dark side of consecutive high performance goals: Linking goal setting, depletion, and unethical behavior," *Organizational Behavior and Human Decision Processes*, vol. 123, no. 2, pp. 79–89, 2014.
10. D. Pink, *Drive*, Edinburgh, UK: Canongate Books, 2011.
11. E. Deci, "Intrinsic motivation, extrinsic reinforcement, and inequity," *Journal of Personality and Social Psychology*, vol. 22, no. 1, pp. 113–120, 1972.
12. M. Treadway, J. Buckholtz, R. Cowan, N. Woodward, R. Li, M. Ansari, R. Baldwin, A. Schwartzman, R. Kessler and D. Zald, "Dopaminergic mechanisms of individual differences in human effort-based decision-making," *The Journal of Neuroscience*, vol. 32, no. 18, pp. 6170–6176, 2012.
13. E. Berkman, "The neuroscience of goals and behavior change," *Consulting Psychology Journal: Practice and Research*, vol. 70, no. 1, pp. 28–44, 2018.
14. K. Murayama, M. Matsumoto, K. Izuma and K. Matsumoto, "Neural basis of the undermining effect of monetary reward on intrinsic motivation," *Proceedings of the National Academy of Sciences*, vol. 107, no. 49, pp. 20911–20916, 2010.
15. C. Cerasoli, J. Nicklin and M. Ford, "Intrinsic motivation and extrinsic incentives jointly predict performance: A 40-year meta-analysis," *Psychological Bulletin*, vol. 140, no. 4, pp. 980–1008, 2014.

16. D. Mobbs and W. McFarland, "The neuroscience of motivation," *NeuroLeadership Journal*, vol. 3, pp. 43–52, 2010.

17. J. O'Doherty, J. Winston, H. Critchley, D. Perrett, D. Burt and R. Dolan, "Beauty in a smile: The role of medial orbitofrontal cortex in facial attractiveness," *Neuropsychologia*, vol. 41, no. 2, pp. 147–155, 2003.

18. B. Knutson, C. Adams, G. Fong and D. Hommer, "Anticipation of increasing monetary reward selectively recruits nucleus," *The Journal of Neuroscience*, vol. 22, no. 9, pp. 3303–3305, 2002.

19. M. Kang, M. Hsu, I. Krajbich, G. Loewenstein, S. McClure, J. Wang and C. Camerer, "The wick in the candle of learning: Epistemic curiosity activates reward circuitry and enhances memory," *Psychological Science*, vol. 20, no. 8, pp. 963–973, 2009.

20. F. Walumbwa, B. Avolio and W. Zhu, "How transformational leadership weaves its influence on individual job performance: The role of identification and efficacy beliefs," *Personnel Psychology*, vol. 61, no. 4, pp. 792–825, 2008.

21. S. Hannah, B. Avolio, F. Walumbwa and A. Chan, "Leader self and means efficacy: A multi-component approach," *Organizational Behavior and Human Decision Processes*, vol. 118, no. 2, pp. 143–161, 2012.

22. W. Grolnick and R. Ryan, "Autonomy in children's learning: An experimental and individual difference investigation," *Journal of Personality and Social Psychology*, vol. 52, no. 5, pp. 890–898, 1987.

23. A. Isen, K. Daubman and G. Nowicki, "Positive affect facilitates creative problem solving," *Journal of Personality and Social Psychology*, vol. 52, no. 6, pp. 1122–1131, 1987.

24. N. D. Volkow, G. Wang, S. Kollins, S. Kollins, T. Wigal, J. Newcorn, F. Telang, J. Fowler, W. Zhu, J. Logan, M. Yeming, K. Pradhan, C. Wong and J. Swanson, "Evaluating dopamine reward pathway in ADHD: Clinical implications," *JAMA*, vol. 302, no. 10, pp. 1084–1091, 2009.

25. O. Manzano, S. Cervenka, J. Aurelija, O. Hellenä, L. Farde and U. Fredrik, "Individual differences in the proneness to have flow experiences are linked to dopamine D2-receptor availability in the dorsal striatum," *NeuroImage*, vol. 67, pp. 1–6, 2013.

26. G. Latham, E. Locke and N. Fassina, "The high performance cycle: Standing the test of time," in *Psychological Management of Individual Performance*, New York, NY, Wiley, 2002, pp. 201–228.

27. A. Hamid, J. Pettibone, O. Mabrouk, V. Hetrick, R. Schmidt, C. M. Vander Weele, R. Kennedy, B. Aragona and J. Berke, "Mesolimbic dopamine signals the value of work," *Nature Neuroscience*, vol. 19, no. 1, pp. 117–126, 2015.

28. A. Kleingeld, H. van Mierlo and L. Arends, "The effect of goal setting on group performance: A meta-analysis," *Journal of Applied Psychology*, vol. 96, no. 6, p. 1289, 2011.

29. G. Seijts and G. Latham, "The effect of distal learning, outcome, and proximal goals on a moderately complex task," *Journal of Organizational Behavior*, vol. 22, no. 3, pp. 291–307, 2001.

30. C. Fernet, S. Austin and R. Vallerand, "The effects of work motivation on employee exhaustion and commitment: An extension of the JD-R model," *Work & Stress*, vol. 26, no. 3, pp. 213–229, 2012.

31. K. Murayama, M. Matsumoto, K. Izuma, A. Sugiura, R. Ryan, E. Deci and K. Matsumoto, "How self-determined choice facilitates performance: A key role of the ventromedial prefrontal cortex," *Cerebral Cortex*, vol. 25, no. 5, pp. 1241–1251, 2015.

32. M. Olbrecht and L. Bornmann, "Panel peer review of grant applications: What do we know from research in social psychology on judgment and decision-making in groups?," *Research Evaluation*, vol. 19, no. 4, pp. 293–304, 2010.

33. N. Kerr and J. Stanfel, "Role schemata and member motivation in task groups," *Personality and Social Psychology Bulletin*, vol. 19, no. 4, pp. 432–442, 1993.

14

Confidence

No one knows who started it, but it originated in basketball. It was the 'hot-hand' concept, the idea that a shooter was more likely to score if their previous attempt had been successful. It was the sense that players would go on scoring streaks when their hands were 'hot', and it seemed they could never miss. To fans and commentators, it made sense, and the idea was so popular it spread to other sports and games.

Then, in the 1980s, researchers got involved. They conducted studies that seemed to show that people were not, in fact, any more likely to succeed at something if they had previously been successful. They dismissed the idea as a myth, and by the mid-1980s, they were developing theories as to how anyone could think that such a thing as 'hot hands' existed. It has been held up as an example of how our brains can trick us into seeing patterns where none exist and was given a new name—the 'hot-hand fallacy'. And under that title, the idea lay for 30 years.

Yet in the stadium seats, the idea persisted. To the fans, it just felt right. And in 2011 two researchers, Gur Yaari at Yale and Shmuel Eisenmann at Humboldt University in Germany, decided to look at it again [1]. Believing that the 1980s studies might not have looked at enough data, they obtained a massive data set of 300,000 National Basketball Association (NBA) free throws from 2005 to 2010. Sure enough, they found a small but significant increase in players' chances of scoring if their previous shot had been successful. In 2013 a study at Stanford University replicated the finding with data from baseball, and in 2014 researchers at Harvard University confirmed it. Hot hands were real.

© The Author(s) 2020
N. Kinley and S. Ben-Hur, *Leadership OS*,
https://doi.org/10.1007/978-3-030-27293-7_14

In retrospect, it should not have been a surprise. Across a wide range of sports, it is a well-known and well-documented phenomenon. People's belief in their ability to do something—their confidence—significantly affects how well they do it [2]. And if you succeed once, you are more likely to feel confident, and so more likely to succeed the next time you try.

It is not just true for sports, either. From the career we choose to our presentation skills, data analysis and creative problem-solving, confidence affects our ability at work as well. This is why it is so crucial that your Leadership OS promotes confidence. In fact, in our research with leaders around the world, having an OS that helps people feel confident was the second biggest differentiator between high- and low-performing leaders. If you want the best out of people, they need to feel good about what they are capable of. They need to believe.

The Many Faces of Confidence

Confidence is called different things by researchers, most commonly, self-efficacy or potency. In general, they all mean the same, but there are a few distinctions. The most important of these is that *self-efficacy* is our belief in our ability to do a particular thing, whereas *self-confidence* (or *generalised self-efficacy*) is our belief in our ability in general. This distinction is important because general confidence seems closely tied to our deepest feelings of self-esteem [3] and, as such, it is relatively stable and hard to change. Our sense of self-efficacy for particular tasks, however, is very changeable.

It is obviously based in part on real differences in how good we are at something. However, it can also be affected by things like the situation we are in, the feedback we receive and the support we feel we have [4]. This means that your Leadership OS can be highly influential in determining a person's confidence. And when you do affect people's confidence, it is their self-efficacy for specific tasks that you are most likely to have an impact on immediately.

Another distinction you might hear talked about is the difference between self-confidence and team confidence. They are different because people might have only little belief in themselves, but lots of belief in the team they are part of or vice versa. However, the impact that individual and team confidence have on performance is very similar, and the things you need to do in your Leadership OS to promote them are essentially the same. So, for the most part, you can think of them as equivalent.

Building Confidence: The Case of Leymah Gbowee in Liberia

Leymah Gbowee was just 17 years old when her life took a dramatic turn. She was living with her parents and sisters in Monrovia, Liberia. She had just begun university, on her way to fulfilling her dream of becoming a doctor. And then civil war broke out (Fig. 14.1).

Her family left Monrovia and became refugees, moving from village to village before eventually fleeing to Ghana. She witnessed unspeakable atrocities of death, destruction, violence and rape. She didn't just witness violence and rape, either; she lived them, at the hands of her then partner. Again, she fled, this time taking her three children back to Monrovia. Now in her mid-20s, she returned to university and began working as a social worker, providing trauma therapy to former child soldiers from dictator Charles Taylor's army. Initially, she hated these children for the war they were fighting. But these boys didn't choose to join the war; their lives were stolen from them

Fig. 14.1 Leymah Gbowee

by older men—dictators, tyrants and warlords—who were using them as pawns to serve their own egos. Gbowee realised that if anything was going to change, she and people like her would have to make the change.

Her drive to bring change and peace to Liberia began as many movements do—by connecting a few women who had shared similar experiences and concerns. Her group did not discriminate. Gbowee, a devout Christian, aligned Christians and Muslims, almost unheard of in Liberia. Women of all religions, ethnic groups, ages and classes had similar experiences, and they all joined her fight. By the summer of 2002, as Taylor's war raged on, Gbowee had aligned thousands of women and was leading peaceful demonstrations outside Taylor's office. They wore white, the colour of peace. They staged a sex strike. They lined the route that Taylor travelled to and from his office. They demanded to speak with him.

Much of what they did was risky. Taylor and his men were renowned for brutality, not patience. But Gbowee led from the front and, with her courage and by connecting people, she gave those around her the confidence to also stand up and be heard. Gbowee's group developed a resoluteness and a belief that they could bring about change.

In the spring of 2003, they achieved a breakthrough. Taylor granted them a meeting, and Gbowee was their designated speaker. When they showed up at his office, they were told that he was sick and couldn't meet with them. But Gbowee didn't care. She marched up the stairs towards his office, determined to him and, eventually, Taylor came out to meet her.

Gbowee had her prepared speech in her hands, ready to be delivered, but she couldn't read it. It was too scripted, too sterile. So she put the speech aside and spoke from her heart. She spoke for the thousands of women who stood behind her. She spoke for the thousands of dead children who couldn't speak for themselves. And she spoke for millions of living children who wanted food, safety and a chance at a future.

In response, Taylor agreed to go to Ghana to engage in peace talks. Gbowee and her thousands of allies met him there. After weeks of lip service and minimal progress in the peace talks, Gbowee was fed up. She led her team into the luxury hotel where the dictators were staying and demanded progress. They locked arms and refused to leave until progress had been made. In an ironic twist, it was now Gbowee and her allies who were holding Taylor and the other tyrants hostage. Leymah Gbowee and thousands of other women would not be denied.

Within weeks, the Liberian civil war was over. In 2011, Gbowee was awarded the Nobel Peace Prize for her work in bringing it to an end.

In 2012, Taylor was convicted of murder, rape, terror and other war crimes committed during his war on Liberia.

Even now, Gbowee knows that her leadership journey is not complete. Yes, the brutal dictator is in prison, but Liberia's future is far from certain. Much of the country's infrastructure—schools, hospitals, businesses—was destroyed during the war. Millions of lives had ended or had been changed forever because of their traumatic war experiences. Millions of children needed a reason to hope. For Gbowee, the mission to bring peace, security and opportunity to Liberia is far from over.

There is hope, though, and not just because the war is over. Gbowee did not just stop a war; she gave a generation of women the confidence to stand up, have a voice and act. She helped them believe in a better future and have faith that they could bring it about.

What Confidence Does

What makes confidence so important is what it does to people. At a broad level, it can improve performance. The hot-hand phenomenon is evidence of this, and research in work settings has confirmed it. People's confidence levels predict both the performance ratings they receive from their manager and 'harder' outcomes such as sales figures [5] and customer satisfaction scores [6]. In fact, confidence is a better predictor of these things than other aspects of people's personality [7]. Those with high confidence for a task tend to perform 28% better at it on average than those with low confidence for it [8]. And this relationship between confidence and performance is so strong that you can reliably predict a person's performance rating in five years' time from their confidence levels today [9].

Confidence does this through four specific effects that it has on the way people work (Fig. 14.2). These four effects are the functions that confidence fulfils in your Leadership OS—the impact it has on people.

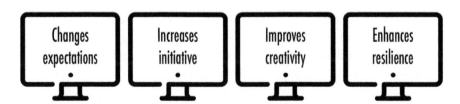

Fig. 14.2 The functions of confidence in a Leadership OS

A. Changes Expectations

The first thing confidence does is to change people's perceptions of how difficult tasks are and their expectations of what they can achieve. Confident people are less likely to see a task as difficult [10] and are more likely to see objectives as opportunities rather than threats [11]. As a result, they tend to choose more challenging tasks [12] and to set higher goals for themselves [13]. In other words, confident people are more positive about their chances of success and so push themselves harder and further.

B. Increases Initiative

The second impact confidence has is that people are more likely to act—and act quickly—if they believe they can do something. Confident people are thus more likely to be proactive and show initiative [14]. They are more likely to speak up in debate and challenge others' thinking [15]. And they are more likely to take risks [16] and be entrepreneurial [17].

C. Improves Creativity

The third thing confidence does is to increase people's creativity [18]. Confident people generate more product innovations [17]. The innovations they produce tend to be more pioneering [19]. And more confident CEOs tend to have more innovative businesses, as measured by R&D expenditure and the number of patents awarded [20].

D. Enhances Resilience

Finally, people with higher levels of confidence tend to report lower levels of stress [21] and have been found to persist longer when they encounter difficulties [22]. They are also more able to stay calm and composed when under pressure and can tolerate more stress before showing a drop in performance [23]. As a result, they are more resilient.

There is also evidence that confident people are more adaptable. Although they persist longer in the face of difficulties, this is only when there are no alternatives. When better alternative strategies exist, confident people are more likely to switch what they are doing, whereas people low in confidence are less likely to adapt their approach [24].

Through these four effects, confidence plays a central role in your Leadership OS, fundamentally changing how people approach their work.

And on the face of it, there is a simple equation: more confidence equals better performance. As we have seen with many of the other OS components, however, things are rarely that straightforward.

The Goldilocks Principle

Named after a nineteenth-century British fairy tale, the Goldilocks principle is the idea that there is an ideal amount of something. That if you have too much or too little of a thing, it can have negative consequences, but that if you have the ideal, 'just right' amount, then it can have a highly positive impact. Confidence is like that. You need a Goldilocks amount.

We have already seen that low confidence can reduce people's performance. Nevertheless, some self-doubt can be useful [25]. It enables us to question ourselves and whether we can do things differently or better [26]. If our confidence levels rise too high, if we become overconfident, then we lose that ability.

When this happens, it can have a detrimental effect on decision-making. Overconfident people have been found to search for less information before making decisions [26], and they have more knowledge blind spots as a result [27]. They are more susceptible to thinking errors [28] and tend to be more extreme in the judgements they make [26]. And as a result of all this, they tend to make worse decisions [29].

This means that you, as a leader, have a balancing act to perform. You need your Leadership OS to build and support people's confidence. But not too much. There is, unfortunately, no definitive amount of confidence that is 'just right', but there are two things you can look out for as warning signs of overconfidence. The first is personal superiority. It is one thing for people to think that they are good at something, but once they start seeing themselves as superior to others in a more general, personal sense, their confidence begins to have a negative impact. The second is a lack of curiosity, since once people become overconfident, they tend to stop asking questions (because they think they know the answers). So, if you see either of these signs, you may need to take action to bring some balance and counter the overconfidence with a little feedback and constructive criticism.

Creating Confidence Through Your OS

Although overconfidence is something that you must look out for, in most situations with most people, your main challenge is going to be building confidence. As with the other components of your Leadership OS, this is

Fig. 14.3 Four techniques to improve confidence

less about you pulling levers that directly change people and more about you creating an environment that enables and supports people to *feel* confident. Similarly, there are differences in what people will respond to. For example, some people need more emotional support—pep talks to boost how confident they feel—whereas others respond best to practical help or advice on what and how to do things.

To manage this, a range of techniques are at your disposal. And the research shows that there are four in particular that you should try to build into what you do as a leader and thus incorporate in your Leadership OS (Fig. 14.3).

Develop People

How confident people feel is influenced by all sorts of factors, but one of the most important is how good they genuinely are what they do. Improving people's skill levels is, therefore, one of the most powerful devices you have for nurturing their confidence [30].

We are not going to expand on this because developing people is a subject worthy of a book in its own right. However, as a minimum, make sure you do the following four things, each of which can improve people's confidence levels [31]:

- Set learning goals, either through formal development plans or informal conversations.
- Provide people with training and make sure they attend it.
- Give people feedback on what they do well and how to improve.
- Comment on and praise people when they improve at something.

None of these is rocket science, but it is easy to forget to do them amid the pressures of daily activity. This is why the leaders we have seen who are

Table 14.1 Developing your team systematically

	Team member A	Team member B	Team member C
Learning goals			
Training provided			
Last time feedback was given			
Last time learning commented on			

best at it are the ones who do it systematically. As a simple start, see if you can complete Table 14.1 for your team. If you cannot, you may need to be more systematic in how you are developing them.

Note Ability

The second technique at your disposal rests on the fact that regardless of how good people genuinely are at a task, telling them they are good at it can improve both their confidence about doing it and how well they ultimately perform it [32]. Perhaps one of the best-known examples of this is with intelligence tests. People who are simply told before starting a test, 'You'll do well on this' do better in the test than people who are not told anything beforehand [33].

We are not suggesting that you tell someone who is not capable of doing something that they are. Nor are we proposing praising people for mediocre performance, since that can have the nasty negative effect of setting low expectations. We are suggesting that if you see someone do something well or demonstrate a particular skill, then be sure to mention it. It sounds obvious, but in the rush of day-to-day activity, it can be all too easy to forget to do it. And if you are a naturally critical person, you may do this less than you should. So, as a minimum, make sure that you regularly do these things:

- When you assign a task or project to someone, tell them why you think they can do it—the strengths they will bring to the task.
- When someone finishes a task and has done it well (or at least parts of it well), tell them what was good about what they did.
- If someone achieves something notable, announce it to the whole team.
- If you believe a person lacks self-confidence, use phrases such as, 'You can do this'. You would not want to do this all the time, since people may begin to see it as inauthentic, but occasional statements like this can have a big impact.

Show Confidence

The next technique for building confidence is to act confident yourself. The research is consistent on this: individuals and teams who work for a leader who acts confident are themselves more confident [34]. So if you show confidence, it breeds confidence in others.

There are a couple of ways to do this. The first is to be optimistic—or at least appear it. If you are not naturally optimistic, this will be something that you have to deliberately and systematically try to do. However, even if you are naturally optimistic, it is worth making sure that you consistently show this optimism to others. Positive comments at the end of one-on-one or team meetings are easy ways to achieve this. But we are not suggesting being positive when it is not warranted—just that you increase the number of positive comments you do make when it is merited.

The other main way to show confidence is to give people autonomy and make sure you delegate effectively [35]. Nothing says 'I believe you can do this' more than giving someone responsibility to do something. Conversely, nothing says 'I do *not* believe you are capable' more than micro-managing people and not delegating things to them. So, make sure you delegate.

One simple tip here is to ask your team whether there is any aspect of your role that they would like you to delegate to them, or that they would like more freedom to do their own way. You do not have to implement their suggestions, but what they say will give you some sense of the degree of autonomy they think they have and may give you some ideas about additional things you could delegate.

Emphasise Locus of Control

The final technique is a psychological phenomenon called *locus of control*, or *LOC* for short. It is the degree to which people believe that they have *control* over the outcome of events in their lives. Someone with an *internal* locus of control believes that what happens in their life is largely the result of them and what they do. When something goes right, they tend to credit themselves, and when it goes wrong, they tend to blame themselves. People with an *external* locus of control, meanwhile, believe that what happens to them is mostly determined by forces outside of them, such as luck or other people. So when things go right, they think it is due to outside forces, and when things go wrong, they tend to blame others.

The relevance of this here is that people with an internal locus of control tend to have higher levels of self-confidence [36]. Moreover, by helping people notice and appreciate the control they have, you can boost their confidence [37]. Doing this is relatively simple, too. You can emphasise to people the choices and options they have. You can ask them for their ideas. And you can ask how they achieved something when things do go right, or what they could do differently next time when things have not gone well.

Reliable Reciprocal Relationships

For most people in most situations, confidence and performance are locked in a reciprocal relationship [38]. High confidence tends to improve performance, and high performance tends to improve confidence. Affect one, and you affect the other. It is not always so, but as a general rule, it is reliable.

There is another reliable reciprocal relationship here, too, between the quality of a person's relationship with their boss and their confidence. When people feel they have a good relationship with their manager, they tend to feel more confident, but when they feel it is less positive, they generally feel less confident [39]. As a leader, therefore, you are uniquely placed to influence someone's confidence. And through this, also their sense of self-worth and self-esteem. Their identity.

This is not to say that you are the only or even the most important influence on these things. But the Leadership OS you create—the daily working environment you form around you—has a significant impact on people that extends beyond how well they perform. You affect how people feel about themselves. As a leader, it is probably not something that you stop to think about often, but the reach you have into the inner lives of the people you lead is an amazing thing. And in the next chapter, we will see how this reach can be extended through the third component of your OS: empowerment.

Summary + Checklist

See Table 14.2.

Table 14.2 Summary of confidence

	OS function	Techniques to build it
Confidence	• Changes expectations • Increases initiative • Improves creativity • Enhances resilience	• Develop people • Note ability • Show confidence • Emphasise locus of control

Checklist

To help you think about whether you have successfully installed confidence in your Leadership OS, ask yourself how the people around you—your direct reports, peers and stakeholders—would respond to the following questions (Table 14.3).

Table 14.3 Have you installed confidence in your Leadership OS?

	✓	✗
Do people feel more confident about themselves when they are around you?	□	□
Do people believe that you consistently appear highly confident about the team and organisation?	□	□
Do people feel that you regularly comment on their achievements?	□	□
Do people believe that you systematically develop them?	□	□
Do people feel that you help them to see the control and choices they have?	□	□

References

1. G. Yaari and S. Eisenmann, "The hot (invisible?) hand: Can time sequence patterns of success/failure in sports be modeled as repeated random independent trials?" *PLoS ONE*, vol. 6, no. 10, 2011.
2. D. Feltz, "Self-confidence and sports performance," *Exercise and Sport Science Reviews*, vol. 16, pp. 423–457, 1988.
3. K. Stanley and M. Murphy, "A comparison of general self-efficacy with self-esteem," *Genetic, Social, and General Psychology Monographs*, vol. 123, no. 1, pp. 81–99, 1997.
4. M. Gist and T. Mitchell, "Self-efficacy: A theoretical analysis of its determinants and malleability," *The Academy of Management Review*, vol. 17, no. 2, pp. 1183–1211, 1992.
5. Y. Gong, J. Huang and J. Farh, "Employee learning orientation, transformational leadership, and employee creativity: The mediating role of employee creative self-efficacy," *Academy of Management Journal*, vol. 52, no. 4, pp. 765–778, 2009.
6. G. Shea and R. Guzzo, "Group effectiveness: What really matters?" *Sloan Management Review*, vol. 28, pp. 25–31, 1987.
7. M. Barrick and M. Mount, "The Big Five personality dimensions and job performance: A meta-analysis," *Personnel Psychology*, vol. 44, no. 1, pp. 1–26, 1991.
8. A. Stajkovic and F. Luthans, "Social cognitive theory and self-efficacy: Implications for motivation theory and practice," *Motivation and Work Behavior*, vol. 126, p. 140, 2003.

9. R. Keller, "Predicting the performance and innovativeness of scientists and engineers," *Journal of Applied Psychology*, vol. 97, no. 1, p. 225, 2012.

10. C. Lee and P. Bobko, "Self-efficacy beliefs: Comparison of five measures," *Journal of Applied Psychology*, vol. 79, no. 3, pp. 364–369, 1994.

11. N. Krueger and P. Dickson, "Perceived self-efficacy and perceptions of opportunity and threat," *Psychological Reports*, vol. 72, no. 3, pp. 1235–1240, 1993.

12. A. Escarti and J. Guzman, "Effects of feedback on self-efficacy, performance, and choice in an athletic task," *Journal of Applied Sport Psychology*, vol. 11, no. 1, pp. 83–96, 1999.

13. E. Locke, E. Frederick, C. Lee and P. Bobko, "Effect of self-efficacy, goals, and task strategies on task performance," *Journal of Applied Psychology*, vol. 69, pp. 241–251, 1984.

14. C. Speier and M. Frese, "Generalized self efficacy as a mediator and moderator between control and complexity at work and personal initiative: A longitudinal field study in east Germany," *Human Performance*, vol. 10, no. 2, pp. 171–192, 1997.

15. K. Emich, "Who's bringing the donuts: The role of affective patterns in group decision making," *Organizational Behavior and Human Decision Processes*, vol. 124, no. 2, pp. 122–132, 2014.

16. N. Krueger Jr. and P. Dickson, "How believing in ourselves increases risk taking: Self-efficacy and perceptions of opportunity and threat," *Decision Sciences*, vol. 25, pp. 385–400, 1994.

17. B. Ahlin, M. Drnovšek and R. Hisrich, "Entrepreneurs' creativity and firm innovation: The moderating role of entrepreneurial self-efficacy," *Small Business Economics*, vol. 43, no. 1, pp. 101–117, 2014.

18. P. Tierney and S. Farmer, "Creative self-efficacy: Its potential antecedents and relationship to creative performance," *Academy of Management Journal*, vol. 45, no. 6, pp. 1137–1148, 2002.

19. M. Simon and S. Houghton, "The relationship between overconfidence and the introduction of risky products: Evidence from a field study," *Academy of Management Journal*, vol. 46, no. 2, pp. 139–149, 2003.

20. A. Galasso and T. Simcoe, "CEO overconfidence and innovation," *Management Science*, vol. 57, pp. 1469–1484, 2011.

21. N. Endler, R. Speer, J. Johnson and G. Flett, "General self-efficacy and control in relation to anxiety and cognitive performance," *Current Psychology*, vol. 20, no. 1, pp. 36–52, 2001.

22. D. Schunk, "Self-efficacy, motivation, and performance," *Journal of Applied Sport Psychology*, vol. 7, no. 2, pp. 112–137, 1995.

23. S. Hanton and D. Connaughton, "Perceived control of anxiety and its relationship to self-confidence and performance," *Research Quarterly for Exercise and Sport*, vol. 73, no. 1, pp. 87–97, 2002.

24. R. Baumeister, J. Campbell, J. Krueger and K. Vohs, "Does high self-esteem cause better performance, interpersonal success, happiness, or healthier

lifestyles?" *Psychological Science in the Public Interest*, vol. 4, no. 1, pp. 1–44, 2003.

25. T. Woodman, S. Akehurst, L. Hardy and S. Beattie, "Self-confidence and performance: A little self-doubt helps," *Psychology of Sport and Exercise*, vol. 11, no. 6, pp. 467–470, 2010.

26. A. Zacharakis and D. Shepherd, "The nature of information and overconfidence on venture capitalists' decision making," *Journal of Business Venturing*, vol. 16, no. 4, pp. 311–332, 2001.

27. D. Ng, R. Westgren and S. Sonka, "Competitive blind spots in an institutional field," *Strategic Management Journal*, vol. 30, pp. 349–369, 2009.

28. D. Moore and P. Healy, "The trouble with overconfidence," *Psychological Review*, vol. 115, no. 2, p. 502, 2008.

29. U. Malmendier and G. Tate, "CEO overconfidence and corporate investment," *The Journal of Finance*, vol. 60, no. 6, pp. 2661–2700, 2005.

30. A. Bandura, *Social foundations of thought and action: A social cognitive theory*, Englewood Cliffs, NJ: Prentice Hall, 1986.

31. D. Schunk and C. Swartz, "Goals and progress feedback: Effects on self-efficacy and writing achievement," *Contemporary Educational Psychology*, vol. 18, no. 3, pp. 337–354, 1993.

32. T. Bouffard-Bouchard, "Influence of self-efficacy on performance in a cognitive task," *Journal of Social Psychology*, vol. 130, pp. 353–363, 1990.

33. T. Bouffard-Bouchard, "Influence of self-efficacy on performance in a cognitive task," *The Journal of Social Psychology*, vol. 130, no. 3, pp. 353–363, 1990.

34. K. Fransen, S. Haslam, N. Steffens, N. Vanbeselaere, B. De Cuyper and F. Boen, "Believing in "us": Exploring leaders' capacity to enhance team confidence and performance by building a sense of shared social identity," *Journal of Experimental Psychology: Applied*, vol. 21, no. 1, p. 89, 2015.

35. Z. Chen and S. Aryee, "Delegation and employee work outcomes: An examination of the cultural context of mediating processes in China," *Academy of Management Journal*, vol. 50, no. 1, pp. 226–238, 2007.

36. T. Judge, "Core self-evaluations and work success," *Current Directions in Psychological Science*, vol. 18, no. 1, pp. 58–62, 2009.

37. D. Schunk and T. Gunn, "Self-efficacy and skill development: Influence of task strategies and attributions," *The Journal of Educational Research*, vol. 79, no. 4, pp. 238–244, 1986.

38. C. Pearce, C. Gallagher and M. Ensley, "Confidence at the group level of analysis: A longitudinal investigation of the relationship between potency and team effectiveness," *Journal of Occupational and Organizational Psychology*, vol. 75, no. 1, pp. 115–119, 2002.

39. F. Walumbwa, R. Cropanzano and B. Goldman, "How leader-member exchange influences effective work behaviors: Social exchange and internal–external efficacy perspectives," *Personnel Psychology*, vol. 64, no. 3, pp. 739–770, 2011.

15

Empowerment

Go back 100 years. In fact, go back just 40 years, and tell an employee you would like to *empower* them. What do you think they would say?

Probably not a lot. The word 'empower' may date back to the 1650s, but before the mid-1980s the idea of empowering people at work was rarely used. Precisely who started this modern trend for empowerment is unclear. But for the past 30 years, there has been a growing belief that if you want the best from workers, you need to give them not only the resources they need but also more autonomy and control over what they do.

What Empowerment Is

At a minimum, empowerment means giving people more discretion over how they do their work. Taken slightly further, it means encouraging and rewarding employees for showing initiative and imagination. It can mean giving more people more information. It can mean pushing decision-making down the organisation, so people don't check with their boss on every issue. And taken to its furthest, empowerment can mean replacing traditional business hierarchies with flatter organisational structures and self-directed teams.

The benefits of empowerment are much heralded. It has been shown to increase not only individual and team performance but also hard organisational measures. For example, in one study of 80 manufacturing companies, firms with higher levels of empowerment were found to have higher levels of productivity and profit [1]. In another study, this time of nearly 500

© The Author(s) 2020
N. Kinley and S. Ben-Hur, *Leadership OS*,
https://doi.org/10.1007/978-3-030-27293-7_15

restaurants, employees who felt more empowered were found to offer better levels of service, leading to better branch results [2]. And in a large study of employees in the chemical industry, empowerment was found to lead to higher levels of workplace safety [3].

Moreover, empowerment's benefits seem to extend beyond performance. It has also been found to improve things like job satisfaction and organisational commitment [4]. And workers who feel more empowered have been found to learn more and more quickly [5], and even appear to have better mental and physical health, with lower levels of heart disease [6]. Little wonder, then, that empowerment is so acclaimed.

The empowerment trend is not just about how we work, either. Politically and socially, we are moving towards an age of empowerment, driven there by information technology and the near real-time sharing of information that it enables. So, empowerment at work is part of a broader societal trend, and there is a sense that as technology changes organisations and the wider world, empowerment is a beneficial and somewhat inevitable necessity. Something every business will inevitably need to do to survive.

Digging Deeper

Look beneath the surface, however, and all is not so rosy. For despite all the claims and hype, an objective academic researcher is likely to tell a different story, because it appears that empowerment does *not* always help and can in fact be hugely detrimental in some situations [7]. For instance, it can be unhelpful in high urgency, high uncertainty situations [8]. It can make it more challenging to coordinate the efforts of multiple teams [9]. It can have a negative effect if teams think a leader is trying to avoid making decisions [10]. And it can increase stress, reducing performance, in some people [11]. Like any other capability or behaviour, then, empowerment is not a guaranteed recipe for success.

Part of this is due to the broader context. For example, there is evidence that empowerment is more important in service industries than in manufacturing [4]. And there is some debate about whether empowerment works best in Eastern or Western cultures [12]. Part of it is also due to individual differences, in that some people—such as those with higher levels of confidence—appear to respond better to empowerment than others [13]. But the bigger issue, the most critical thing determining whether empowerment helps or hurts, is your broader Leadership OS. Because for empowerment to work, other things need to be in place around it, otherwise you risk undermining performance and so achieving the opposite of what you intended. Before exploring this further, though, we need first to understand *how* empowerment works.

What Empowerment Does

When we talk about leaders empowering people, we usually mean one of two things. There is *structural empowerment*, which involves changing something about the nature of a person's environment, role or skills base—for example, delegating authority and responsibility, ensuring people have the training and physical resources they need to do their jobs, or creating flatter organisational structures and self-managing teams. Then there is *psychological empowerment*, which is more about changing people's attitudes, approach and mindset. This includes encouraging people to take the initiative, be innovative and contribute more broadly. And, of course, for both types of empowerment, the important thing is not so much what you do, but what people experience and believe—whether they feel that they have a greater degree of autonomy or control in what they do.

Whichever type of empowerment we mean, when you create a Leadership OS in which people feel empowered, it drives their performance through five key effects it has on them (Fig. 15.1).

A. Enhances motivation and effort

The first function empowerment serves is to increase people's motivation. When someone feels empowered, they have a greater sense of autonomy [9] and, as we saw in the chapter on motivation, improving a person's sense of autonomy increases their motivation and thereby also the effort they put into things.

We can see this in their brain activity, in that when people are told they can make a decision about something, parts of the brain known to be

Fig. 15.1 The functions of empowerment in a Leadership OS

involved in motivation light up [14]. We can also see it in their behaviour. For example, in a global study led by researchers from Tel Aviv in Israel, experienced kickboxers (including a world champion) were asked to perform a series of punches. First, they were asked simply to perform a variety of punches in a pre-set order. Then, they were asked to perform the punches again, but this time in any order they liked. Simply empowering people in this small way—just giving them a little choice—increased their speed of punching by 10% and the strength of the punches by 11% [15]. Empowered people try harder.

B. Increases creativity

The second thing empowerment does is to make people more creative. People who say they feel empowered both report feeling more confident in their ability to be creative [16] and then actually show higher levels of creativity in tasks [17]. As a result, teams with higher levels of empowerment tend to be more innovative, delivering, for example, greater levels of new product development [18].

C. Improves agility

The third thing empowerment does is to improve the ability of businesses, teams and individuals to respond to events and changing environments. It does this in two ways. By driving decision-making down the organisation, closer to the frontline of delivery, empowerment reduces the time it takes to make decisions and solve problems [19]. It also increases people's willingness and ability to be proactive and take action [20]. So, empowerment promotes quicker decisions and faster action and, as a result, greater agility.

D. Increases confidence

The fourth function of empowerment enables and supports the previous three things. It increases people's sense of confidence [21]. And when people feel more confident, they are more likely to feel motivated, be creative and be proactive.

When you empower someone, you are effectively saying that you trust their ability to do something and, unsurprisingly, this can have a positive impact on how they view themselves and their ability. This is not just a quick-hit, short-term impact, either. Studies show that people who work in an empowering Leadership OS have higher levels of confidence than people who work in a more authoritarian environment even two years later and even after they have left it [20].

E. Enhances collaboration

The final thing empowerment does in your OS to improve performance is to enhance collaboration. You might think that empowering individuals would make them more individualistic. But studies show that empowerment increases the level of trust between people and, as a result, also improves teamwork, knowledge sharing and the amount of support people give each other [22]. Moreover, this appears to be particularly true when teams are dispersed or have less face-to-face time [23].

Empowerment, then, has a broad effect. Perhaps its most striking feature is that, although it works at an individual level—in that it is individuals who feel empowered—its impact is particularly strong at the team level. So, with empowerment, you get a 'twofer': two benefits—improved individual and team performance—for the price of one component.

Empowering People: The Case of Gerry Anderson and DTE Energy

From 2007 to 2010, more than 340,000 Michigan residents lost their job. None of the 10,000 employees at Michigan-based DTE Energy lost theirs, however (Fig. 15.2).

In 2008, the president and chief operating officer of DTE Energy was Gerry Anderson. The global financial crisis was in full force and many of Michigan's largest employers—including General Motors—were months away from declaring bankruptcy.

DTE, whose operating units included electric and gas utility suppliers, had more than 2.2 million customers—many of whom would lose their jobs and homes during the crisis. As a result, the company lost more than $200 million of revenue in 2008 alone. Operating in a highly regulated industry with rigid fixed costs, it seemed that the only way to offset the lost income was to downsize. But Anderson wanted to find another way.

Anderson had started his career as a consultant with McKinsey & Co. He joined DTE Energy in 1993 as a vice president, before becoming president

Fig. 15.2 Gerry Anderson

and COO in 2005. In his early years at the company, he focused almost exclusively on costs and efficiency. He worried about the numbers, not the 'soft stuff'. But when he became president, something changed.

In 2005, DTE's employee engagement and customer satisfaction scores were terrible. Anderson made it his mission to improve them. He became convinced that culture and morale were vital to the company's financial success. And he worked tirelessly to convince the DTE employees of how important they were.

Then the financial crisis hit. Faced with big losses, Anderson could have focused exclusively on the short term and covered the loss through downsizing. But he knew that what he did at this moment would determine the culture—and the financial performance—of the company for decades to come.

So, in December 2008, Anderson made a video for all 10,000 DTE employees. He did not promise that there wouldn't be any layoffs, but he was clear he wanted to avoid that. He told them that it would be the last thing the company did, but in return, he needed people to bring their energy, focus and intensity to work like never before. And he told them that if all 10,000 of them they did that, they could overcome the challenges facing the firm.

Anderson later admitted that he did not really have a plan for how this would play out. He did not know what the economy was going to do, and he did not know how his employees would respond. But respond they did.

It may not have been planned, but Anderson's call to arms acted as an invitation for initiative. Employees began coming up with innovative solutions to both big and small problems. For example, a project team responsible for replacing the power-plant system initially estimated the cost at $30 million. But encouraged to think like owners and empowered to come up with solutions, they realised they could make one simple change to a logic board, harvest the obsolete equipment, and bring the cost down to $3 million. Another team using the equivalent of 100 full-time external consultants decided to rethink this relationship. By restructuring their work and processes, the team was able to eliminate the need for all 100 consultants. Ideas like this created enormous momentum within the company. The more word spread of these initiatives, the more it encouraged and empowered others to act in the same way. Employees even began competing with each other to see who could help the company more.

Throughout 2009, as the financial crisis devastated much of the US economy, DTE's results were better than anyone could have expected. Revenues did fall by 14%, but net income only fell by 2%. Just surviving 2009 felt like a major victory for the 10,000 employees, and it gave them great momentum going forward. From 2009 to 2011, revenue increased by 10% and net income by 34%. And the company still had 10,000 employees.

Creating Empowerment

Research on how leaders can empower people points to three actions you can take. You can delegate authority to your employees, ask for input and ideas, and encourage people to take the initiative and make their own decisions [10]. Do these three things, and your employees are likely to say that they feel empowered. But then again, they might not, because for these attempts to empower people to work reliably and have the maximum impact, there are things you need to put in place around them. You need to ensure that your Leadership OS supports empowerment.

Fig. 15.3 Three techniques to support empowerment

Specifically, there are three techniques—all shown by research to be important foundations for empowerment—that you can use (Fig. 15.3). As before, the suggested techniques are options to try, and how you approach them will depend on your own personal style and the individuals involved.

Create Clarity and Accountability

Cynics sometimes dismiss empowerment as leaders lacking the confidence to make decisions, as lacking the courage to lead. At its worst, empowerment *can* be like that. But it shouldn't be. For empowerment to add value, it needs to be guided, and that means two things. First, it means setting some direction or giving some goals [24]. Examples of this would be assigning a person a clear task, but giving them leeway on how to do it; or giving someone the authority to approve credit up to a certain limit, but making sure you leave them to make the decisions up to that ceiling.

The second thing required is accountability. People respond best to having autonomy when they feel they are responsible for achieving something with it. A recent study showed the importance of this. It followed fast-food restaurant managers and found that managers who reported feeling empowered had higher-performing restaurants than managers who did not feel empowered, but only when the empowered managers also felt a strong sense of accountability [25].

So, empowerment done well is about giving autonomy, but with direction and accountability. This is particularly important when you need to empower someone whose ability you are not fully confident of when you want to empower someone to do something as a way of stretching or accelerating their development. By empowering within the boundaries of clear goals and accountability for results, you create a kind of safety net to ensure the empowerment succeeds.

Protect Against Stress

One of the risks with empowerment is that it can create unhelpful levels of stress. This can be because of the individual involved and their confidence levels or attitude towards responsibility. It can be because people feel they lack the skills or training required. Or it can be because people feel they do not have the resources they need. Whatever the reason, it must be dealt with, since overly high stress kills empowerment and cuts performance.

One simple way to do this is to ask people how they feel about the task or role they are being empowered to do: how confident they feel; what support they might need; and whether they have the resources they require. It is a quick, simple and crucial conversation, yet also one that it is all too easy to forget. So, take the time to have it, and make sure people are protected against unnecessary stress.

The other thing you can do to protect against stress is to make sure people feel informed and that they have the information required to make the decisions they have to [18]. There are a few simple rules to guide you here. Since sharing too much or too complex information can hinder empowerment [26], make sure the information you give is quick and easy to understand. And when you share information, do it early in the process. A recent study of flight crews in moments of crisis showed how important this can be. The captains of high-performing flight crews were the ones who explicitly shared information and stated plans and strategies as soon as a crisis began. The captains of low-performing flight crews, however, were far more reactive, only giving information in response to events. So, to protect against stress, give simple information as early as possible.

Give Feedback and Coach

The final technique at your disposal to ensure that empowerment works is to give people feedback and coach them. Studies show that feedback not only increases people's sense of empowerment but also makes sure that the empowerment is successful [27]. This is because when you give people constructive feedback, they tend to be clearer about their goals and better able to do tasks well [28]. And when you build on this feedback by coaching people—by giving them advice or helping them think through how to do things differently—you also increase the support you are giving to empowerment [29].

Empowerment in Context

These, then, are the core things you need to do to ensure that empowerment works. As with every other component of your Leadership OS, the key is to try different techniques, monitor your impact and adjust your approach as necessary. It may be harder to create in some circumstances, such as in strongly hierarchical cultures, where people may initially be less willing to be empowered [30]. And it might not work immediately. There is evidence that whereas autocratic and directive leaders usually have an immediate effect on people, empowerment can take time to work [31]. So patience may be required.

As we have seen with the other Leadership OS components, empowerment needs the right environment to flourish. Some of this is about more structural things, such as role clarity and accountability. However, some of it is also about more psychological things, such as confidence and stress. Most importantly, empowerment needs trust. If you want to empower people, it will only work if people feel they have a good, supportive and trusting relationship with you [32]. Like all the other aspects of your OS, *the* biggest determinant is individuals' relationship with you.

And it is to people's relationships that will we now turn—to the last component of momentum, connection.

Summary + Checklist

See Table 15.1.

Table 15.1 Summary of empowerment

	OS function	Techniques to build it
Empowerment	• Enhances motivation and effort • Increases creativity • Improves agility • Increases confidence • Enhances collaboration	• Create clarity and accountability • Protect against stress • Give feedback and coach

Checklist

To help you think about whether you have successfully installed empowerment in your Leadership OS, ask yourself how the people around you—your direct reports, peers and stakeholders—would respond to the following questions (Table 15.2).

Table 15.2   Have you installed empowerment in your leadership OS?

	✓	✗
Do people feel that you encourage them to take the initiative?	□	□
Do people believe they are free to decide how best to do their jobs?	□	□
Do people believe that you are an effective delegator?	□	□
Do people feel clear about their goals?	□	□
Do people feel accountable for their objectives?	□	□
Do people believe that you regularly give them feedback and coach them?	□	□
Do people feel informed?	□	□

References

1. M. Patterson, M. West and T. Wall, "Integrated manufacturing, empowerment, and company performance," *Journal of Organizational Behavior*, vol. 25, no. 5, pp. 641–665, 2004.
2. G. Gazzoli, M. Hancer and Y. Park, "The role and effect of job satisfaction and empowerment on customers' perception of service quality: A study in the restaurant industry," *Journal of Hospitality & Tourism Research*, vol. 34, no. 1, pp. 56–77, 2010.
3. R. Hechanova-Alampay and T. Beehr, "Empowerment, span of control, and safety performance in work teams after workforce reduction," *Journal of Occupational Health Psychology*, vol. 6, no. 4, p. 275, 2001.
4. S. Seibert, G. Wang and S. Courtright, "Antecedents and consequences of psychological and team empowerment in organizations: A meta-analytic review," *Journal of Applied Psychology*, vol. 96, no. 5, p. 981, 2011.
5. F. Bond and P. Flaxman, "The ability of psychological flexibility and job control to predict learning, job performance, and mental health," *Journal of Organizational Behavior Management*, vol. 26, no. 1–2, pp. 113–130, 2006.
6. H. Bosma, S. Stansfeld and M. Marmot, "Job control, personal characteristics, and heart disease," *Journal of Occupational Health Psychology*, vol. 3, no. 4, pp. 402–409, 1998.
7. B. Harley, "The myth of empowerment: Work organisation, hierarchy and employee autonomy in contemporary Australian workplaces," *Work, Employment and Society*, vol. 13, no. 1, pp. 41–66, 1999.

8. J. Houghton and S. Yoho, "Toward a contingency model of leadership and psychological empowerment: When should self-leadership be encouraged?" *Journal of Leadership & Organizational Studies*, vol. 11, no. 4, pp. 65–83, 2005.

9. G. Stewart, "A meta-analytic review of relationships between team design features and team performance," *Journal of Management*, vol. 32, no. 1, pp. 29–55, 2006.

10. A. Lee, S. Willis and A. Tian, "When empowering employees works, and when it doesn't," *Harvard Business Review*, 2 March 2018.

11. M. Cheong, S. Spain, F. Yammarino and S. Yun, "Two faces of empowering leadership: Enabling and burdening," *The Leadership Quarterly*, vol. 27, no. 4, pp. 602–616, 2016.

12. C. Robert, T. Probst, J. Martocchio, F. Drasgow and J. Lawler, "Empowerment and continuous improvement in the United States, Mexico, Poland, and India: Predicting fit on the basis of the dimensions of power distance and individualism," *Journal of Applied Psychology*, vol. 85, no. 5, p. 643, 2000.

13. M. Biron and P. Bamberger, "The impact of structural empowerment on individual well-being and performance: Taking agent preferences, self-efficacy and operational constraints into account," *Human Relations*, vol. 63, no. 2, pp. 163–191, 2010.

14. L. Romaniuk, A. Sandu, G. Waiter, C. McNeil, X. Shen, M. Harris, J. Macfarlane, S. D. I. Lawrie, A. Murray, M. Delgado, J. Steele, A. Mcintosh and H. Whalley, "The neurobiology of personal control during reward learning and its relation to mood," *Biological Psychiatry*, vol. 24, no. 2, pp. 190–199, 2018.

15. I. Halperin, D. Chapman, D. Martin, R. Lewthwaite and G. Wulf, "Choices enhance punching performance of competitive kickboxers," *Psychological Research*, vol. 81, no. 5, pp. 1051–1058, 2016.

16. X. Zhang and J. Zhou, "Empowering leadership, uncertainty avoidance, trust, and employee creativity: Interaction effects and a mediating mechanism," *Organizational Behavior and Human Decision Processes*, vol. 124, no. 2, pp. 150–164, 2014.

17. X. Zhang and K. Bartol, "Linking empowering leadership and employee creativity: The influence of psychological empowerment, intrinsic motivation, and creative process engagement," *Academy of Management Journal*, vol. 53, no. 1, pp. 107–128, 2010.

18. G. Spreitzer, "Psychological empowerment in the workplace: Dimensions, measurement, and validation," *Academy of Management Journal*, vol. 38, no. 5, pp. 1442–1465, 1995.

19. E. McDonough III and G. GloriaBarczak, "Speeding up new product development: The effects of leadership style and source of technology," *Journal of Product Innovation Management*, vol. 8, no. 3, pp. 203–211, 1991.

20. S. Parker, H. Williams and N. Turner, "Modeling the antecedents of proactive behavior at work," *Journal of Applied Psychology*, vol. 91, no. 3, pp. 636–652, 2006.

21. M. Kim and T. Beehr, "Self-efficacy and psychological ownership mediate the effects of empowering leadership on both good and bad employee behaviors," *Journal of Leadership & Organizational Studies*, vol. 24, no. 4, pp. 466–478, 2017.

22. X. Jiang, H. Flores, R. Leelawong and C. Manz, "The effect of team empowerment on team performance," *International Journal of Conflict Management*, vol. 27, no. 1, pp. 62–87, 2016.

23. B. Kirkman, B. Rosen, P. Tesluk and C. Gibson, "The impact of team empowerment on virtual team performance: The moderating role of face-to-face interaction," *Academy of Management Journal*, vol. 47, no. 2, pp. 175–192, 2004.

24. P. Hempel, Z. Zhang and Y. Han, "Team empowerment and the organizational context: Decentralization and the contrasting effects of formalization," *Journal of Management*, vol. 38, no. 2, pp. 475–501, 2012.

25. J. Wallace, P. Johnson, K. Mathe and J. Paul, "Structural and psychological empowerment climates, performance, and the moderating role of shared felt accountability: A managerial perspective," *Journal of Applied Psychology*, vol. 96, no. 4, pp. 840–850, 2011.

26. R. Liden, S. Wayne and R. Sparrowe, "An examination of the mediating role of psychological empowerment on the relations between the job, interpersonal relationships, and work outcomes," *Journal of Applied Psychology*, vol. 85, no. 3, p. 407, 2000.

27. G. Zhenxing, Z. Jian, Z. Yujia and Y. Lei, "The relationship between feedback environment, feedback orientation, psychological empowerment and burnout among police in China," *Policing: An International Journal*, vol. 40, no. 2, pp. 336–350, 2017.

28. E. Gonzalez-Mulé, S. Courtright, D. DeGeest, J. Seong and D. Hong, "Channeled autonomy: The joint effects of autonomy and feedback on team performance through organizational goal clarity," *Journal of Management*, vol. 42, no. 7, pp. 2018–2033, 2016.

29. J. Arnold, S. Arad, J. Rhoades and F. Drasgow, "The empowering leadership questionnaire: The construction and validation of a new scale for measuring leader behaviors," *Journal of Organisational Behaviour*, vol. 21, pp. 249–269, 2000.

30. N. Khatri, "Consequences of power distance orientation in organisations," *Vision*, vol. 13, no. 1, pp. 1–9, 2009.

31. N. Lorinkova, M. Pearsall and H. Sims, "Examining the differential longitudinal performance of directive versus empowering leadership in teams," *Academy of Management Journal*, vol. 56, pp. 573–596, 2013.

32. G. Spreitzer, "Taking stock: A review of more than twenty years of research on empowerment at work," *Handbook of Organizational Behavior*, vol. 1, pp. 54–72, 2008.

16

Connection

In the summer of 1954, twenty-two American boys were picked up by buses and transported to a 200-acre Boy Scouts camp in the Robbers Cave State Park in Oklahoma. The boys were all similar: 11 years old with good school grades and above-average intelligence, and from a Protestant, two-parent background. And although they didn't know it, they were about to become part of one of the most famous experiments in psychology [1].

Before arriving at the camp, the boys were randomly assigned to one of two groups. On arrival, the two groups were kept apart and not told of the other's existence. During the first phase of the experiment, each group was encouraged to bond together through activities such as hiking, swimming and problem-solving games that required the boys to cooperate. The boys quickly developed an attachment to their group, choosing a name for it—the Eagles and the Rattlers—and writing the name on shirts and flags.

Then phase two started. The groups were introduced to each other and asked to take part in a series of competitive games, like bean-tossing and tug-of-war. The idea was to create friction between the groups to see what would happen. It didn't take long. At first, the groups just taunted each other, in a more or less friendly fashion. But as the competition continued, things became less friendly. The taunting turned into more aggressive name-calling. Each group became more negative in its views of the other; they became more mistrustful, suspecting each other of cheating. Then they started raiding each other's camps. The Eagles burned the Rattlers' flag. The next day, the Rattlers broke into the Eagle's cabin and ransacked it, overturning beds and stealing property. Finally, after the Eagles won the

© The Author(s) 2020
N. Kinley and S. Ben-Hur, *Leadership OS*,
https://doi.org/10.1007/978-3-030-27293-7_16

tournament, the Rattlers stole their prizes. In the ensuing confrontation, boys from both sides began punching each other and looking for rocks to throw. At that point, with real bloodshed beckoning, the researchers stepped in to end the experiment.

The study has been criticised over the years for its methods, but other experiments have produced similar findings. The experiment is famous because it showed how rapidly relationships could deteriorate between two groups, and how far this could go even in well-educated, well-adjusted groups of people.

It showed something else, too. That when you gather a group of people and give them an activity to do together, an activity to cooperate on, something happens to them. They begin to develop a sense of connection, of something shared. And when that happens, being part of the group becomes part of them, part of their identity. They *become* an Eagle or Rattler.

This sense of connection can be powerful because when we feel connected to someone or something, we become protective of them. We try harder for them.

This is why connection is so important. It is the social glue that pulls motivation, confidence and empowerment together and binds them into momentum.

What Connection Is and Does

Connection, then, is *not* just about having relationships with people. It is the sense of togetherness that comes *from* relationships. It is the feeling of being part of something, the feeling of 'we're all in this together'. It is what puts the 'we' into 'I'.

There is a small proportion of people who do not need a sense of connection. But for the vast majority, feeling connected to others is important, and not just for happiness. Connection appears to be good for our health, too, as studies show that socially isolated people tend to have poorer mental and physical health [2].

What is perhaps less well known is *just* how important connection is at work. It is probably not a big surprise that people who feel strongly connected to their boss or colleagues are happier in their job and have lower levels of absenteeism [3]. But these people are also more efficient and productive [4]. This leap in performance improvement can be found in both production and service teams [5]; it is particularly strong in small groups [6] and also where people are dependent on each other to deliver their

Fig. 16.1 The functions of connection in a Leadership OS

objectives [7]. For example, project teams with a high sense of connection are more likely to meet their goals in budget and on time [8].

The reason connection has such a big and reliable impact on performance lies in *how* it affects people: creating a Leadership OS in which people feel a strong sense of connection to others appears to do three things to them (Fig. 16.1).

A. Increases trust and collaboration

We saw in Chapter 2 that interacting with others in a positive way stimulates our biological trust system, which leads us to be more positive, sociable and collaborative. Well, just *feeling* connected to others has the same effect, stimulating the release of oxytocin in our brains [9]. Moreover, when we do not feel connected to others—for instance when we feel lonely—our brains interpret this as an unsafe situation. The threat-detection system is triggered, and the trust system is shut down, and we become more alert, negative and distrustful [10]. So, feeling connected improves trust, which in turn makes us more collaborative.

As a result, people who feel a strong sense of connection are more likely also to feel a sense of responsibility for the welfare of colleagues [11] and are thus more likely to go out of their way to help them [12]. They are also more likely to share information [13] and discuss issues more openly [14]. As a result of this, they are more likely to be creative [15]. For example, research and development teams have been shown to be more innovative when the people in those teams feel a strong sense of connection to each other [16].

B. Enhances commitment and effort

The second thing connection does is to increase people's sense of commitment to others, which in turn leads them to be more engaged, work harder and contribute more [17]. We see this effect across all sorts of jobs, with one of the more memorable examples being that soldiers are more willing to put themselves in danger and fight if they feel a strong sense of connection to the other people in their unit [18].

There are a variety of reasons why connection can breed such strong commitment. One is that people feel more obligated to others when they feel connected to them. Another is that when you feel connected to a group, team interest becomes self-interest [19]. And there is also evidence that for some people, feeling connected to others makes work feel more meaningful for them, thereby increasing their motivation [20].

C. Reduces stress

The third thing connection does to people is to increase their resilience and tolerance for stress [21]. We see this across all sorts of jobs, including particularly high-stress ones such as nursing [22] and the military [23]. There seem to be a couple of reasons for this protective effect. Greater social support may be available to people who feel well connected to others. Feeling connected can also increase people's confidence levels, and thus their ability to cope [24]. And when people do *not* feel connected, it can suppress the function of all sorts of body systems associated with their health, including their immune and cardiovascular systems, and thereby reduce their resilience [25]. So, connection protects against stress and burnout.

Connecting People: The Case of Herb Kelleher and Southwest Airlines

Southwest Airlines took off in 1971, with four aeroplanes and a simple approach: low fares and no frills. For most of Southwest's history, Herb Kelleher was the heart and soul of the company. During his tenure as CEO and chairman of the board, Kelleher was always clear about the philosophy that he believed would lead to success. Time and again, he told his leaders to put employees first. If they did that, he said, the employees would treat customers well, the customer would come back, and with them the necessary business results. Ultimately, they were producing value for shareholders, but the first and most important step was to treat employees well (Fig. 16.2).

Company policy reinforced this attitude, as the words 'Employee' and 'Customer' were always capitalised. But Kelleher's approach wasn't just words. He lived it. He was an incredible listener, who when he was with people could make them feel that he was totally focused on them. He had

Herb Kelleher (SWA)

Fig. 16.2 Herb Kelleher

an uncanny ability to remember names. Many Southwest employees have stories that they had met Kelleher once, then met him again a year later and he remembered their name. He treated everyone with dignity and respect. He did not treat people differently because of their class or level and made it clear that he viewed titles and positions as mere adornments that were not important. He joined in company events, mixing with all levels of employee and encouraging people to be themselves at work. He led the way in this regard, too, whether by singing at the annual party, always seeming to have a cigarette and glass of bourbon in hand, or wearing a pink dress to a company event. And he constantly showered his people with praise—in his one-on-one meetings, speeches and annual reports—showing them how much he admired and valued them.

Kelleher was not just about being nice, though. As any competitor would testify, he could be tough as well. He was utterly clear in his vision for the business and completely inflexible in his commitment to it. And with his people, he set high expectations, did not accept second best, and continually pushed and encouraged them to dig deeper and reach for more. So, there was a real edge beneath all the positivity.

Through his behaviour, Kelleher set the tone for everyone around him. He cultivated a culture of real focus, yet also friendly openness and trust, in which people felt an almost family-like bond and sense of togetherness. Kelleher may have been the fulcrum of everything at Southwest—the centrepiece that everyone felt connected to—but the culture he created also enabled people to feel more connected to the colleagues they stood beside and to the business as a whole. The result was deep commitment and exceptional loyalty. Engagement scores on staff surveys were consistently high, and voluntary turnover sat at around 2%.

Critically, this unique culture has helped the company thrive like no other in the industry. From 1973 all the way through to 2017, Southwest Airlines was profitable. That is 45 consecutive years, an incredible feat in an industry characterised by intense competition, difficult union relationships and fuel price volatility.

Kelleher passed away on January 2019, but his legacy will be lasting. He did not just build an exceptional business, he transformed the entire airline industry. He established the low-cost business model that has since become the industry standard. He introduced employee profit-sharing as early as the 1970s, a time when it was unheard of in the industry. And he created a near 60,000-strong family of employees whose loyalty to the firm, him and each other was unrivalled in the industry.

Kelleher liked to say that he managed with his heart, not his head. By doing so, and by putting people first, he created a unique experience for employees and customers alike.

Creating Connection

For you as a leader—as the creator of a Leadership OS—this means that if you can help others feel a sense of connection, you can help boost their performance. There is plenty of evidence that people form connections rapidly and naturally. Thus, there is a degree to which, if you bring people together and give them something to work on as a team, they will start feeling a sense of connection. But this connection does not always happen and, unfortunately, work is one of the key reasons why.

Recent research in neuroscience suggests that the parts of our brains that deal with tasks are different from the parts that deal with relationships. And

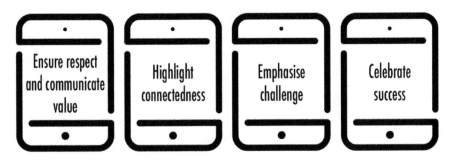

Fig. 16.3 Four techniques to create connection

critically, these two brain systems interfere with each other, so that when one is activated, the other becomes suppressed. This means that the more task-focused we become, the less able we are to pay attention to our relationships with other people. Obviously, some tasks involve dealing with people, but the rule still holds in these situations. We may be dealing with others, but the more focused on outcomes we are, the less empathetic we will be [26].

Amid the rush and focus of everyday work demands, then, our sense of connection can disappear. So, it is not enough simply to put people in the general vicinity of each other and hope for the best. If you want to build a connection in your OS, you need to act to ensure it happens. And the more task-focused your environment is, the more important it is that you act to support connection [27].

Like many of the other components of your Leadership OS, connection is far more likely to occur if you deliberately and systematically set out to create it. And as with the other components, there is no one way to do this. People differ in their need for connection and which drivers of connection they respond to best. So, a degree of trial and error will be required on your part.

When we look at the research, there are four techniques in particular that can help build connection (Fig. 16.3). They will not all work with everyone, but each is an option you can try.

Ensure Respect and Communicate Value

The first technique at your disposal is to ensure that people feel respected and valued [28]. It is important because people are far more likely to feel connected to a team or business when they feel they are appreciated by it [29]. So, publicly praising people can help here. Ensuring that conflicts between team members are resolved can also help, as can stepping in to address the behaviour of anyone who does not show proper respect to a colleague. And finally, reminding people of the contribution and personal investment they make to the team and business can also reinforce feelings of respect and value.

Highlight Connectedness

The second technique simply involves reminding people of how connected they are to each other and the degree to which everyone relies upon each other for the business to do well. This works because the more people perceive themselves as reliant on each other, the more likely they are to be collaborative and help each other, and in turn feel connected.

Asking people in one-on-one meetings who they are most reliant on, and who is most reliant on them, can help here. Setting shared objectives or giving people tasks to do together can also help [30]. Praising collaboration where you see it can be important. Involving people in discussions, asking their opinion and encouraging them to speak up also communicates that you value them. And while in diverse groups emphasising everyone's distinctiveness can help increase connection, in more homogenous groups emphasising similarities works better [31].

One final option you have for highlighting connectedness is social functions—using team-building events or parties to help foster team chemistry. There is evidence this can work [32], but it comes with a big caveat: although extraverts may respond really well to it, introverts may not. Not everyone likes a party.

Emphasise Challenge

The third technique available is to emphasise the challenges facing people. Studies show that when you give people more complex or difficult tasks, it can increase their sense of connection, since it encourages them to seek out help to overcome problems [30]. So talking with people about the challenges they face in achieving objectives, and who might be able to help them overcome them, can be a useful tactic here.

One thing to be wary of, however, is creating competition with other parts of the business. We have seen some leaders try to create a stronger sense of connection within teams by encouraging competition between teams. This can work but brings with it the risk that teams will not cooperate with each other and may become isolated. Therefore, it is only really effective in the rare situations where teams are truly independent and not reliant on each other for anything.

Celebrate Success

Like many of the other components of your Leadership OS, connection has a reciprocal relationship with performance [33]. When connection goes up, so does performance, which in turn increases connection even further, and so on. And you can use this fact to help build connection by ensuring that you celebrate success.

Simply put, teams who feel successful are more likely to feel a strong sense of connection to each other. So, updating people on progress towards key goals, through visible scoreboards, regular emails or even big thermometers (for a fund-raising campaign) can all help here. Similarly, following Herb Kelleher's example by recognising significant accomplishments and milestones and thanking people for their contributions can help breed connection. Essentially, anything you can do to make progress and success more visible will help to encourage connection.

A Social Glue

There has been debate over the years about whether connection has a dark side. For example, it has been suggested that if people feel too strongly connected to others, it can create group conformity, resulting in a lack of proper discussion and poor decision-making. Yet studies show that connection alone is unlikely to cause this [34]. Instead, conformity and poor decision-making only happen when connection is coupled with overly hierarchical or authoritarian leadership [35].

That does not mean that connection always has a positive impact. For example, if there is little accountability for results, connection is unlikely to yield much better performance [36]. And if a leader does not set a clear ethical tone, then employees who feel strongly connected to the leader may follow their example and also engage in more unethical behaviours [37].

Connection alone, then, is never enough. It is not enough to either drive performance or ensure failure. Instead, it derives its power from what it is combined with and how it fits into your broader Leadership OS. It is, however, no less critical for that.

This is because connection is the social glue that binds the other elements of momentum together. When people feel connected, they are more likely to feel motivated, confident and empowered. And this is what generates momentum in your OS—the capacity for action, the drive to get things moving and make things happen.

Summary + Checklist

See Table 16.1.

Table 16.1 Summary of connection

	OS function	Techniques to build it
Connection	• Increases trust and collaboration • Enhances commitment and effort • Reduces stress	• Ensure respect and communicate value • Highlight connectedness • Emphasise challenge • Celebrate success

Checklist

To help you think about whether you have successfully installed connection in your Leadership OS, ask yourself how the people around you—your direct reports, peers and stakeholders—would respond to the following questions (Table 16.2).

Table 16.2 Have you installed connection in your Leadership OS?

	✓	✗
Would others say that you take measures to ensure people feel that they are all in this together?	☐	☐
Do you put in place processes or events to help people feel connected to their peers?	☐	☐
Do people feel a sense of connection with you?	☐	☐
Do people believe that you make sure that everyone treats each other with respect?	☐	☐
Do people feel that you help them to understand the value they add to the organisation?	☐	☐
Do the people around you feel appreciated for what they do?	☐	☐

References

1. M. Sherif, O. Harvey, B. White, W. Hood and C. Sherif, "Intergroup conflict and cooperation: The Robbers Cave experiment," in *University of Oklahoma book exchange*, Norman, OK, 1961, pp. 155–184.
2. E. Cornwell and L. Waite, "Social disconnectedness, perceived isolation, and health among older adults," *Journal of Health and Social Behavior*, vol. 50, no. 1, pp. 31–48, 2009.

3. E. Lee, T. Park and B. Koo, "Identifying organizational identification as a basis for attitudes and behaviors: A meta-analytic review," *Psychological Bulletin*, vol. 141, no. 5, pp. 1049–1080, 2015.

4. B. Mullen and C. Cooper, "The relation between group cohesiveness and performance: An integration," *Psychological Bulletin*, vol. 115, pp. 210–227, 1994.

5. F. Chiocchio and H. Essiembre, "Cohesion and performance: A meta-analytic review of disparities between project teams, production teams, and service teams," *Small Group Research*, vol. 40, no. 4, pp. 382–420, 2009.

6. B. Mullen and C. Copper, "The relation between group cohesiveness and performance: An integration," *Psychological Bulletin*, vol. 115, no. 2, p. 210, 1994.

7. S. Gully, D. Devine and D. Whitney, "A meta-analysis of cohesion and performance: Effects of level of analysis and task interdependence," *Small Group Research*, vol. 26, no. 4, pp. 497–520, 1995.

8. R. Keller, "Predictors of the performance of project groups in R & D organizations," *Academy of Management Journal*, vol. 29, no. 4, pp. 715–726, 1986.

9. A. Jobst, A. Albert, C. Bauriedl-Schmidt, C. Mauer, B. Renneberg, A. Buchheim, L. Sabass, P. Falkai, P. Zill and F. Padberg, "Social exclusion leads to divergent changes of Oxytocin levels in borderline patients and healthy subjects," *Psychotherapy and Psychosomatics*, vol. 83, pp. 252–254, 2014.

10. J. Cacioppo and L. Hawkley, "Perceived social isolation and cognition," *Trends in Cognitive Sciences*, vol. 13, pp. 447–454, 2009.

11. J. Dovidio, J. Piliavin, S. Gaertner, D. Schroeder and R. Clark III, "The arousal: Cost-reward model and the process of intervention: A review of the evidence," in M. S. Clark (Ed.), *Review of personality and social psychology, Vol. 12. Prosocial behavior,* Thousand Oaks, CA, Sage, 1991, pp. 86–118.

12. S. Haslam, C. Powell and J. Turner, "Social identity, self-categorization, and work motivation: Rethinking the contribution of the group to positive and sustainable organisational outcomes," *Applied Psychology*, vol. 49, no. 3, pp. 319–339, 2000.

13. S. Taggar, "Individual creativity and group ability to utilize individual creative resources: A multilevel model," *Academy of Management Journal*, vol. 45, no. 2, pp. 315–330, 2002.

14. J. Mathieu, S. Tannenbaum, M. Kukenberger, J. Donsbach and G. Alliger, "Team role experience and orientation: A measure and tests of construct validity," *Group & Organization Management*, vol. 40, no. 1, pp. 6–34, 2015.

15. T. Craig and J. Kelly, "Group cohesiveness and creative performance," *Group Dynamics: Theory, Research, and Practice*, vol. 3, no. 4, p. 243, 1999.

16. C. Huang, "Knowledge sharing and group cohesiveness on performance: An empirical study of technology R&D teams in Taiwan," *Technovation*, vol. 29, no. 11, pp. 786–797, 2009.

17. R. Mitchell, B. Boyle, V. Parker, M. Giles, V. Chiang and P. Joyce, "Managing inclusiveness and diversity in teams: How leader inclusiveness affects

performance through status and team identity," *Human Resource Management*, vol. 54, no. 2, pp. 217–239, 2015.

18. R. Gal, "Unit Morale: From a Theoretical Puzzle to an empirical illustration—An Israeli example," *Journal of Applied Social Psychology*, vol. 16, no. 6, pp. 549–564, 1986.

19. D. van Knippenberg and N. Ellemers, "Social identity and group performance: Identification as the key to group-oriented effort," in S. A. Haslam, D. van Knippenberg, M. J. Platow, and N. Ellemers (Eds.), *Social identity at work: Developing theory for organizational practice*, New York, NY, Psychology Press, 2019, pp. 29–42.

20. T. Schnell, T. Höge and E. Pollet, "Predicting meaning in work: Theory, data, implications," *The Journal of Positive Psychology*, vol. 8, no. 6, pp. 543–554, 2013.

21. H. Okamura, A. Tsuda and T. Matsuishi, "The relationship between perceived loneliness and cortisol awakening responses on work days and weekends," *Japanese Psychological Research*, vol. 53, no. 2, pp. 113–120, 2012.

22. R. AbuAlRub, "Job stress, job performance, and social support among hospital nurses," *Journal of Nursing Scholarship*, vol. 36, no. 1, pp. 73–78, 2004.

23. J. Williams, J. Brown, R. Bray, E. Anderson Goodell, K. Rae Olmsted and A. Adler, "Unit cohesion, resilience, and mental health of soldiers in basic combat training," *Military Psychology*, vol. 28, no. 4, pp. 241–250, 2016.

24. F. Walumbwa, B. Avolio and W. Zhu, "How transformational leadership weaves its influence on individual job performance: The role of identification and efficacy beliefs," *Personnel Psychology*, vol. 61, no. 4, pp. 793–825, 2008.

25. Y. Luo, L. Hawkley, L. Waite and J. Cacioppo, "Loneliness, health, and mortality in old age: A national longitudinal study," *Social Science & Medicine*, vol. 74, no. 6, pp. 907–914, 2012.

26. R. Boyatis, K. Rochford and A. Jack, "Antagonistic neural networks underlying differentiated leadership roles," *Frontiers in Human Neuroscience*, vol. 8, p. 114, 2014.

27. A. Tziner and Y. Vardi, "Effects of command style and group cohesiveness on the performance effectiveness of self-selected tank crews," *Journal of Applied Psychology*, vol. 67, no. 6, p. 769, 1982.

28. C. Reade, "Antecedents of organizational identification in multinational corporations: Fostering psychological attachment to the local subsidiary and the global organization," *International Journal of Human Resource Management*, vol. 12, no. 8, pp. 1269–1291, 2001.

29. J. Fuller, K. Hester, T. Barnett, L. Frey, C. Relyea and D. Beu, "Perceived external prestige and internal respect: New insights into the organizational identification process," *Human Relations*, vol. 59, no. 6, pp. 815–846, 2006.

30. D. Man and S. Lam, "The effects of job complexity and autonomy on cohesiveness in collectivistic and individualistic work groups: A cross-cultural analysis," *Journal of Organizational Behaviour*, vol. 24, no. 8, pp. 979–1001, 2003.

31. L. Jans, T. Postmes and K. Van der Zee, "Sharing differences: The inductive route to social identity formation," *Journal of Experimental Social Psychology*, vol. 48, no. 5, pp. 1145–1149, 2012.

32. R. Bakeman and R. Helmreich, "Cohesiveness and performance: Covariation and causality in an undersea environment," *Journal of Experimental Social Psychology*, vol. 11, no. 5, pp. 478–489, 1975.

33. J. Mathieu, M. Kukenberger, L. D'innocenzo and G. Reilly, "Modeling reciprocal team cohesion-performance relationships, as impacted by shared leadership and members' competence," *Journal of Applied Psychology*, vol. 100, no. 3, p. 713, 2015.

34. B. Mullen, T. Anthony, E. Salas and J. Driskell, "Group cohesiveness and quality of decision making: An integration of tests of the groupthink hypothesis," *Small Group Research*, vol. 25, no. 2, pp. 189–204, 1994.

35. L. Dyaram and T. Kamalanabhan, "Unearthed: The other side of group cohesiveness," *Journal of Social Sciences*, vol. 10, no. 3, pp. 185–190, 2005.

36. C. Langfred, "Is group cohesiveness a double-edged sword? An investigation of the effects of cohesiveness on performance," *Small Group Research*, vol. 29, no. 1, pp. 124–143, 1998.

37. J. Mpeera Ntayi, W. Byabashaija, S. Eyaa, M. Ngoma and A. Muliira, "Social cohesion, groupthink and ethical behavior of public procurement officers," *Journal of Public Procurement*, vol. 10, no. 1, pp. 68–92, 2010.

Part IV

Your Leadership OS

17

The Imprint You Make, the Legacy You Leave

There are schools in India that have stopped teaching handwriting. They teach keyboard skills instead. There are schools that place less emphasis on children spelling correctly, as the kids all use spell checkers. And our own children are taught on iPads, learn how to present information on PowerPoint, and are given the choice of whether to write essays or present their work through audio files or videos. One of them even has a tutor they have only ever met on Skype. School has changed since we were there.

As parents, we look on, glad to see education evolving with the times, but unsure whether all the changes will better prepare our children for their futures. We wonder what the connectivity enabled by social media will do to them, and how the constant distractions of an always-on internet will affect how they process information and think.

This lack of clarity extends to home, too. We try to create an environment for our children that will equip them with the character and values they will need to thrive in tomorrow's world. But not only are we often unsure about the impact we are having on them but we are also uncertain about what tomorrow's world will look like and demand of our children. So we do what we can, guided by a mixture of core values, concerned judgement and trial and error. And in that respect, parenting isn't that much different from leadership these days.

The world of work is also changing, its future form is also uncertain. New technologies are digitising economies and businesses and enabling new ways of working. There are more freelancers and part-time workers than ever before, and around a quarter of US employees now say they work

© The Author(s) 2020
N. Kinley and S. Ben-Hur, *Leadership OS*,
https://doi.org/10.1007/978-3-030-27293-7_17

from home some of the time. Spans of control have grown larger through delayering, and teams are bigger, more diverse and increasingly virtual. Globalisation has also ensured that leaders have more stakeholders, with more diverse values and attitudes. And all these changes are occurring alongside ever-greater levels of market uncertainty, as the economic context continues to be volatile and the pace of technological change shows no signs of slowing down.

As a result, the demands on leaders are greater than ever before. The job of leadership is simply more complex than it used to be 20 years ago. And in the face of this, leaders can be forgiven for sometimes feeling—like many parents—that they are pulling levers in the dark. Our purpose in this book has been to try to shine a light on what leaders need to do to succeed in this changing and uncertain world, and highlight which levers are the most effective.

Unreliable Levers in Uncertain Times

We started by showing that many of the traditional levers leaders have been taught to use are no longer fit for purpose. The guidance offered for the past 50 years has come in the form of leadership models that describe the core components leaders need in order to succeed—the competencies they need to have and the behaviours they need to show. Be like this and do these things, they say, and you will be successful.

Although there is no doubt that many of these models have genuinely helped improve the practice of leadership, they are increasingly unsuited to the age we live in. This is because they ignore the role of context. They do not say, 'In this situation be like this, and in that scenario be like that'; they just say, 'Be like this'. In doing so, they ignore the fact that factors like business challenges, culture and the characteristics of the people around you can all change the impact you have. And as a result, you can be as these models say and do as they direct you to, yet not have the impact they promise or that you wished for.

For many years, this was okay, because these models were meant as general rules and still worked seven or eight times out of ten. But as the context leaders operate in has become increasingly complex and changeable, the odds of the behaviours advocated by these traditional models actually working have fallen. As a result, leaders can no longer trust them to work as reliable guides. To identify how to succeed in today's more complicated and uncertain world, they need a new and different kind of guidance.

A New Kind of Guide

The solution lies in the fact that as leaders rise to more senior levels, the mechanics of *how* they impact the business changes. As frontline, first-level managers, it is quite easy for people to have a direct impact on business performance. They can do things like drive sales or improve service either personally or by directing their teams. But the further up the organisation a leader rises, the further they move from the frontline. And as a result, their impact becomes more indirect. It becomes less about doing things themselves, and more about driving and supporting other people to do things. It becomes more about the environment or operating system they create.

This Leadership OS encompasses relationships and ways of working. Yet it is not just what leaders do with people when they are with them, but what remains in the room after the leader has left. It is the impact they have, the imprint they make. And it is at work, changing how people think, feel and act, long after the leader has left the room.

It functions in roughly the same way as the OS on any computer. It affects leaders' ability to manage people and interact with stakeholders—their ability to get the best from others. It affects their ability to make sure that work streams and projects run smoothly. And it sets the tone for how people interact, work together and treat each other.

Moreover, crucially, unlike competencies and behaviours, an OS is not changed by context. It is what is produced by the interaction between a leader's competencies, characteristics and behaviours and the context they operate in. And as such, because it is an output rather than an input, an OS is a better, more reliable guide for leaders.

What About Competencies?

The leadership industry's capability-based approach, which has been the foundation of leadership selection and development over the past half century, is ill-suited to deal with today's more complex business environment. It is too focused on the internal qualities of leaders, too oblivious of context and too simplistic.

However, this does not mean that we think competencies are unimportant. Some of the skills they describe—in particular, those that are mainly internal qualities, like strategic thinking, financial understanding and technical skills—are useful and necessary. Instead, we are saying that capabilities and 'just-do-this' behaviour models are no longer *on their own* a useful guide for how leaders can succeed in today's world. Just like a smartphone, leaders need both quality core components *and* a good OS.

The New Levers of Leadership

In this book we have laid out a new kind of guide for leaders. Based on a review of over 1000 studies and articles and our research with more than 2500 leaders around the world, we identified three elements of a Leadership OS that are critical for performance. These three elements—*trust, clarity* and *momentum*—all need to be in place for leaders to succeed.

Think back to the example of Elon Musk in Chapter 1. Is he successful? Undoubtedly. Is he as successful as he could be? That's another matter. He's great at inspiring people with his vision—creating both clarity and momentum. But his unpredictable tweeting habits undermine trust, limiting his ability to get the absolute best from the people around him, including important stakeholders like the regulators.

For each of the three elements, we have described four components. These components are the new levers of leadership for the modern age. They are what you need to focus on and hone to get the perfect balance of the three elements for the situation you are in. Since these components are the product of both what you do and the context you operate in, they are not completely in your control. But as the main contributor to them, you can significantly affect them.

A More Honest Type of Leadership Model

Knowing which levers to use and when is not straightforward, but as a rule, we suggest starting with trust as a foundation, then moving on to clarity before looking at momentum.

Our research shows that high-performing leaders have OSs that are rated highly for all three elements, but beyond this, which element is most important can vary between roles. In a turnaround scenario, clarity and momentum might be particularly important. In a situation demanding creativity and entrepreneurialism, trust and momentum might be more vital. In addition, the most effective way to build trust, clarity and momentum can vary between situations. In some circumstances, *care* and *psychological safety* might be the keys to building trust. In others, they might be *reliability* and *fairness*.

This, then, is one way in which these new levers of leadership are fundamentally different from the old, traditional ones. They do not promise, 'Be like this and you will succeed'. They say, 'This is the impact you need to have, but how you produce it will take some trial and error'. This may be less simple to achieve, but we also believe it is a more honest type of leadership model—one that acknowledges the reality that for most leaders, just like most parents, creating the right environment is a matter of trying things and seeing what works. To help, we have described techniques you can use to pull each of the levers, but it is up to you to see which ones work best for you.

For many years, leaders have been presented with an oversimplified picture of how leadership works, a picture in which competencies and behaviours produce certain results. However, that is not how leadership really works—certainly not at senior levels. The real mechanism through which leadership works is the Leadership OS produced by the mix of competencies and context. Get your OS right and you have a chance; fail and, sooner or later, you'll be in trouble.

Doing this—getting your OS right—requires three things of a leader. It requires a deliberate and systematic approach. It requires you to be more aware of the impact you have on other people. And it requires you to strengthen your understanding of the context you operate in, the differences between specific challenges, people and cultures, and how these can affect the impact you have.

This book represents the end of a road for us. Seven years and three books later, the end of an accidental trilogy. But it is also the beginning of something new. The issues we have pointed out with traditional leadership models are only going to intensify. And the new approach we have identified has significant implications for how businesses select and develop their leaders. That is for another day. Our intent here has been to shine a light on a more reliable set of levers that leaders can use to build effective OSs. Our hope is that you will use them to develop your impact, drive better performance, and enhance the experience and quality of life of the people around you. After all, these are the building blocks of a leadership legacy, the ones that really matter for the future of our organisations, our communities, and indeed the wider world.

Index

Printed by Printforce, the Netherlands